50
YEARS OF
CARRY
ON

Also by Richard Webber

The Complete One Foot In The Grave

That Was the Decade That Was: Best of Sixties' TV

Porridge: The Complete Scripts and Series Guide

Fifty Years of Hancock's Half Hour

The Complete A-Z of Dad's Army

The Complete A-Z of Only Fools and Horses

Rising Damp: The Complete Scripts

Some Mothers Do 'Ave 'Em

*Dad's Army: Walmington Goes to War –
The Complete Scripts for Series 1–4 (Scripts)*

Porridge: The Inside Story

Rising Damp: A Celebration

A Celebration of The Good Life

Dad's Army: A Celebration

Whatever Happened to the Likely Lads?

Are You Being Served?: A Celebration of Twenty Five Years

The Life and Legacy of Reginald Perrin: A Celebration

50 YEARS OF CARRY ON

RICHARD WEBBER

CENTURY

Published by Century 2008

2 4 6 8 10 9 7 5 3 1

First published in Great Britain in 2008 by
Century
Random House, 20 Vauxhall Bridge Road,
London SW1V 2SA

www.randomhouse.co.uk

Addresses for companies within The Random House Group Limited can be found at:
www.randomhouse.co.uk

The Random House Group Limited Reg. No. 954009

A CIP catalogue record for this book
is available from the British Library

ISBN 9781844138432

The Random House Group Limited supports The Forest Stewardship
Council (FSC), the leading international forest certification organisation. All our
titles that are printed on Greenpeace approved FSC certified paper carry the FSC logo.
Our paper procurement policy can be found at www.rbooks.co.uk/environment

Mixed Sources
Product group from well-managed
forests and other controlled sources
www.fsc.org Cert no. TT-COC-2139
© 1996 Forest Stewardship Council
FSC

Typeset in Adobe Garamond by Palimpsest Book Production Limited,
Grangemouth, Stirlingshire

Printed and bound in Great Britain by
CPI Mackays, Chatham ME5 8TD

Picture credits: 1, 2, 3, 4, 5, 6, 15, 16, 17, 18, 20, 21, 22, 23, 24, 25, 28, 29, 30, 31
© Mirrorpix; 7, 8 © Robert Teele; 11, 12, 13, 14, 26, 27 © The Maidenhead Advertiser;
19 © Freemantle Media

For Hollie and Peter, with love

Contents

Acknowledgements   ix

Introduction   1

Part 1: In the Beginning   9

Part 2: The Rothwell Era   71

Part 3: The Beginning of the End?   141

Part 4: False Starts and Fresh Hopes   183

Epilogue   193

Extra . . . Extra . . . Extra   199

Notes   335

Bibliography   343

Index   345

Acknowledgements

Whenever you write a book like this there are always countless people who help in innumerable ways. There are too many to name individually so I'd like to take this opportunity to thank everyone who, in whatever capacity, helped get this book up and running – it wouldn't have been possible without you.

But there are some people, however, I would particularly like to mention by name, beginning with Peter Rogers who, once again, helped in many ways, including allowing me to publish internal documents, script extracts and an unfinished script for an unmade film in the latter stages of the book. Then there is Norman Hudis, who has become a friend through the various chats and exchanging of e-mails during the time that I have been working on the book. Thank you, Norman, for answering so many questions in depth, which has given me the chance to appreciate the Hudis era more fully than would otherwise have been possible. I had the pleasure of meeting Norman and his lovely wife Rita on one of their recent visits to Dorset: it was an enjoyable day and a get-together that I hope to repeat in the near future.

Others I would like to mention include all the actors and crew members and the relatives of the deceased who gave up their time to answer queries and talk about the *Carry On* days. These include Alan Hume, Jack Douglas, Dilys Laye, Jacki Piper, Suzanne Danielle, the late Patsy Rowlands, Patricia Franklin, Kenneth Cope, Fenella Fielding and Angela Douglas. I also owe thanks to writer Vince Powell for sharing memories of the scripts he worked on and, again, for granting permission for me to publish his *Down Under* script herein, and to Lance Peters for discussing *Carry On Emmannuelle* and allowing me to publish extracts from his original script.

Last, but certainly not least, my thanks to John Goldstone; to my agent Jeffrey Simmons; to Hilary Johnson for, again, providing her valuable advice; to Brett Tremble, Andy Davidson, Gwilym Hughes, Beryl Vertue and John Antrobus; to Gill Kenyon, for transcribing so many tapes; to those helpful souls at the BFI, especially Carolyne Bevan, and to everyone at Random House, particularly Hannah Black for commissioning the book and Katie Duce. And, of course, to my wife, Paula, who's always been there to lend an ear during the trials and tribulations of writing the book.

Thank you all.

Introduction

The summer of 1958 saw the birth of a cinematic legend which continues to entertain millions even today, five decades later. The indefatigable *Carry On* films, a catalogue of 31 low-budget productions, have spawned numerous spin-offs, including television series, stage shows, myriad videos and DVDs, a plethora of merchandise and countless happy memories. No matter which film you watch – the duffs or the gems – you're guaranteed a barrage of quips, double entendres and innuendoes, along with moments of sheer slapstick flying all over the place – all par for the course in the world of the *Carry On*s.

The *Carry On*s were hardly Oscar-winning material. Why then do so many people hold them in such high esteem? Turn on a DVD, press the fast-forward button and no matter where you stop, the chances are that you'll arrive at a point close to a memorable scene – memorable in its abundance of corny gags, obvious situations and predictable punchlines.

Think *Cleo*: an alarmed Julius Caesar, played by Kenneth Williams, comes running into view, spouting those immortal lines: 'Infamy! Infamy! They've all got it in for me!' If ever a one-liner or snatch of dialogue epitomised what the *Carry On*s were all about, it's this, which, in recognition of its popularity, topped a recent poll of funny one-liners conducted by Sky Movies Comedy. But if it hadn't been this line there were thousands more to choose from. Trawling through the archives, *Cowboy* finds the Rumpo Kid (Sid James) talking to the Indian chief, Big Heap (Charles Hawtrey): 'Once talked peace with the Sioux but you can't trust them. One moment it was peace on, the next peace off.' Then there's Peter Butterworth extracting information from Kenneth Williams in *Screaming!*: 'Name?' 'Dr Watt.' 'Dr who?' 'No, Watt, Who's my uncle' – the list is endless.

One might regard the *Carry On*s' style and form of humour as

3

anachronistic in today's world but, love them or loathe them, no one can deny that together they form by far the most successful big-screen comedy series, in terms of longevity and audience appeal, ever produced.

No one associated with the *Carry On* movies ever expected them to be celebrated for their artistic merit, and some film historians would dismiss the claim that the comedy series was more than a mere footnote, albeit a popular one, in the history of the British film industry. Some critics were persistent in decrying the merits of the films. Yet others were less dismissive, valuing the product more highly and believing that it should be accorded the respect and credit it deserved. Most of the films provide perfect examples of team playing at its best. With Peter Rogers's insistence that no one, however high their profile, could have their name above the title *Carry On*, everyone had to pull together; each actor played their part, with women being given equal standing in such matters as character billing. Yes, there were some real individuals – after all, there could only ever be one Kenneth Williams or Charles Hawtrey – but when the camera began to roll egos disappeared and everyone performed for the benefit of the product – otherwise they were out on their ear.

In a climate when many complain about a surfeit of repeats on our screens, or see the discarding not only of repeats but of proven classics, too, these timeless little films from the Rogers-Thomas stable continue to entertain. Forgetting the obvious entries that didn't come up to scratch, what is it in the *Carry Ons*' make-up that makes them as accessible and as rip-roaringly funny as the day they were released?

When producer Peter Rogers and director Gerald Thomas set out to make the first film, *Carry On Sergeant*, they hired scriptwriter Norman Hudis to mine comedy from a familiar situation: the army. The film's unexpected popularity led to another instalment, *Carry On Nurse*, again based around a recognised institution. Even more success followed and before long, Rogers and Thomas found themselves entertaining the masses by spotlighting areas of life audiences understood and could relate to. Although the Talbot Rothwell era – Rothwell wrote the *Carry On* screenplays from *Cabby* in 1963 to *Dick* in 1974 – brought a change in direction, with all the main institutions having been given the treatment, by then the familiarity which engendered a sense of cosiness and security within the films had become established in the faces of the characters. By using, primarily for practical reasons, a nucleus of players who would move from film to film, resembling to all intents and purposes a repertory company, the film-makers ensured that the familiar performers came almost to be regarded as friends by fans who couldn't wait to find out what Kenneth Williams, Charles Hawtrey, Sid James or their own particular favourite would be doing in the next picture. The scene was identical around the British Isles: the cinema lights would dim, the audience would be eating ice creams and munching popcorn in anticipation of the first notes of the unfailingly happy music score that would transport them, briefly, into a world that one could only associate with the *Carry On* films.

Cheap and cheerful they might have been, but the *Carry On*s have become ingrained in the national psyche. Now accorded cult status, even though many of those who helped make it happen are no longer around, they're as much a part of the British culture as fish and chips, Donald McGill's seaside postcards and Kiss Me Quick hats. Critics may have labelled the jokes obvious, the plots thin and the puns excruciating, and many fans, if honest, would agree in some cases. But that didn't matter one bit because such elements swiftly became part of the films' charm as they established themselves as national treasures. As critic Penelope Gilliatt wrote: 'The usual charge to make against the *Carry On* films is to say that they could be so much better done. This is true enough. They look dreadful, they seem to be edited with a bacon slicer, the effects are perfunctory and the comic rhythm jerks along like a cat on a cold morning. But if all these things were more elegant I don't really think the films would be more enjoyable: the badness is part of the funniness.'[1]

In the history of British comedy, *Carry On* films are something of a naughty institution, brimming with the risqué antics of a unique set of actors whose jokes lie somewhere between the old gags of Max Miller and the modern-day musings of *Viz* magazine. While views on society are transient, unwavering attitudes towards the

Carry On films have helped them survive the decades, blissfully unshaken by the winds of change. We still love them because they make us feel part of a bygone era, a simpler time when political correctness was unheard-of and people wanted to smile rather than complain. Everyone likes to feel naughty now and again and watching a *Carry On* film still gives us that sense of wicked fun. The *Carry Ons* were continuing a tradition of British humour that had first emerged on the stages of music halls and variety theatres; when such places began closing up and down the country, largely due to the advent of television which meant that fewer people were interested in trudging down to their local venue, there was a desperate need for good, old-fashioned laughter and the *Carry Ons* filled that void. Much of the style and sense of humour evident at such locations influenced, in particular, the Rothwell-scripted *Carry On* films; and it was no coincidence that some of the leading actors had experience in this area of live theatre and were schooled in the belief that simplicity – and getting a laugh – was all-important.

Equally remarkable for a product that has withstood the test of time so well is the fact that the *Carry On* films were productions made on a shoestring budget at breakneck speed. There was no time for dallying and retakes were only sanctioned if absolutely essential because everyone was rushing towards the finishing line on an extremely short production timetable. The pace at which Peter Rogers, Gerald Thomas and the team whipped through the schedule astounded even contemporaries who didn't believe that films could be made so quickly. Of course, there were those who scoffed at such swiftness, believing nothing but sub-standard material could be produced in a rush. How wrong they were.

The films may not have been outstanding examples of the best in film-making; they did, however, mould the viewing habits of generations of people who grew to hold the films close to their hearts. With their fingers never far from the national pulse, producer Peter Rogers and director Gerald Thomas forged a formidable partnership that saw them laugh all the way to the bank as they scored highly at the box office.

Everyone has their favourites in the genre and mine are the earlier creations, written by Norman Hudis. Yes, I thoroughly enjoy most

of the other films, particularly Talbot Rothwell's fine scripts for
Camping, Abroad, Loving and the various hospital-based offerings,
but Hudis's scripts were more gentle, with moments of mirth and
merriment laced with pathos, proving that you could bring a tear
to the eye even in a *Carry On*. I missed this approach when Hudis
headed for a new life in the States and was replaced by Talbot
Rothwell, with the focus shifting towards packing scripts with as
many double entendres as possible. However, the public lapped up
the saucy humour and each production displayed an indefinable
charm.

There are many components that need to reach their potential
if a film is to be a success; bearing in mind that there was more
than just the one *Carry On*, the team obviously got it right. A suitable script and precise directing are just two factors, but much praise
must be bestowed upon the cast, whom the audiences grew to love.
A reviewer in *Variety*, while extolling the virtues of *Carry On Nurse*,
wrote about the 'long string of popular British players who enter
into this romp as if it were a Christmas party.'[2] That statement
sums up the entire catalogue of films – well, most of the entries –
because whenever the gang got together for another film it was like
schoolkids returning from their summer holidays, glad to be seeing
their friends again. This happiness and warmth infused the films.

In many respects this film series has almost sidestepped the
surge of criticism aimed at other efforts in the media world and
has become a bastion of good old British comedy, comprising
simple, cheap slices of laugh-a-minute humour, fêted, subsequently
if not at the time, throughout the film industry for what they are:
unpretentious instalments of fun.

When deciding what approach to take with this book, I realised
that there have been a number of volumes, including my own
Complete A-Z of Everything Carry On, that have charted the history
of the *Carry On* empire – films, television episodes, stage shows; reach
for those if you want a chronological study of, well, everything
Carry On. I've given myself some latitude in how I have structured
this book. Instead of marching relentlessly through each film,
beginning with *Sergeant* and ending with *Columbus*, I've allowed
myself the chance to make it a personal journey, wandering where

I want in terms of the *Carry On* history. For starters, I've focused only on the films because, to me, *Carry On* is all about the movies; so, if you're looking for information about the various small-screen and stage offerings, apart from straightforward cast lists, you'll be better served elsewhere. Then, I've decided to work through the films, largely in chronological order because that seems the logical route, but stopping off along the way to visit certain aspects of a particular film that are of particular interest. Perhaps the event or film was significant in the development or decline of the series, marking a milestone, or, simply, it's of interest to me personally. For example, I've dedicated a lot of space to the Norman Hudis era, partly because of its obvious importance to the series inasmuch as it set the ball rolling, but also because it happens to be my favourite segment. Hudis was a skilled writer with an ability to mix tears with laughter, which I wanted to explore in more depth, hence the amount of words dedicated to the first six pictures.

As well as the Hudis era, the final three films – excluding *That's Carry On* – namely *England, Emmannuelle* and *Columbus* needed plenty of attention. Personally, they're my least favourite films, particularly the dreadful *England,* but they're significant because they marked the beginning of the end for the *Carry On* franchise.

As well as the 'life story', I've included all the essential extras that any fan deserves and expects from a book about the films, including cast lists and synopses. Then there are the added extras, in this case some original production notes and, published for the first time, a script for an unmade film that was abandoned when the expected funds weren't forthcoming – more of that later.

So, before you is a personal and public journey back through the years of *Carry On.* I hope you enjoy it as much as I did. Happy reading!

Richard Webber
Minehead, January 2008

Part 1

In the Beginning

I

It was a partnership that begot the most successful series of British comedies ever, and whatever your views about the cinematic qualities of the thirty-one films crafted no one can deny the impact their offerings have had on the history of our home-grown industry: after all, here we are fifty years later still celebrating the success of *Carry On*. Books and DVDs exploring the canon continue to sell and the films still receive regular airing on terrestrial and satellite television – not a bad feat for producer Peter Rogers and director Gerald Thomas, considering it was circumstance that led to the series.

When cameras began rolling at the Queen's Barracks, Guildford for the first day's recording on the inaugural film, *Carry On Sergeant*, a wry and comical look at National Service, Rogers and Thomas – whose styles and skills complemented each other perfectly – never had the slightest inkling that they were embarking on a seemingly never-ending journey that would incorporate not just thirty-one pictures but small-screen and stage adaptations, too.

'You don't make a series, you start with one film,' states Peter Rogers, in his matter-of-fact manner. 'You don't know you're going to make more than one, and to assume any different is taking too much for granted. Luckily, *Carry On Sergeant* was very successful and the distributors requested another. I wanted to make other films, and had scripts ready, but was told: "No, give us another *Carry On*." So it just went on and on, and I reached the point where I thought: "Let's stick in our own backyard."'

It was a 'backyard' that Rogers and Thomas cultivated adroitly, creating a formula that worked time and time again. The schedules were tight, the budgets low and everyone was expeditious in carrying out their duties, and although critics frequently churned out the derogatory comment that offerings from the Rogers-Thomas stable were cheap and lowbrow, it didn't vex any member of the

Carry On production team in the slightest because cheap, cheery, laugh-a-minute comedy was what they wanted.

In Rogers and Thomas, we didn't have two green film-makers dipping their toes in the shark-infested waters of the British film industry – they were experienced individuals who brought with them a solid background in various aspects of the industry. Thomas's grounding and expertise was in film editing, a major benefit when stepping up to direct the first *Carry On* film: retaining an editor's hat while executing his directing duties meant he strived for a sharpness and tightness that would aid the editing process. Rogers's background was in scriptwriting, which proved valuable when liaising with the various writers, primarily Norman Hudis and Talbot Rothwell, who were commissioned to pen the screenplays; he was also a proficient organiser, controlling and overseeing every aspect of the film-making. 'Being a scriptwriter myself, I always worked on the scripts – it was my greatest pleasure,' recalls Rogers. 'I loved interfering with other people's scripts; I never took credit for it, but I did lots of work on them. I don't believe in putting credits everywhere. Let's face it: you've already got "A Peter Rogers Production" and "Produced by Peter Rogers" in there so you don't want another one, for God's sake. People would get fed up with it.'

Born in Gillingham, Kent, in 1914, Rogers began nurturing his writing talents from a young age. Recognising a propensity for dialogue, he wrote plays while at school, but a lack of confidence in his output prevented him revealing his work to anyone. On hanging up his school bag for the last time, he joined his father's business, valuing licensed property. But his love for writing never waned and he holed up in his bedroom, spending most evenings hunched over his typewriter, tapping out endless streams of plays. But working into the small hours finally took its toll. During the day, Rogers became ineffectual at work and his father, despite reservations about his son's fascination with writing, realised that the current situation couldn't continue. Reluctantly, Rogers senior, respecting his son's desire for a career in the arts, decided to pay Peter a small allowance to stay home and make a concerted effort to sell his plays. However, the breakthrough that Rogers junior craved eluded him. The continual flow of rejection slips caused such distress within his family that Peter's father pulled a few strings and persuaded a friend, the owner of the *Kentish Express* newspaper, to hire his son as a cub reporter.

Although quickly realising the journalist's life wasn't for him long-term, Peter knuckled down and filed his articles during the day, knowing he was free to return to his real love, writing plays, in the evening. Frustrated by the lack of success that he was experiencing, his spirits were lifted somewhat when he discovered American theatre producer Auriol Lee was visiting London to produce a play. Grasping the opportunity, Rogers mailed one of his efforts to her, and although she rejected the play she subsequently invited him to work as an assistant on her upcoming production of J. B. Priestley's *People at Sea*.

Although Rogers's working relationship with Lee was short-lived, he established a clutch of contacts which paid dividends when, aged twenty-one, he saw two of his own plays, *Human Straws* and *Mr Mercury*, staged. Having work accepted was the breakthrough he'd sought for so long; but a barren spell, artistically, followed, before Rogers received his call-up papers in 1941. Just when a period in khaki beckoned, he contracted a severe case of cerebral spinal meningitis and was hospitalised for a year, preventing him joining up.

During the war, Peter Rogers returned to writing, this time concentrating on radio. Before long he tasted success when the BBC transmitted some of his radio scripts, including *The Man Who Bounced*, *Mr South Starts A War*, *Cross Questions* and *Cards On the Table*. His experience broadened later when, as a consequence of his radio plays, he received an offer to join J. Arthur Rank's religious film company as a scriptwriter.

The unit's subsequent closure resulted in Rogers's eventual return to journalism with the trade paper *World Press News*. Responsible for the publication's film section, an assignment saw him interview British writer-producer Sydney Box, older brother of Rogers's wife-to-be, Betty. Sydney Box invited Rogers to submit ideas for his upcoming comedy drama, *Holiday Camp*, and was so impressed with his efforts that he offered him a full-time contract as screenwriter at Gainsborough Studios, based at Lime Grove. During this period Rogers's relationship with film producer Betty Box flourished and in 1948 they married.

Between 1947–57, Rogers penned myriad screenplays and contributed to other scripts, including *When the Bough Breaks, Dear Murderer, Here Come the Huggetts, To Dorothy a Son, Circus Friends* and *Time Lock*. But by the early 1950s he was running Beaconsfield Film Studios and busy producing his own films.

Between them, Peter and Betty were producing some of the most popular British films of the period, although as Rogers points out, they never discussed each other's projects. 'We were friendly rivals,' he laughs. 'For a long time, my films were on the ABC circuit, not Rank's. Often, our films were playing opposite each other in towns. If I drove down to the country to see my father, we'd drive through south London and as we were going along, Betty would say things like, "I think I've got more in my queue than yours." As the money went into the same pocket, it didn't matter much.'

Noticing that his wife's decision to work with a dedicated director, namely Ralph Thomas, proved fruitful, Rogers decided to follow suit. Having been impressed with Betty's regular editor Gerald Thomas, Rogers sought his wife's blessing to approach him, so beginning a highly profitable 40-year working relationship.

Rogers had already met Ralph Thomas's younger brother. 'We used to go around together because Betty and Ralph were often on location abroad for long periods,' recalls Rogers. 'On those occasions, Gerald, being Ralph's brother, used to take his wife out to lunch to keep her happy whilst her husband was away, and he'd nearly always invite me. One day I said: "Why don't we make a partnership like Betty and Ralph?" So we did.'

Gerald Thomas was born in Hull in 1920. After finishing his schooling in Bristol, it looked as if a medical career was on the cards until his studies to become a doctor were interrupted by the outbreak of war, which saw him join the Royal Sussex Regiment and serve in Europe and the Middle East. After the cessation of hostilities, he ditched plans to resume his medical training and targeted a career in the film industry. Obtaining his break in Denham Studios' cutting rooms with Two Cities Films, he quickly climbed the ladder and was appointed assistant editor on films such as *Hamlet*, which starred Laurence Olivier, and the Roy Ward Baker-directed *October Man*, with John Mills.

Thomas stepped up to editor in his own right with the 1948 drama *Madness of the Heart* before leaving Denham and editing *The Twenty Questions* and *Murder Mystery*, followed by a spell as associate editor on Carol Reed's much-acclaimed *The Third Man* and *Pandora and the Flying Dutchman*. A return to Pinewood saw him edit, among others, *Tony Draws a Horse, Appointment With Venus, Venetian Bird, Day to Remember, Doctor In The House, Mad About Men* and the naval epic *Above Us The Waves*, on which he also directed the second unit.

In 1953 Thomas was Hollywood-bound, travelling across the pond to edit Disney's *The Sword and The Rose*, but on returning to home shores he left the Rank Organisation to accept Peter Rogers's offer to form a partnership at Beaconsfield, cutting his director's teeth on the Children's Film Foundation drama *Circus Friends* in 1956. But, as Rogers recalls, it took a while before he was acknowledged by contemporaries in the industry as a fully fledged director. 'It was a couple of years before people accepted him. We did one or two children's films together, which he directed, but no one seemed to worry about those non-profit-making ventures. It was only when we made *Time Lock*, which I scripted and I believe cost no more than £20,000, that people realised he could direct.'

The partnership blossomed as Rogers and Thomas clocked up numerous films, including *The Vicious Circle, The Duke Wore Jeans, Chain of Events, The Solitary Child, Please Turn Over, Watch Your Stern, Raising the Wind, Nurse On Wheels* and *Twice Round The Daffodils*. But their futures were sealed when an inconspicuous film titled *Carry On Sergeant* and scripted by Norman Hudis – now based in California – met with many plaudits upon its release in 1958. The all-important title for the film was the brainchild of Anglo Amalgamated's Stuart Levy, and film and title had no relation to the Val Guest-directed comedy *Carry On Admiral*, which had been released in 1957. 'At that time, the British Film Corporation [BFC] had what they called "story rights",' explains Peter Rogers. 'You could register your story for a small fee and make sure no one else did it. George Minter, who produced *Admiral*, wanted to do another *Carry On* but the BFC wouldn't let him. They said: "No, Peter Rogers has got all the *Carry On*s."' It was unfortunate for Minter so, trying to benefit from the success of *Sergeant*, he reissued *Admiral*. 'It died a death.'

Norman Hudis, who proceeded to write the next five *Carry On* scripts before accepting a generous invitation to try his luck in the United States, got to know and respect Rogers and Thomas during his years working for them not just on the early *Carry Ons* but on, among others, *Twice Round the Daffodils* and *Nurse On Wheels*. He says: 'Professionally, Gerald Thomas was a successful film editor before outstripping that acclaim as the *Carry On* director. He prided himself on completing a film on budget and schedule, but preferably under both. Finer production-time-consuming details of staging and presentation were not allowed to interfere with these objectives.

'As a man, Gerry knew when he was deeply needed, and saw it as his chance to become rich. He took it with both hands. He protected my incredible blinkered innocence and soothed my hurts as far as he could which, of course, never trespassed on his own interests. The thrust of his life was towards what was necessary to fulfil it totally: once, urging me to hurry up a draft, he said: "We need the script fast, Norman. We're making pictures. That is why we live."'

Turning his thoughts to Peter Rogers, Hudis says: 'Professionally, as a producer, Peter took the broad view, with executive sweep. He had a practical yet imaginative flair for casting. He became ruthless, quickly, at story meetings and ended them with: "You can write anything. Go away and do it." When the script was delivered, however, he paid close and critical attention to a few points he considered key. In short, he seemed happier commenting on actual pages than in trying to shape their content in advance.

'As a man, to me, Peter was unknown. A very private person, he drew a firm and guarded frontier between studio and home – he never took business calls at the latter. Devoted to his wife Betty Box, they were the king and queen of Pinewood. Of them, it could be said, with respect: "Making films. This is why we live." Despite success as a movie producer, my belief is that Peter would have preferred to be known, fundamentally, as a writer.'

Peter Rogers, now in his 90s, still travels to his office at Pinewood daily. Even now, he's busy dealing with all things *Carry On*, including the stream of fan letters that continues to flow in, and the latest proposed *Carry On* project – *London*.

II

The original inspiration behind *Carry On Sergeant* can be traced back to the summer of 1955, three years before Norman Hudis's taut and finely tuned script finally hit the screens. Correspondence held in the Rogers-Thomas archive reveals that writer-producer Sydney Box authorised distinguished writer R. F. Delderfield to prepare an original story and screenplay on the theme of National Service. With a working title, *National Service Title*, Delderfield set to work on 22 August and anticipated submitting an outline for discussion within ten days. A 14-page outline was subsequently delivered but the idea was abandoned in September, even though Delderfield had, by this time, also written nearly 50 pages of a developed treatment.

In January 1957 Box and Delderfield's agent Felix de Wolfe were back in touch, with Box again commissioning the writer to pen another draft screenplay focusing on National Service, for which he would receive £2,000. For the first time the title *The Bull Boys* appeared in correspondence, but although the script was completed Box failed to interest a financial backer and the film was never made. The basic premise, however, interested Peter Rogers, as he explains. 'The script was hanging about for so long and nobody wanted it, so Sydney [Box] said to me: "I don't want this, can you do anything with it?" I told him I'd take a look, thinking the thing to do was make it funny.' Delderfield's idea wasn't a comedy at all – it concerned two ballet dancers torn apart by conscription. 'We moved completely away from the original idea and just did a comedy about conscription.'

In need of a writer to turn his idea into reality, Rogers approached Associated London Scripts [ALS], home of such writing luminaries as Ray Galton, Alan Simpson, Spike Milligan and Eric Sykes. While Milligan and Sykes reportedly declined the opportunity, another writer in the ALS stable, John Antrobus – suggested by ALS's secretary and general manager, Beryl Vertue – was commissioned in September 1957 to pen a script for £750. By mid-September, Vertue, an old school chum of Alan Simpson's (she has since become a distinguished producer in her own right, with credits including *Men Behaving Badly*, *Is it Legal?* and *Coupling*) sent Rogers preliminary material from Antrobus. Rogers, however, wasn't enamoured of the script when it arrived and started looking for another writer.

Before the end of March 1958, aware that Antrobus's script had to be revised, Vertue wrote to Rogers, asking to see a copy of the revised screenplay. In his rather blunt reply, Rogers stated: 'I have been unable to send you a script of this film for John to read until now because we have been rewriting a good deal. One thing that worries me is the possibility of some of the script finding its way into *The Army Game* TV programmes [Antrobus wrote two scripts for the series]. Perhaps this is an unfair thing to suggest but bearing in mind the time lag in film releases it would be very serious for us.'[1] In early discussions it was agreed that Antrobus would receive 2.5% of the profits, over and above his fees for writing the script, but Rogers felt that due to the amount of rewriting required this should be reviewed. As he pointed out: 'Quite frankly, there is not a great deal of Antrobus in the script because what he wrote was really a radio script and I want him to read the present script as much for his guidance as anything. If after reading it he still insists on the percentage we suggested as an encouragement, I will be very surprised.'[2]

Digesting the contents of Rogers's letter at the desk of her office in Cumberland House, Shepherd's Bush, Vertue soon had a reply winging its way to the producer, pointing out that she found some of his comments 'a little mystifying in that you found it necessary to remind us that John is not allowed to use any of the film script in an *Army Game* script.'[3] Vertue reassured Rogers that Antrobus was aware of his responsibilities and that copyright in the work was vested in Beaconsfield Films Limited. As for the profit percentage, on reading the revised script, Vertue confirmed that 'now that he [Antrobus] has read the script he is quite willing to review this. He leaves it entirely to you either to make the percentage smaller, or to drop it all together. He realises that you have had to do a lot of work on the script, which has probably necessitated more fees being incurred as a result.'[4]

Rogers replied on 9 April 1958, apologising for 'any lack of understanding shown in my letter ... it was not intentional.'[5] He confirmed that Gerald Thomas also felt that Antrobus's script read more like a radio script than a screenplay and offered, when he had a moment, to discuss the script in detail and show Antrobus what he meant.

Reflecting on the correspondence to-ing and fro-ing during that period, John Antrobus says: 'I suppose it was just his [Rogers's] anxiety to protect the material. He wasn't using most of it anyway.' Upon rereading his original work for *Carry On Sergeant* – his first film script – it's clear that Antrobus didn't agree with Rogers's assessment that it was more suited to radio. 'What I thought was strong in the script was the visual comedy: when the recruits arrive at the station, on the gun range – it's all visual comedy, but they didn't use any of that. But the character that Eric Barker played, with his unusual speech pattern, *was* based on what I wrote. Overall, I thought it was a pleasant script.'

Writers often look back on their first piece of work with slight embarrassment, identifying with the benefit of hindsight glaring errors and a multitude of ways in which the script could have been improved, but Antrobus regards *Sergeant* as 'a fairly good effort, really'. He adds: 'In those days, you never went to writing schools, you just got on and wrote the script.' Antrobus was able to write from experience. 'I'd been in the army doing military service, and my father was a sergeant major so I'd been brought up in an army camp. I'd done two and a half years in the army and I'd worked my way up through the ranks. Then I joined Sandhurst but left because I didn't want to kill people. But my background helped when writing the script.'

Meanwhile, the search for a writer who could deliver a script to satisfy Rogers's requirements continued and he eventually found his man, someone he'd known for years: Norman Hudis. Their paths had crossed when Hudis had been working in the Pictorial Publicity Department of the Rank Organisation, based at Islington Studios, while Rogers was scriptwriting and, subsequently, working as an associate producer. 'I took him on as a contract scriptwriter, passed him the script [Delderfield's] and said: "I think we can make this funny." I had some ideas, as I always do – I interfered with the scripts as much as possible!' says Rogers, smiling. 'I couldn't resist it, probably because I started life as a scriptwriter.'

Hudis, who was already a freelance scriptwriter when he joined the fold, recalls first meeting Rogers. 'I was a publicity man for a long time and it was in my capacity as a publicity representative that I first met Peter.' Tasked with writing a potted biography of the producer for inclusion in publicity material issued for any films he worked on, the assiduous Hudis visited Rogers's office. 'He seemed a modest, interesting young man,' recalls Hudis, who admits that he probably stayed in publicity too long. 'Perhaps because it was a beguiling occupation. It may sound arrogant, but it was easy for me. Unlike newspapermen who have to fight for their stories, everyone wanted to talk to me because they wanted publicity. It was fun mixing with journalists and movie stars. But I finally became a writer when I had one of my plays produced.

'I wrote a stage play, *Here Is The News*, which was about something I knew – being a newspaperman, which I'd been from the age of 16 before the war, followed by two years on the RAF's own *Air Force News*, based in Cairo.' It was produced by the Under Thirty Theatre Group at the Leatherhead Repertory Company, Surrey, and received 'reasonably good notices'. Earl St John, then executive producer at Rank, read them and contacted Hudis, offering him the chance to become a screenwriter. 'I didn't tell him I'd been yelling about this around Pinewood for seven years, I simply said: "Thank you very much, sir." That was how I started, although I took a pay cut from being a publicity director to get my break as a screenwriter.'

Hudis worked on various ideas for several producers without any of his efforts being filmed and, after two years, he quit and turned freelance. He finally cut his screenwriting teeth on B-features for reputable producers, including Robert S. Baker and Monty Berman. 'They were chiefly thrillers and taught me what made a screenplay and what didn't,' Hudis explains. 'It was a good apprenticeship because those films cost practically nothing and if they were flops it didn't hurt anyone; no one's career got destroyed because they went out under the shadow of a big feature.'

Hudis's first taste of working for Peter Rogers was on 1957's *The Tommy Steele Story*, spotlighting the rise to fame of the young rock'n'roller. It was distributed as a second feature to the film *After the Ball*, starring Patricia Kirkwood and Laurence Harvey, which detailed the life and career of musical artist Vesta Tilley. It didn't stay a second feature for long, as Hudis recalls: 'I'm ashamed to say that when Peter phoned and asked me to write a screenplay about Tommy Steele, I replied: "Who's he?" His rise to fame was that meteoric; in fact, he shot to the top in about three weeks, about as long as it took to make the picture! How do you write the life story of someone who's only 20 years old, I wondered. So I went to see Tommy at his house in Bermondsey and listened to his story. I wrote the script with spaces for the songs to go in, and it became a historic picture because it ran away with the public and became one of the few films to switch and become the main feature in mid-release. It cost just £20,000 and took an incredible amount of money, none of which I saw, I'm afraid, because I was on a straight fee of £250! On the strength of that, we made *The Duke Wore Jeans*, again with Tommy, which Gerald Thomas directed. After this, Peter took me under contract.'

Now on the payroll, the first assignment he was handed was to rewrite the National Service story which had been conceived by R. F. Delderfield. They kept the original premise in Delderfield's script of a man conscripted into the army on his wedding day, thereby ruining his honeymoon because he's required to report immediately. Hudis says: 'Two reels or so of the film were based on what Mr Delderfield wrote. I didn't mind because I had enormous respect for him – he was way ahead of me in terms of material success: I didn't have a play on in the West End for five years, nor had I written a best-selling novel. He's somebody about whom you don't say: "Oh, I rewrote him." It just worked out differently, that's all. I was simply fortunate enough, in the course of being a journeyman writer, to come up with a notion that worked well for the first six *Carry On*s: the notion of a group of incompetents – people who didn't know what they were doing, but whose hearts were in the right place and who came up trumps in the end.'

The incompetents-muddle-through concept wasn't scrupulously applied to all six films. 'I had no interest in or intention of getting dubious laughs out of incompetent nurses: first of all, they wouldn't last long on active duty and, second, comedy or not, the under- lying reality was that they frequently held life and death in their young hands and screwing up was no laughing matter. If I may mount a sanctimonious platform for a moment, I've never believed in laughs at any cost: such a desperate and unfeeling tactic demeans everyone involved, including the audience. Yet while the nurses weren't incompetents, they worked under the archaic discipline of the British nursing system at that time: the battleship of a matron.'

Hudis acknowledges that he was fortunate inasmuch as the majority of the topics used in his scripts were easy targets from which to mine comedy. 'They were within the general experience of the cinema-goers – especially the British; most people had been in the army during the war or subsequently, everybody had either been in hospital or knew jokes about nurses, everyone had been to school and had their perceptions of a loving teacher or headmaster – and, of course, the police force was another easy target. They were all beloved and familiar institutions, all with preconceived public images begging to be affectionately pilloried.' But the team was careful not to pillory the institutions themselves. As Peter Rogers once explained, their aim was to simply portray some of the un- conventional personalities found not just within those institutions but in every walk of life.

For *Sergeant*, the subject was National Service and it was from the tensions the characters' situation precipitated that Hudis compiled his script. 'This was an awkward platoon, and to the misfortune of the sergeant, who was coming up for retirement, he'd never had a star squad; so he takes a £50 bet with his fellow sergeants that he's going to lick the next one, his final squad, into shape. Then, what does he get? This bunch of hopeless misfits. But when they discover that he's put his rugged old heart into this, they decide to be terrific overnight and pass out as number-one platoon. It's all very sentimental.'

It was this sentimentality, coupled with Hudis's ability to blend pathos with humour, that distinguished his work on the first six films – as well as other screenplays he wrote for the Rogers-Thomas partnership. Writing comedy is complex enough, but being able to weave in moving scenes without affecting the script's general comedic tone is a skill unmastered by many. Hudis explains: 'The fusion of laughter and tears, as in real life, has always struck me as essential in storytelling which has any pretence of relevance to real life, even when said life is being lived at a farcical level.' But Hudis admits that the mix has to be carefully controlled, both in terms of content and timing. In *Twice Round the Daffodils*, written for Rogers and Thomas, he observed the lives of patients in a TB sanatorium; the cast included such familiar faces as Donald Houston, Ronald Lewis, Donald Sinden, Lance Percival, Andrew Ray and Kenneth Williams. Juxtaposing both elements of dialogue into the script works beautifully but, as Hudis points out, the timing was wrong. 'That film suffered from its unfortunate timing. We felt the comedic treatment was justified because TB was no more; in fact, five thousand people died of it in Britain in the year of the film's release, giving rise to such headlines as: "Carry On Coughing"!'

The use of pathos became a trademark of Hudis's and one appreciated by, among others, Peter Rogers. 'Norman was sentimental in heart. I said to him: "I fancy a Chaplin style of comedy." That is a laugh and a tear-jerker at the end, which he was able to write.'

Any discussions about the scripts took place in Rogers and Thomas's office at Pinewood Studios, Buckinghamshire. First meetings on a project were brief. 'We talked about the premise and fluttered around it for a little while,' recalls Hudis. 'Peter then usually said: "You can write anything. Just go away and do it."'

Norman Hudis listened and absorbed what his employers wanted before returning to his three-bedroom house on London Road, Rickmansworth, Hertfordshire. Holing himself up in his office in front of his typewriter, he lit a cigarette and set to work. 'I was a heavy smoker in those days,' admits Hudis. 'I was smoking 80 a day, to the point where it was a substitute for air! At one point, my wife Rita made curtains for the small office I had overlooking the backyard. After a few months, the time came to wash them and they fell apart! There were nicotine stains in the folds and the fabric had rotted.' Hudis always worked in silence and resented interruptions breaking his train of thought. 'It sounds pompous but when you're a professional writer it's important,' says Hudis. 'I always work in quiet, never with music. My method is to get to the desk early in the morning and start writing longhand. I sometimes make notes on my bedside nightstand or similar. Otherwise, even when inspiration isn't flowing as it usually does, I take Somerset Maugham's advice and "sit at the desk until something happens". After the longhand, I type what I've scribbled on an old Selectric II, edit with pencil and Rita transfers it all to the computer. Of course, in the days of the *Carry On*s, we didn't have such things as computers.'

When a first draft was complete, Hudis returned to Pinewood to present the script. 'Almost invariably, Peter would say: "We're very disappointed." I'd written the scripts with little guidance and would react by asking why he didn't tell me what he'd wanted? Given a brief I'd have delivered much closer to what he'd been looking for.

'Elsewhere, I've stated that this became a joke between the three of us. Well, it wasn't an uproarious one. The swing from total trust in me to total disappointment with my effort was hurtful and inexplicable – something like the Chaplin situation where Charlie has a friend who, at night, is all over him with generosity and affection but next morning scarcely acknowledges his existence. But I soon discovered that Peter was much more at ease discussing an existing script than going through the preliminary process of shaping one in discussion. Many experienced, successful and articulate men find it difficult to say what they want and arrive at that by instantly recognising what they *don't*. But once this was established, in that sunlit Pinewood office, then, as Frank Richards's old *Gem* and *Magnet* schoolboy stories used to say, "All was merry and bright."'

Whereas Gerald Thomas was happy to sit down with Hudis and work through a script, Peter Rogers preferred to study it alone, in the comfort of his home. Hudis recalls discussing the different approaches while dining at Thomas's house during the period he was writing *Carry On Again Nurse*, a film that never made it to the screen and is discussed later in this book. 'I read the script to Gerry, which he liked, and I said it was a pity I couldn't do this with Peter as well. Gerry explained that he'd never do that, he liked to go back to his house, with a coffee beside him, and work through it in his own methodical way, making notes.'

Rogers is fully aware of how Hudis felt about their script meetings. 'Norman used to say that in all his experience as a scriptwriter, he never had such short interviews as he had with me!' he says, smiling. 'But when the script arrived I'd work on it for about a week, going over the dialogue, putting in a few gags and so on. Then I'd bring it back. I thoroughly enjoyed that bit.'

Sergeant afforded Hudis the opportunity to write his first comedy, although he admits to treating scriptwriting as a business contract and, therefore, was prepared to write anything that came his way. 'Films are fundamentally a business and I'm what you'd call a "Friday-night writer". If I don't think something is absurd or beyond my reach or talent, I'll write anything that has a cheque attached to it – after all, I have to make a living. I defend my ideas and don't take lightly to harsh criticism, but what it amounts to is I'll say what I have to say vehemently, forcefully, courteously and if I'm outvoted, I turn my gift of writing to adapt to the style they want. So I felt fine when Peter offered me *Sergeant*.'

Although he'd never written comedy before, Hudis was grateful for the trust that had been put in him and produced a first treatment with development ideas, which are reproduced later in this book. With two previous scripts (by Delderfield and Antrobus respectively) filed away in Rogers's office, it was inevitable that elements would be integrated into Hudis's material; however, the lion's share of the story was original. 'There might have been a couple of things that trickled into the film,' says Hudis. 'I'm not being disingenuous, I simply don't remember the detail because it's a long time ago. I do recall, though, that the only aspect which we carried over from R. F. Delderfield's original script was Bob Monkhouse's character being called up on the day of his marriage and, deprived of his wedding-night consummation, smuggling his bride into the army camp. An example of my personal taste, and in no way a criticism of master comedy-writer Delderfield, I found this idea a little unreal when judged against the actualities of the rest of our script.' Although John Antrobus's work didn't influence Hudis's product, the script reveals the character names 'Bailey' and 'Copping' (played by Kenneth Williams and Bill Owen in the film), while 'Herbert' appears early on as an incompetent dullard who continually fails basic training, the character played by Norman Rossington.

As Hudis completed the script, attention turned to casting. Peter Rogers says: 'I didn't particularly want high-flying characters; that wouldn't have been right because they wouldn't have fitted in. They had to be part of a team, with nobody above the title – ever. The star of the film was *Carry On* – everybody came underneath it.'

The producer assembled a cast that would eventually resemble a repertory company, moving between films. Although costumes and character names changed, the inherent characteristics in their performances would remain. Two names pencilled in by Rogers were William Hartnell and George Cole; although Cole's recruitment didn't happen, Hartnell – who'll forever be remembered for playing the first *Doctor Who* – was signed up as tough-talking Sergeant Grimshawe. Playing gruff, snapping middle-ranking military men had become a speciality of Hartnell's during his long career. 'He was a well-known, thoroughly professional artist. He was ideal for the job of sergeant – nobody else could have done it better,' states Rogers, who believes Hartnell probably didn't want to be typecast and therefore wouldn't have become a regular in the team. 'We weren't to know back then, of course, but the *Carry Ons* did become something of a repertory company and I don't think William Hartnell would have wanted to be part of that.' Hartnell's granddaughter, actress and businesswoman Jessica Carney, commented in her biography of the veteran actor that Grimshawe was perhaps 'the culmination of all Bill's roles as hard NCOs.'[6]

Another veteran of stage and screen who would appear in three other *Carry Ons* was Bill Owen, who played Grimshawe's loyal Corporal Copping. The actors' interaction was seamless, which didn't surprise Rogers who had known Owen for years. Meanwhile, making his sole *Carry On* appearance – as the romantic lead – was Bob Monkhouse, whose presence in the film was at the behest of the distributors, Anglo-Amalgamated. 'That's not to say I wouldn't have had him, he was very good and played his part well,' remarks Rogers. But when other *Carry On* films were requested Rogers didn't consider using Monkhouse again. 'It was simply because I think he stuck out too much as an individual to be part of a team.'

Playing Monkhouse's new bride, Mary Sage, was Shirley Eaton, who first worked with Rogers in an uncredited role within a harem scene in the 1954 comedy *You Know What Sailors Are*. Playing alongside her in most of the scenes was Dora Bryan, making her solitary *Carry On* appearance as Nora, the dotty NAAFI cook who's besotted with feckless hypochondriac Horace Strong, adroitly portrayed by soon-to-be-regular, Kenneth Connor. If circumstances had been different Bryan might have become a regular, too: her services were requested for further instalments but a busy schedule in the theatre and family commitments rendered her unavailable.

Other actors hired for *Sergeant* who would become synonymous with *Carry On*s were Kenneth Williams and Charles Hawtrey, who both donned khaki to play recruits, and Hattie Jacques as Captain Clark, a doctor at Heathercrest National Service Depot whose patience is severely tested when Horace Strong appears on the scene. Having a female play a doctor at a National Service centre posed a few questions, which Norman Hudis resolved with a quick call to the War Office. 'Peter [Rogers] said he was going to cast her as the medical officer, so I told him I'd check on the feasibility of such a thing happening. I called the War Office's public-relations department who confirmed there was no reason why a female doctor shouldn't be the medical officer of a unit composed of men.'

The larger-than-life figure of Hattie Jacques would become an integral part of future *Carry On*s. A comely, perceptive woman, she was equally adept at portraying stern, uncompromising characters as she was at depicting those revealing a vulnerability or lack of confidence. Despite her large physique limiting the variety of roles that she was offered she forged a successful stage and screen career.

Born in Sandgate, Kent, in 1924, she trained as a hairdresser before serving with the Red Cross during the Second World War and, later, at a factory in north London. She made her acting debut at the Players' Theatre, London in 1944. Her big break, however, was on radio, as part of the team behind the highly successful and popular series *ITMA*, followed by long associations with equally popular radio series such as *Hancock's Half-Hour* and *Educating Archie*. By the time she appeared as Captain Clark in *Sergeant* she had already clocked up several big-screen credits. Her polished performance as the no-nonsense medical officer met with approval from writer Norman Hudis. 'She played it very sympathetically and sweetly.'

Such was Jacques's standard of performance, as well as that of those of Williams, Connor and Hawtrey, that when Hudis was commissioned to write the next *Carry On* script Peter Rogers asked him to write specifically for these particular actors because he was determined to form a team, bringing back a nucleus of familiar faces each time he was asked to make a film in this vein. The *Sergeant* actors and those who established themselves in subsequent films, including Joan Sims, Peter Butterworth, Bernard Bresslaw, Barbara Windsor and Sid James, interplayed beautifully, with such sparkle and precision; they cultivated a team spirit which emanated from each production.

Peter Rogers enjoyed working with his rep company. 'I have happy memories of them all – they were very nice people and I was pleased to be with them; Gerald and I couldn't have been luckier. I was with them all the time because I had a little portable office on the set; wherever they were shooting, I was there. I could always see what was going on.' Of those appearing in the inaugural film who would become mainstays of future films, Kenneth Connor was regarded as a 'very funny man' by Rogers, who regularly saw him perform alongside Ted Ray in his radio show *Ray's A Laugh*, a domestic comedy which ran between 1949–61. 'He brought to the films whatever the script called for; he always made a lot out of his role.'

It was a sublime piece of casting which saw Connor playing Horace Strong, a character who was mortified to be passed fit for National Service. The role set the tone for the diminutive actor's *Carry On* career, and if ever someone was required to play a dithering, nervous, angst-ridden character Connor was usually the man for the job, portraying such characters with aplomb.

Born in London in 1918, Connor was appearing regularly on stage by the age of eleven, performing in various revue shows with his brother. Realising acting was the life for him, he trained at the Central School of Drama and undertook his first professional job at His Majesty's Theatre, London in 1936. He gained valuable experience in repertory theatre before the outbreak of war saw him serve with the army's Middlesex Regiment and for a period enjoy an attachment to George Black's company, 'Stars in Battledress'.

Returning to civvy street, he soon became a regular on stage, screen and radio, forming a long-standing relationship with Ted Ray. So when he joined the *Carry On* cast this rock-solid professional brought a wealth of experience. Considering the actor's merits, Norman Hudis recalls Connor as 'the most balanced, warm and gentle actor' he ever met. He adds: 'Yet, that terrible insecurity of the breed: I was in the office alone, at Pinewood, when I'd returned to the UK to write the script for *Carry On Again Nurse*. He'd read that I was writing the script and asked, with a humility which stabbed me through the heart: "Will there be a part for me?" He was a fully rounded, instinctive, thoughtful comedian and a warm, wholesome human being.'

Kenneth Williams, meanwhile, was the complete antithesis of the more reserved Kenneth Connor. Nostril-flaring and highly expressive mannerisms combined with an extensive repertoire of funny voices were tools that the outrageous Williams exploited during his 20-year association with the films. Initially, Williams was employed for supercilious roles, such as the recalcitrant James Bailey in *Sergeant* and the studious bookworm Oliver Reckitt in *Nurse*, but as the years passed his characters, while retaining an air of arrogance and vaingloriousness, became more laughable and asinine.

Riddled with uncertainty over his own identity and sexuality, Kenneth Williams was a complex and contradictory man. His qualities as a performer, however, were unique. Early in his life, he made decisions about how he would present himself to the outside world, only discovering the consequences of his choices later. Often regarded as a forlorn character, he guarded his private life intensely, choosing not to form intimate relationships, believing he couldn't provide the vulnerability required. But as the years passed he became trapped by his choice, and however much he longed for intimacy and companionship the chance to attain it had gone.

Born in London in 1926, son of a barber, Kenneth Williams left school at 14 and was accepted for training as a litho draughtsman at Bolt Court, the School of Lithography, in London's Fleet Street. While he studied during the day, his evenings were spent performing in amateur dramatics with the Tavistock Repertory Theatre. By the time of his conscription into the army he was apprenticed to a cartographer, a line of work he continued in the forces by compiling maps for the Royal Engineers before he transferred to Combined Services Entertainment where he performed a double act with Stanley Baxter, touring the Far East.

After the war Williams returned to civvy street and resumed his career as a draughtsman until he decided his future lay not in front of a drawing board but on stage. Pursuing his dream, he joined a rep company in Newquay, marking the beginning of a successful career in all the media of the time. Sadly, however, work opportunities tailed off towards the end of his life and he found himself restricted largely to guest appearances on television. Later in life Williams developed a serious ulcer and was prescribed medication to fight the pain, but on 15 April 1988 he was found dead in his London flat after overdosing on barbiturates. He was 62. Debate still rages over whether or not Williams committed suicide, a line of speculation fuelled by the publication of his diaries in which there are references to suicide and claims that, having nothing to live for, he longed for death.

Norman Hudis doesn't believe that Williams took his own life, 'except in the sense that his self-destruction probably began the day he was born.' Reflecting on his association with Williams via the *Carry Ons*, he says: 'Ken irritated me with his tormented self-hate over his fastidious homosexuality and, more annoyingly still, his calling as an actor. Ignoring the tangled psychology behind his stance, I can only urge such self-tormentors: if acting is irredeemably trivial, impermanent, reprehensible and all things insignificant, save yourself the postured angst and don't bloody well do it.' Hudis regarded Williams as a 'tragic figure', adding: 'He existed in the darkness of his constant negative and frequently contradictory impression of himself:

gay but ashamed of it and repelled by physical contact; dismissive of his comedic gift and wishing he could switch to straight acting; yet, essentially, contemptuous of that activity, too, as fundamentally false. He felt superior to almost everyone, yet found no serenity in his patently broad-based intellect. He made some extravagant comments, such as that the *Carry On*s were stupid, and that he wouldn't do this or that, although in most cases he did them in the end. Maybe it was to accentuate his importance; but he was vital to all of us and could have done a great deal more with his life and career. It was a shame that such a talent should end up doing talk shows.'

All the actors who became *Carry On* regulars possessed unique foibles and idiosyncrasies, but Williams was, arguably, the most outrageous and capricious: one minute he could immerse himself in a conversation about abstruse topics, the next he'd be acting like a naughty schoolboy, spouting comments wrapped in acerbity or griping about something of which he didn't approve. His at times bizarre behaviour was witnessed by Donald Toms, who was employed as unit manager on *Cabby, Jack, Spying* and *Cleo*. While making *Cleo* Toms was walking along a corridor at Pinewood with production manager Frank Bevis when he spotted Williams walking towards him. 'Kenneth was dressed in a toga and as he approached, he lifted it up. He had nothing on underneath, and showed what he hadn't got, saying: "What about that, fellas, don't you wish you had one like that?" Frank replied: "No, if I had one like that I'd cover it up." The office girls around couldn't believe what they were seeing. He was such a character,' says Toms, smiling.

Another member of the production team who recalled an encounter with the demonstrative Williams was the late Nora Rodway, who assisted her husband, make-up designer Geoffrey Rodway, on many *Carry On*s. She explained how Williams became her favourite among all the people she worked with. 'He was completely different in real life from all the overacting and false voices that, of course, made him so funny. Frequently his wit could be cruel and he was aware of this and bitterly regretted it – but he was always extremely funny.

'I was so afraid of doing something idiotic, I didn't want anyone to know I was Geoff's wife. Of course, they quickly found out.' Nora's nerves weren't helped when she discovered she had to make up Kenneth Williams, and it wasn't long before she became a victim of the free-tongued performer. The first film Nora Rodway worked on was *Don't Lose Your Head* and she tried her utmost to keep a low profile. 'On the second day, he [Williams] was late returning to the set after lunch. The actors in the next shot were supposed to have their make-up checked after lunch, but he didn't come, so after all the others had been I went down on the set hoping to "do" him there, but he wasn't around; when he did arrive the second assistant said: "Mr Williams, you're holding us all up and I don't believe you have been to have your make-up checked." Kenneth replied: "Well, I did go up to the make-up room but both their doors were locked because they were having it off as they do every lunchtime." Now, you may not believe this but at 47 I was still learning the facts of life – well, the slang version. I didn't know what "having it off" meant so I turned to Geoff and asked, "What does he mean, having it off?" Lots of people heard and I could detect stifled laughter. Geoff said very quietly, "Well, what do you think it means? If Kenneth says anything it's bound to mean only one thing." I made it all much worse and more amusing for everyone by going bright red and saying to them all, "We weren't doing anything of the kind, I swear we weren't."'

Gerald Thomas, seeing the embarrassment Nora Rodway was enduring, strolled over and, patting her hand, apologised on Williams's behalf before turning to the mischief-making actor and delivering a few sharp words. Realising the discomfort he'd caused Nora, Williams later apologised. 'Just before he left that evening, he came to the make-up room, shut the door and said, in his real voice: "I'm deeply sorry, I can't imagine what made me say it – well, I can because I'm afraid I'll do anything for the sake of getting a laugh. It's all I know how to do." We became friends from that minute.'

Despite Williams's obvious eccentricities, Peter Rogers didn't regard him as an overly complicated individual. 'He might have been a complex character to himself but not to me. As far as I'm concerned, he was a natural person and I got on well with him. He'd come to dinner on occasions and I regarded him as a very serious, erudite person.' Williams's diaries, when published, caused a stir among the industry but Rogers admits he's never read them. 'I've been told about them, and what he got up to when he wrote them, I don't know, because things he wrote about me were quite untrue. I think Kenneth's problem was that he saw himself as a serious theatre actor and mixed with such people; I think they used to say to him: "What on earth are you doing those bloody awful films for?" I think it used to worry him. But he always returned and used to say how much he loved them.'

Rogers, however, was aware of Williams's antics and recalls an occasion he had to go searching for the absent actor. 'He was a lovely show-off. One day, he fell off a rostrum on the stage between two flats and said he'd grazed his penis. So he went along to the medical department and was gone a while. I said to my director [Gerald Thomas] that I'd better go and see what was the matter with him. And there he was, stretched out on the bed, and this extraordinary nurse – I wouldn't say she was a pin-up by any means – was smearing some cream on his penis while Kenneth was almost half asleep, thoroughly enjoying it. So I told him that was enough and he came back, giggling and laughing.'

Usually cast in effeminate roles, bespectacled Charles Hawtrey was a veteran of stage and screen by the time he joined the fold. 'He was a wonderful character, although a bit of a loner and inclined to raise the elbow!' admits Rogers, grinning. 'But, again, he played his part and when you watch the films you wouldn't have known. Sometimes, though, we had to pour black coffee in him or stand him between two people. He was a bit of a lonely character and we noticed that when he had a boyfriend with him he didn't drink. You must remember, these artists had to get to the studios for about seven for make-up, hairdressing and all sorts of things; it was a hell of a long day – and a lonely one, at times.'

One of the most popular *Carry On* faces among fans and critics, Hawtrey's initial appearance on screen was often enough to induce anticipatory laughter and smiles. He once remarked: 'In a way it's terrible. Often my first line of dialogue, funny though it may be, is completely lost. On the other hand, it's nice to be able to make people laugh so I can't really complain.'[7]

Spotting the impact of Hawtrey's entrance early on, director Gerald Thomas exploited it thereafter. He explained in 1966: 'In the beginning, Charles's shock entrance was an accident, but realising the potential I set out deliberately to shock and now his first appearance is carefully planned – it has been for the last ten pictures. Apart from the comedy value of the unlikely role he plays, I'm careful to arrange the right timing for his actual appearance, so that the two factors combined surprise the audience into instant risibility.'[8]

Hawtrey was born in Middlesex in 1914; he entered the entertainment world as a boy, making recordings for Columbia and Regal Gramophone Records. He made his stage debut aged eleven before training at the Italia Conti School. By the age of 18 he was performing in the musical *Marry Me* and had even started producing plays before embarking on his film career in the 1930s with parts in *Good Morning, Boys* and various other Will Hay films, including *The Ghost of St Michael's* and *The Goose Steps Out*. Other early film credits included *You're Only Young Once* and *A Canterbury Tale*. Forays into other media saw him working with Patricia Hayes in many radio plays for BBC's *Children's Hour* and, like Norman Rossington, William Hartnell and, of course, Bernard Bresslaw, subsequently appearing in *The Army Game* in 1957.

'It seemed to me that everything positive in his life went into his instinct as a comedian,' suggests Norman Hudis. 'The drinking and other things were simply tragic. He wasn't the most pleasant of human beings, but he was very professional in his work and always thought carefully about what he did. He was a fine comedian but had a colossal ego.' It was this that so very nearly ended his *Carry On* career, when *Cruising* came along.

Actor Peter Byrne – who appeared with Hawtrey in *Cabby* and later directed the actor's last pantomime in Swindon during Christmas 1979 – experienced first-hand the effect that alcohol had on the actor's life. 'He was very uncooperative and caused all sorts of problems, including exposing himself in the street to a WPC. I said: "Charlie, for Christ's sake, if you must expose yourself please do it in front of a civilian, not a policewoman!"' Byrne witnessed Hawtrey's sad decline. 'He wasn't a well man and was hitting the bottle. He refused to do very much in the pantomime. The leading man, Spencer K. Gibbons, had just won the *New Faces* competition; on the first day of rehearsals he tried introducing himself to Charlie. It was 11 a.m. and already Charlie was lying around drinking a bottle of brandy.' Gibbons received a waspish response. 'He said: "I understand you're one of these new mohair-type comedians – fuck off!" That was the end of the conversation. He didn't endear himself to people, which saddened me because I'd always admired him.

'There were certain films in which he was jolly good, but if you analyse it they had the minimum of dialogue and you tended to laugh *at* him rather than *with* him, whereas in the past, when he was younger, some of his roles were aggressive, streetwise characters, which he played extremely well.' Byrne acknowledges Hawtrey as a lonely man who, perhaps, used the profession as a comfort blanket. 'There is one great thing I like about our profession – it's a classless society. So long as you deliver the goods, that's it. A lot of lonely people tend to seek refuge in the profession, I think.' Byrne was accused of making excuses for Hawtrey's problems. 'Some of the cast would stick pins in effigies of poor old Charlie. I know they thought I was being easy on him, but I felt desperately sorry to see such great talent being frittered away.'

As well as assembling the cast for *Sergeant*, Peter Rogers and Gerald Thomas set about forming a production team, many of whom would forge long relationships with the producer and director, including hairdresser Stella Rivers – who would clock up 20 *Carry Ons* – Nora Rodway's husband, Geoffrey, who was in charge of make-up on 23 of them and 34-year-old Alan Hume who would work on 20, the first four as camera operator, then as director of photography. Putney-born Hume left school and followed in his father's footsteps by joining the London Underground but, quickly realising that he disliked the job, he secured a position as a clapper boy at Denham Studios in the early 1940s.

While serving with the Fleet Air Arm during the war, Alan Hume worked as a photographer until he returned to Denham after demob. Rather than slot back into his former role as a clapper boy he became a camera assistant until he grasped an opportunity to train as a camera operator. His career soon blossomed and he has since worked on over one hundred films, including three James Bond movies.

Hume had already worked with Gerald Thomas on other projects when he was invited to join the *Sergeant* team. He recalls: 'I worked for Gerald and Peter for ten years without a contract; if they didn't have a movie on, I'd go off and do other things and return when they did their next film. I was very fortunate because they asked me to do every picture they made.'

The War Office allowed the filming of exterior scenes at the Queen's Barracks, Guildford and the cameras began rolling on 24 March 1958, beginning with interior shots at Pinewood. The final scenes were in the can by early May, a whirlwind turnaround which became one of the *Carry On* trade marks. Equally surprising was that the film's final cost was just under £78,000, a modest sum even in the 1950s, again setting the tone for future productions. Even the pre-production meeting on Thursday, 20 March 1958 opened with the chairman stressing that 'this [*Sergeant*] was a low-budget production.'9 Gerald Thomas reiterated the chairman's comment, explaining that it translated to, on average, three minutes' screen time being completed each day; as Roy Goddard, then assistant production manager, added, it afforded everyone the chance to show that films could be made on low budgets, for which the *Carry On*s became known. Concerning the cost, Rogers states: 'We couldn't have spent more on the budget if we tried; some people could have but I didn't see the point in spending money unnecessarily. You might as well say: "All right, we won't spend £5,000 on an artist, we'll spend £50,000." What's the point? What are you doing it for? If you want to go mad and spend more than the budget, that isn't very good film-making to my mind.'

Of course, stories of how the cast were, arguably, poorly paid have become folklore, but as Peter Rogers says, the actors were, at one point, offered a potentially bigger slice of the pie. 'In order to keep budgets low, after about the fourth film I offered everyone the chance to participate in the profits of the film, while pegging their salaries, but they all turned it down – or their agents did.' The only person, according to Rogers, who admitted they'd made a mistake in not accepting the offer was Kenneth Williams. 'The agents wanted guaranteed money. In hindsight, they would probably have realised it was a big mistake.'

Whenever one of the chief *Carry On* performers has published their memoirs, invariably the subject of fees has arisen. Joan Sims, in her autobiography, set the tone by stating that pay 'was a constant bugbear for all the actors.'[10] She wrote: 'The concept of inflation simply didn't register as far as our paymasters were concerned, and the fact that most of the technicians were earning more than we were did not make us any less restive. Moaning to Peter Rogers never got us anywhere.'[11] Regarding the proposed profit-sharing, Sims remarked: 'I never heard any of the actors talk of that proposed profit-sharing venture, and my agent Peter Eade would certainly have told me had any such proposition been made to him with regard to me. If it was, I knew nothing of it.'[12]

But Kenneth Williams was, arguably, a lone voice when he defended the pay structure in an interview with *Film Review*. He acknowledged how he liked the 'economic independence engendered by belonging to the *Carry On* team.'[13] Williams took comfort from the fact that he didn't have to accept purely for the money a part in a play that would be professionally unfulfilling or thankless hard work. He added: 'I shall always be grateful to Peter Rogers for letting me conduct my career without being rushed into anything. That's why I get angry when I hear people say that the *Carry On* cast should have some share in the vast profits from the films. I say: "Why the hell should they?" The man who makes the initial investment in a film and takes that kind of risk deserves everything he makes. You still get paid if it makes nothing.'[14]

Top of the wages bill for *Sergeant* was William Hartnell who earned £2,000, followed closely by Bob Monkhouse on £1,500 and Kenneth Connor on £1,250. Other soon-to-be-regulars Charles Hawtrey and Kenneth Williams were paid £1,000 and £900 respectively, with Hattie Jacques pocketing £150 for her cameo as the medical officer. Although as the films matured into a series, actors like Frankie Howerd were paid £9,000 for *Up the Jungle* and Phil Silvers £30,000 for *Follow That Camel*, the ceiling for the actors such as Williams and James was £5,000 and for the actresses £3,000. But while those affected bemoaned the financial aspects of being a

Carry On performer, the consolation was that anyone becoming a mainstay of the team could enjoy the prospect of two films a year, which the Rogers-Thomas stable churned out when it became an established product. And, let's face it, the actors weren't press-ganged into accepting the roles: if they felt the fee was insufficient they could have declined the offer. Another reason – a vitally important one – why the regulars continued to sign their names on the dotted lines was the camaraderie and family atmosphere engendered by the cast and crew alike. Joan Sims describes the joy of the team when they assembled back at Pinewood for the next film. 'Gathering at the studios for each new picture was like going back to school after the hoildays – meeting old chums and sharing all the jokes and gossip. We knew we had a few weeks of fun ahead of us.'[15]

The day after the first scenes of *Sergeant* were shot Peter Rogers received a letter from John Nicholls, Secretary of the British Board of Film Censors [BBFC] between 1956 and 1958. Formerly a member of the Foreign Office's Cultural Section, he'd read the script and drew Rogers's attention to some minor points that he wanted addressed, which he felt were 'rather much for the "U" category'.[16] Alterations requested included omitting references to 'rape', the phrase 'the nuptials', the line 'Man does not live by sausage rolls alone' and references to 'looking pregnant' and 'having been mucked about'. Rogers reported to Stuart Levy, chairman of Anglo-Amalgamated Film Distributors, in a letter dated 31 March 1958 that he'd made all the corrections bar two, including the line 'heap of chits' which had already been shot and, in Rogers's view, was 'quite inoffensive'.[17] 'We always had to be careful as far as censorship was concerned,' admits Rogers. 'The censor's idea was that if a family went to the cinema and the father was too embarrassed to tell his little boy what he was laughing at, there was something wrong; that was the yardstick the censor used. Nowadays, boys seem to know more than the fathers!

'Even for an "A" certificate we had to be careful. The bit in *Carry On Camping* where Barbara Windsor's bikini top flies off is a well-remembered scene. We used a fishing rod and line to tug it at the right moment, but you never saw her bare bosoms.' By 3 April, though, the BBFC confirmed that they were happy to wait until viewing the film before making a final decision on the 'heap of chits' line but stressed, again, that use of the word 'rape' was unacceptable in a 'U' film. Left with no alternative, the film-makers deleted the offending sequence from the picture.

While such matters were being resolved away from the set, Hawtrey, Williams, Connor and the other actors playing reluctant soldiers called up for National Service were being drilled on the parade ground by a real-life sergeant major. For six hours he barked his orders while knocking the actors into shape so that they would look effective in the film: after all, they had to appear realistic because the concluding scenes saw Able Platoon, under the command of retiring Sergeant Grimshawe, achieve the most remarkable transformation into star performers, providing their gruff-voiced sergeant with the perfect send-off as he waves goodbye to Heathercrest National Service Depot. Cameraman Alan Hume recalls watching everyone doing their square-bashing and coming increasingly to resemble soldiers as the days passed. 'To start with, trying to gear the shot was almost impossible because they couldn't march in step, couldn't about-turn, couldn't do this or that. But they responded as actors. I could sense they were enjoying doing it and trying to be good at it. When they marched as a platoon at the end, they were really very good.'

With early scenes in the can, Peter Rogers thought he'd let Nat Cohen and Stuart Levy, chiefs of Anglo-Amalgamated in London, view the rushes. What he wasn't expecting, however, was their reaction. 'They said: "I don't know what you are doing, but this is not at all funny." Undaunted, I replied: "Don't worry, I won't show you any more rushes – wait until it's finished." And that was what I did: they waited until the end, then agreed it *was* funny!' Whereas green producers and directors might have taken umbrage at such a negative response, or even decided to consider reshooting the scenes, Rogers had confidence in his judgement and what he was doing. 'They didn't, of course, because they hadn't been in production and didn't know what rushes were all about.'

With the final scenes complete, a private viewing of the film was arranged at Pinewood Studios, attended by many who'd worked on the picture, as well as staff at the studio. It was standing room only as the lights dimmed and the first few black and white scenes of what would, unknowingly, kick-off the legendary film series flickered on the screen. Many of Rogers's contemporaries in the industry didn't conceal their disdain for the team's efforts, especially as it was made at Pinewood, arguably the industry's most prestigious studio and where many lavish, expensive blockbusters and masterpieces had been created. Here, though, was an unassuming little black and white picture with a modest, albeit talented, cast in a project costing less than £100,000. Rogers was aware how people regarded his films – and it didn't end with *Sergeant*. 'First of all, with *Sergeant*, they were looked upon as a load of rubbish; people frowned upon our low-budget pictures. They thought: "My God, what's happening here? Fancy letting a picture like that into Pinewood on that budget." I remember one of the technicians coming onto the floor one day and saying to the continuity girl: "You're lumbered working here!" So I made sure when we made the next *Carry On* that he was on the film, and he stayed with us after that. But that's how people viewed them, even though on *Sergeant* we had Alex Vetchinsky, one of the finest art directors in the country. I always made sure we had the best technicians, which is the secret: don't skimp on technicians, have the best, and we did.' But when Rogers and Thomas eventually showed the film to, among others, heads of department at Pinewood, it was a 'riot'. Rogers adds: 'After that, they thought we were wonderful.'

It was August before finishing touches had been applied and *Sergeant* was released. Response from the press and industry journals was mixed, which would become the norm. A reviewer in the *Monthly Film Bulletin* pinpointed William Hartnell and Dora Bryan – as Nora, the eccentric love-lorn cook at Heathercrest's NAAFI – for praise, saying their professional skill 'lends some reality and humour to this conventional farce, in which all the characters come from stock.'[18] The reviewer classed the film as a 'traditionally English mixture of old farcical situations, well-worn jokes and comic post-card characters.'[19] While in the review Hawtrey and Williams were also singled out for providing genuine laughs, the rest of the humour was deemed 'either overdone or half-baked.'[20] A critic at *The Daily Cinema*, meanwhile, was more upbeat about the film's prospects, saying it was 'on parade for lots of laughs in a Service farce the way we like 'em. Cannot fail to hit the bull's-eye in popular houses.'[21] While it was felt that the 'picked cast of British comedy favourites make the most of their opportunities'[22] Hawtrey and Williams were highlighted again as making the grade. Fellow trade publication *Kinematograph Weekly* dubbed the film a 'bright and breezy Service extravaganza'[23] with the gags 'shrewdly varied and interleaved by romance'.[24] And the journalist at *Variety* who was given the task of assessing *Sergeant* classed it a 'modest, unimportant film'[25] but one that for at least '75% of its way will have ordinary family audiences in a cheerful state.'[26] He predicted that it would 'make a cash-killing in the British sticks and probably die almost everywhere else.'[27] How wrong he was, because not only was it a hit with audiences in the provinces, its success spread throughout the UK as it became one of the three top-grossing films at the box office for 1958.

Commercial mainstream newspapers were mixed in their assessments, too, with Hollis Alpert in *Saturday Review* terming it 'not terribly funny'[28] and Campbell Dixon at the *Daily Telegraph* classing William Hartnell a 'sad human being lost in a charade'[29] while the rest of the cast were 'stock figures speaking lines rising from the smutty to the banal.'[30] But the *Observer*'s Penelope Houston believed it was 'commendably brisk and played with great determination'.[31] A journalist at the Sunday tabloid *News of the World* rated it his favourite release of the week, believing that 'every old sweat and every young sweat doing his Service will revel in it.'[32] Unlike Dixon at the *Telegraph*, many critics didn't fail to mention in their review of *Sergeant* the quality and assurance that William Hartnell brought to the production via his portrayal of the old-time sergeant who bellows, with some asperity, his commands until he adroitly tries a new tack. As Ernest Betts reflected in *The People*, 'our old friend Billy Hartnell'[33] while playing Sergeant Grimshawe was 'looking more than ever like the real thing'.[34]

Viewing the film today, half a century since it first hit the big screen, it is clear that *Sergeant* has aged well, unlike so many other films from the same period. The warmth and subtle humour which emanates from Norman Hudis's script, combined with fine performances and slick production, help retain the film's accessibility; watching it now is just as entertaining as it was for the millions who crammed into cinemas up and down the country back in 1958. Perhaps this is because it was the first film, but in any case it's a delightful picture that has a vitality and cosiness that endures to this day. The final assessment, perhaps, should be reserved for the scriptwriter himself. Hudis says: '*Sergeant* was, for me, burdened by an inescapable age gap which bothered no one else. The conscripts in this National Service story, as cast, and, to a man, seasoned comedians, were demonstrably too old to be summoned to the colours. Fortunately, the characterisations I gave them (Kenneth Connor's hypochondria; Terence Longdon's easy, aristocratic charm; Kenneth Williams's intellectual loftiness; Charles Hawtrey's indestructible feyness; Norman Rossington's amiable acceptance of his fate, etc.) were vivid and entertaining enough to overcome this unreality. But, overall, I regard it as a lovely film and I'm glad the sentiment worked at the end of a lot of rough comedy. I thought William Hartnell was clever: I didn't give him a line at the end, when the guys give him the cigarette lighter. I thought an actor might ask for one but he didn't. I think he realised that a man of that type, when it came to sentiment, was inarticulate. If people like that let themselves go, they lose the authority they must have when dealing with recruits.'

Considering the success of *Sergeant*, it's hardly surprising that the distributors were chomping at the bit for another film in the same mould.

III

When deciding on the subject matter for the next film – and most of Peter Rogers's ideas came to him while in the bath – thoughts turned towards the medical profession. In June 1956 Sydney Box's Anglo-American Associates Limited had acquired film rights in a play, *Ring for Catty*, written by Patrick Cargill and Jack Beale, for £1,000 and a percentage of the producer's gross. Box wasn't the first to show interest in the play: prior to its initial stage production at the Lyric Theatre the Boulting brothers had considered it as a vehicle for Richard Attenborough but nothing had materialised. Rogers's

plans to adapt the play for the big screen lay dormant for nearly
two years before he turned his attention to a follow-up for *Sergeant*,
by which time he'd registered provisional titles – *Carry On Nurse*,
Nurse and *Ring for Nurse* – with the British Film Producers' Association, in May 1958. When Rogers told Nat Cohen about the *Catty*
acquisition, Cohen was far from chuffed, as Rogers recalls. 'He said:
"That's a terrible play." I told him it didn't matter because we'd
make it funny. And we turned it into *Carry On Nurse*. In fact, from
Patrick Cargill and Jack Beale's play we made two films because we
did *Twice Round the Daffodils*, too.'

Norman Hudis was assigned the task of completing a screenplay.
Recalling settling down in his office to create the second *Carry On*,
he's quick to point out: 'There was no similarity between *Ring for
Catty* and *Carry On Nurse*, other than both stories centring on
nurses. My *Nurse* was an historic blockbuster, *Daffodils* a sad flop
– in no way Cargill's fault, though. I think the reason it failed was
because we were under the impression that tuberculosis had been
conquered but, in fact, people were still dying of it in the UK. The
Great God Freelance decreed that I should spend a good deal of
my time writing scripts about the medical profession – *Carry On
Nurse, Nurse On Wheels* and *Twice Round the Daffodils* in the UK,
and, in Hollywood, a dozen or so episodes for TV's *Marcus Welby
MD*. In addition, I had the inestimable great fortune to marry a
nurse who is so absorbed in her dedicated profession that, years
after retirement, she was technical adviser on the *M.A.S.H.* series.'

Recalling the moment he was asked to write *Nurse*, Hudis says:
'All I remember is Peter telling me that everyone wanted another
Carry On, fast. He said: "Your wife is a nurse, why don't you have
a word with her? She'll tell you some funny things. Go to it with
Carry On Nurse."'

So, with a medical comedy to write, Hudis did, in fact, turn to
his wife Rita for situations that he could exploit in his script. 'I had
nothing in my head and most of the practical incidents I wrote up
and exaggerated were from her experience as a student nurse.' He
beavered away on the script and when he required an additional
incident or a little inspiration, he'd call his wife from his office: 'I'd
shout: "I'm stuck, tell me something else that happened."'

However, Hudis was soon able to draw upon his own experience of hospital life when he was rushed to the Peace Memorial Hospital, Watford, with appendicitis. 'I started writing the script with certain sentimental attitudes; suddenly I got this pain and was taken to hospital – so I got free research at the cost of a bit of pain. The ten days in hospital meant I saw what it was all about with my own eyes.'

Rita Hudis was instrumental in the script's authenticity: although incidents and experiences were exaggerated for comic effect most of them could have occurred for real. 'Nearly all the scenes and attitudes were correct for nursing at that time,' admits Rita. 'And most actually happened to me, friends or contemporaries during our training.'

However, two scenes in particular failed to make it onto the screen. The first was omitted because Peter Rogers didn't believe in it, even though it was another true-life event that befell Rita and her colleagues. 'We were supposed to be back in the dorm area before midnight,' she recalls, smiling. 'A friend of mine went to a party and had a lot to drink. She came back late and the only way into the hospital was through a window in the locked morgue. But she fell asleep on one of the gurneys and scared the life out of a technician when he entered the morgue the next morning and she sat up with a start!'

'I think the scene was judged too gruesome,' adds Norman Hudis, 'or maybe those judging it simply didn't believe it. For me, it was a classic and salutary example of the truth being far better – and funnier – than the fiction, while acknowledging that each, in its own way, was incredible.'

The second sequence that didn't get beyond script-editing saw Hudis exploring a moment of sadness in a hospitalised patient's life: the patient's relationship with his partner is faltering, but it is hoped that if there is one consolation for his illness, it is that it will bring the couple closer again. 'Peter and Gerald felt they might need more material so I thought some of the reality of hospital life wouldn't be out of place. When I started on the script, I began in very sentimental terms. I had to write a comedy but invented a lonely character in the ward who's visited by a hospital visitor, the kind of person who picks out people who don't have relatives to visit them; I looked at the whole question of who gets more out of that: the visitor or the person visiting? The scene was much too serious and was dropped with my complete agreement,' says Hudis. 'I thought, initially, that it would be a nice contrast to the comedy, but Peter said: "Forget it, make them laugh."'

The scene which replaced it is set in the operating theatre. Jack Bell is annoyed when his bunion operation is delayed, scuppering plans for a dirty weekend away with his girlfriend, who happens to smuggle some champagne into the hospital. Bell decides to drown his sorrows in alcohol with the other patients, but when Oliver Reckitt (Kenneth Williams) mentions he is reading a book about practical surgery a tipsy Bell asks an equally tipsy Reckitt to operate on his bunion.

It was the film's one big comedy sequence and got plenty of laughs from audiences. Although he appreciates the humour in the operating-theatre shenanigans, Hudis regards it as an 'absurd scene that didn't work.' The operating scene couldn't have happened. But no one objected, not even the 200 delighted off-duty nurses who packed the balcony at the press show. He explains: 'As a technical comedy assignment, I enjoyed writing it up; it also worked very well, so what's my reservation? It was unreal. A great pity because all other incidents were based on actual nursing possibility. And one, the skirmish with Matron about patients not being allowed to lie atop the bedclothes, was an elaboration of an incident from my stay in hospital, though I wasn't as fluent and effective in my spluttering objections as the cutting and defiant lines I gave Ken Williams.'

For some inexplicable reason, one line that received more than its fair share of laughs was 'sew a button on it', uttered by Reckitt while playing the surgeon under the influence of laughing gas. 'I stole this from Mr Cohen, part-owner of the tailoring factory where my father was production manager,' confesses Hudis. 'Faced with any problem, the unflappable Mr Cohen uttered this line immediately, and only then went on to a practical solution.'

With Rogers and Thomas wanting Hudis to write the script as quickly as possible, he set to work, delivering the first draft of the screenplay on 18 June 1958. It had taken ten days to write. Set in Haven Hospital, *Nurse* centred on life in the men's surgical ward and the interplay between patients, staff and hospital visitors. Among those warming the beds were Oliver Reckitt, a bookworm studying nuclear physics; the combative boxer, Bernie Bishop; snobbish Henry Bray; eccentric music-lover Humphrey Hinton; amiable flirt Jack Bell and mild-mannered journalist Ted York. Played by Terence Longdon, who notched up four *Carry On* appearances, York was loosely based on Hudis inasmuch as the character was a journalist and while hospitalised was carrying out research, in this case for newspaper articles rather than, as in Hudis's case, a screenplay. 'In comedy, I like to have a focal point, a purpose. A series of brilliant gags is fine but in the best comedy there is always a point to things, and Ted York provided that.' But Hudis suggests that it was a peripheral element, with the journalistic content limited to one brief expository scene involving Ted York and his editor.

A memorable scene saw boxer Bernie Bishop (played by Kenneth Connor) visited – and slapped – by his son Jeremy, played by Connor's real-life son. 'With my stage mum, I had come to collect my father from hospital,' recalled Jeremy Connor. 'He has his arm in a sling and says: "Jeremy, have you got something for me?" He goes to me as if I'm going to give him a kiss and I give him a left hook. We had been rehearsing it in the bath for about three nights beforehand, and when we went for the actual take I hit with the right and we had to do it again.'[35]

Arguably the most famous incident in the film involved veteran actor Wilfrid Hyde-White's character, The Colonel, and the unfortunate planting of a daffodil in a certain part of his anatomy – namely his posterior, although there wasn't actually any nudity and shots of the actor lying on his stomach and the daffodil standing erect were separate. The story's origin stems from Hudis and his Irish mother-in-law, the late Ethel Robinson, swapping jokes. 'Actually, it's not much of a joke if told straight so, though risible in its own right, it *may* have been a real or apocryphal incident in an Irish hospital,' confirms Hudis. 'Anyway, following the principle that a vital quality for a writer is a good memory, I used it in *Nurse* after telling it to Peter [Rogers] and Gerry [Thomas].'

The placing of the daffodil was inopportune for the Colonel. 'It was actually unfitting, because Hyde-White's character hadn't been irascible and unpleasant, only saucy and a little demanding,' says Hudis. 'He didn't deserve this appalling indignity and the nurses came out of it as meaninglessly malicious.'

Hyde-White's presence in the film, for which he was paid £2,000, was a welcome addition and was appreciated by the screenwriter. 'Wilfred enjoyed a long, warm career in the UK and the US by never varying his expression or tone, no matter what role he was playing. He was always the amiable clubman, his accent unvaried, with not a thought in his head beyond the next hand of chemin de fer. I believe he only ever read his own lines because it didn't matter a jot to him what the story was about, or his character's relationships with the other players: he was always going to play and sound like himself anyway. He did a show for me in America, *It Takes A Thief*, with Robert Wagner. They cast him as a Russian agent because he was a name. But I had to write in that he trained in Russia to be super-British so that he could blend into America or Britain as an effective spy, simply because he wouldn't play it any other way – he always played himself.'

For the infamous daffodil scene, Hyde-White was filmed simply lying on his stomach on the hospital bed, uttering the feed line to Matron, unaware that a scene showing the flower would be inserted to give the impression that the Colonel had become the unknowing victim of an embarrassing prank. It's alleged that when Hyde-White saw the finished film, he was outraged and threatened legal action. 'He didn't like it and thought he'd been insulted,' recalls Peter Rogers. Originally, it was intended to close the film with a routine fade-out showing Shirley Eaton, as Nurse Denton, and Terence Longdon embracing as their characters become smitten with each other; but while viewing the rough cut of the picture, Rogers and Thomas believed there was no better way to close the film than with the daffodil scene.

Not everyone was enamoured of the rough cut, though: Hudis was horrified when he sat down to watch it at Denham Laboratories. 'I was inexperienced and nervous and thought it was dreadful; I wanted to throw myself under a bus because it seemed unfunny, dull, slow – awful! But Peter and Gerry, old hands when it came to these things, said: "Don't worry, we should never have asked you along." Of course, they were right. When the music was added and everything was completed, it was totally different.' The next time Hudis caught the picture was at the trade show, a different experience, albeit rather fraught. Because he didn't own a car, he accepted the offer of friends to drive him and his wife to the cinema in London's Oxford Street. After being picked up late from their house in Rickmansworth, their morning deteriorated as they were delayed further by heavy traffic. Minutes before the film was due to start the Hudises alighted from the car and raced to the Tube. 'We came flying out of the Underground and ran along to the cinema where my father was waiting for us,' recalls Norman Hudis. 'He was a coronary patient at the time and practically having a heart attack standing on the sidewalk waiting for his ticket.' Eventually making it to the jam-packed cinema, the Hudises finally took their seats. 'There I was, the author, seated down the front, horizontal, looking up at the screen.' This time, though, feelings of disappointment were replaced by jubilation. 'Emotionally, it was one of the most satisfying times I've ever experienced. Some genius at Anglo-Amalgamated had circulated several London hospitals and given tickets to 200 off-duty nurses. They'd just come off night duty and were dead with fatigue; they packed the circle and saw every joke coming and were screaming, setting the audience alight. It was probably the best audience the movie ever had and I was there, in the front row, hearing the laughter. It's quite tear-jerking even now, remembering it.'

When casting later *Carry Ons* Peter Rogers retained the services of as many faces from *Sergeant* as possible, but one of the major pluses was Hattie Jacques's elevation from her cameo appearance as Captain Clark, the medical officer, to that of the archetypal matron, a role she would make her own and revisit. Having this adept comedienne and actress propelled to a more substantial role was propitious as she became an essential member of the team whose repartees with the likes of Kenneth Williams and Sid James in, among others, *Doctor*, *Camping* and *Loving* were priceless. Jacques forged a successful stage and screen career, although her large build

restricted the variety of roles she was offered, a sad fact acknowledged by Hudis. 'Inside Matron there was a sensitive and gifted
Juliet, Lady Macbeth and Desdemona. ABC once asked me to write
a dramatic role for her: I chose, not very inventively, a Madame
Pimpernel situation, getting threatened kids out of World War Two
Europe. The upshot: "Nice script, Norman – but on second thoughts,
who'd believe plump, jolly Hattie in such a role?" I have a very
vivid recall of Hattie in *Teacher*, delivering the final speech in which
she passionately explained and defended the children's touching, if
misguided, actions. Proof that a finely honed comedic instinct was
only one component of her talent. Compelled because of her
physique to "be funny" she never got the chance, in a sustained
role, to unleash the sensitive serious actress within.'

Meanwhile, embarking on her *Carry On* debut, the first of 24
appearances, making her the most employed actress in the series,
was Essex-born Joan Sims, daughter of a stationmaster. By the time
she completed her education she had already cultivated an interest
in acting by performing with the Langdon Players, a local amateur
dramatic society. After four attempts she was accepted by RADA, and
on graduating began a long career at various repertory companies
before breaking into films in the early 1950s.

Equally at home playing roles from the green, rip-roaringly funny,
accident-prone Nurse Dawson in *Nurse* to the nagging, straight-
faced Daphne Barnes in *Behind*, Sims was an instinctive comic
performer and always value for money, turning in sterling performances. In one way, however, her debut was marred by an accident
on Tuesday, 2 December: while filming a scene, she fell against a
trolley and cut her leg, a wound that required two stitches. It's an
amusing scene on screen with the hapless Stella Dawson colliding
with the trolley and causing mayhem; but the anguish on Sims's
face was real, as she recalled in her autobiography. 'The sharp edge
of the trolley left a deep gash in my shin, and I was rushed off
to the Pinewood medical room. It was not much consolation to
me, as I lay there having stitches sewn into the wound, that the
take had been given the OK, and my injury had not caused any
hold-up.'[36]

Like many of the *Carry On* faces, Sims's performances often portrayed a confidence and assurance which masked a woman full of doubt and vulnerability. Assessing the actress, Norman Hudis says: 'She was probably the most vulnerable of the entire rep company. Like all of them, she had a superb comic gift; privately, she relied on her agent, Peter Eade, and Hattie [Jacques] for almost everything from arranging her savings to emotional advice. The amateur analyst in me thinks she sought to be dependent so as to rebel against her mother being so demanding on her. When Peter and Hattie died, she conceived the notion (she told me, at any rate) that she was "abandoned by life and surrounded by death". Not unusual for comics to weave such melodramatic webs around themselves. Overweight, sipping on champagne and orange juice, and lonely: what, indeed, a Carry On.'

Peter Rogers describes Sims as a 'very lonely person. She never seemed to have anybody – that's why she drank so much, of course. She would ring me up in the evening and go on forever and ever. On one occasion, she said: "Hang on, Peter, while I go and get another bottle of brandy."'

Filming for *Nurse* started on 3 November and was scheduled to finish on 12 December. The final cost of making the film totalled £82,500 and by the time of its release in March 1959 the next film, *Teacher*, was already in production. *Nurse* became the biggest box-office hit in Britain that year; its success, however, spread far beyond British shores. *Nurse* travelled across the Pond and was warmly received by American audiences, despite James Powers, a reviewer in *The Hollywood Reporter*, suggesting that 'most of it is local in nature and the sectional speech will be a handicap for American audiences.'[37] The film's première at Dallas's Granada Theater saw cinema-goers presented with plastic daffodils upon arrival. Nat Cohen confirmed in December 1961 that the film had grossed an impressive $2 million in the US and Canada alone, one of the highest grosses ever achieved by a British comedy on the American market; it was later suggested that *Nurse* had, in fact, been the highest-grossing British comedy shown in the States until *Four Weddings and a Funeral* appeared on the scene in the mid-1990s.

On the strength of *Nurse* alone, Norman Hudis was later invited to Hollywood to write for American audiences, where he experienced first-hand the impact that his screenplay had had on the people. He recalls one occasion when he was waiting to meet Nicholas Schenck at MGM Studios. 'I arrived early and was in the waiting room at his Los Angeles office. There was another person waiting. When my name was called, the other guy leapt from his seat, raced across and grabbed me, planting a kiss on my mouth – he was the distributor of *Carry On Nurse* in America. He'd been very badly stung by other ventures, then picked up *Nurse* quite inexpensively and made his fortune!'

Perceptive critics predicted *Nurse's* success, with a correspondent in *Variety* terming it a 'rollicking hospital farce that will raise the laughs with all but complete eggheads . . . a sure-fire box office winner here.'[38] The writer also predicted a 'golden series.'[39] A contemporary on the *Monthly Film Bulletin,* however, wasn't so confident, classing *Nurse* as a 'somewhat stale farce, mixing slapstick, caricature and crudely anatomical humour'[40] – unaware, of course, that this blend would become the trade mark of the *Carry On*s, particularly with Talbot Rothwell in the chair.

Back in the UK, the *Daily Mirror* was bowled over and felt that the lack of plot didn't matter, while the *Evening Standard* expected the film to make a 'mint'[41] at the box office; concurring with the *Standard,* the *Daily Herald* was also predicting a big success and in confirming that Norman Hudis had achieved what he had set out to do, the reporter wrote: 'Strangely enough, it also has the ring of truth. Of course, it is a caricature, but one drawn from real life.'[42] Nina Hibbin, who would later write a book about the *Carry On*s, discussed the 'latest in a new and welcome trend towards unpretentious, down-to-earth comedy, it is the funniest (and earthiest) I've seen for a very long time.'[43] And the reviewer in the *Daily Express* was equally impressed, admitting that he 'laughed at all the jokes, all of which were in the worst possible taste.'[44] But the final word in terms of reviews must come from the much-respected critic Dilys Powell, who wrote that *Nurse* brought 'a welcome breath of good, vulgar, music-hall fun, no connected plot to speak of and, in its series of comic or farcical incidents, some excellent playing.'[45]

IV

After the unprecedented success of *Nurse*, Norman Hudis moved on to the remaining four films that he would script in the series, beginning with *Teacher*, a screenplay that he had completed three months before *Nurse's* official release, such was the conveyor-belt approach. The storyline concentrated on the classroom struggles at Maudlin Street Secondary Modern School. When acting head William Wakefield spots his dream job and plans to apply, the children – not wanting him to leave – hatch a plan, involving a series of pranks and incidents, to ensure that Wakefield doesn't realise his dream. Looking for the opportune moment to wreak havoc, the visit of school inspector Felicity Wheeler and eminent child psychologist Alistair Grigg seems the ideal occasion, although in Norman Hudis's preliminary notes the visiting officials were intended to be Mr Ellis Hackenschmidt and Miss Cornelia Wheeler, young teachers from the United States who were concluding their study tour of British educational establishments. His subsequent character descriptions, however, reveal that in Hackenschmidt's case he wasn't far from the character he became. Hudis wrote: 'Earnest, bespectacled, analytical. Has theories about education, most behaviourist and psychological, all wildly impractical and only just this side of crackpot. Totally mystifies his English hosts.'[46]

Seizing on the visit as a way of effecting their plans, the kids win the day and prevent Wakefield from leaving, but not before more touching Hudisesque moments with the acting head learning that the kids' unruly behaviour was an attempt to keep him at the school. Cast as Mr Wakefield, the highest earner on the film with a wage slip of £2,500, was Wigan-born all-round entertainer Ted Ray. It was to be his only *Carry On* performance, into which he injected a wholesome and human quality. 'He was a very good artist, one of the funniest comics there was. He was also a wonderful man and I was very fond of him,' says Peter Rogers, who received instructions to exclude Ray from any future plans. 'He'd been under contract to ABC [Pictures] for two years and had never been used, so the casting director was embarrassed, as were the rest of the ABC hierarchy. ABC got very upset and told Stuart Levy, at

Anglo-Amalgamated: "We don't want to see any more of Ted Ray's films – tell Peter to knock him out of *Carry Ons*." I was sorry to lose him but if I wanted to make any more films I had to. They were furious that they'd had two years with this man and now he suddenly appeared in a *Carry On* – and ran away with it, too. It was a combination of embarrassment and sour grapes. I could understand it but didn't agree with it.'

Leslie Phillips was cast as Alistair Grigg, the second of his four appearances, and he regarded *Teacher* as his favourite *Carry On*. 'The cast and director were very confident by then, and the franchise was still fresh. Norman Hudis had drawn on his experience in the earlier titles to good effect,'[47] he wrote in his autobiography. Of the remaining cast, returning this time as teachers were Kenneth Connor, Charles Hawtrey, Hattie Jacques, Kenneth Williams and Joan Sims, who booked herself into a health farm in Hertfordshire to lose weight, not surprising when you consider the tight shorts she had to squeeze into for her role as the PE teacher. Fluctuating weight was something which dogged Sims during her career. Later, in *Nurse on Wheels*, produced by Rogers and released in 1963, Sims was offered the lead role of Joanna Jones. Soon after, the role was recast and Juliet Mills was given the job. A disappointed Sims, reflecting on the decision, stated: 'I had been letting myself go a bit over the past couple of years, and the trim figure of Nurse Stella Dawson had been somewhat swamped by the effects of a few too many buns and gin and tonics: the blunt fact was that I was simply too round to play the glamorous female lead.'[48]

In his preliminary notes, Hudis suggested, among others, Wilfrid Hyde-White to play Wakefield, Dora Bryan as Miss Allcock, Harry Locke as Alf the caretaker, and Terence Longdon as one of the teachers, later revised to Bill Owen. Michael Medwin was suggested as one of the American visitors, along with Hattie Jacques. Although Hudis's suggestions were largely dismissed, it was clear that a series was now in Rogers and Thomas's minds, and that its success was partly dependent on using the services of a select group of actors, proven by Rogers's letter dated 26 November 1958 to John Terry at the National Film Finance Corporation, which was formed via the Cinematograph Film Production (Special Loans) Act 1949. The subsequent Cinematograph Film Production Act 1952 gave the Corporation the authority to borrow financing for films from sources other than the Board of Trade. In his letter to the Corporation, Rogers wrote: 'It has become increasingly evident that the *Carry Ons* will depend more and more for their success upon a handful of feature artistes.'[49] Acknowledging the difficulties of securing the services of popular feature players who, he said, were in more demand than 'so-called stars',[50] Rogers suggested that the only way to keep the team together was to 'offer them some kind of contract or promise for their services at some future date'.[51] Rogers provided a breakdown of what the actors concerned had cost for his previous films, classing the figures as 'low for artistes who virtually carry a film.'[52] Referring to Connor, Williams, Hawtrey, Sims and Cyril Chamberlain in particular, Rogers asked the Corporation to assist in the proposed expenditure, at least for the next *Carry On* [*Constable*]. Although there is no record of Terry's response, this communication reveals that Rogers had acknowledged that *Carry On* had a life beyond just one or two films.

Filming began on 9 March 1959, in the studio, with internal shots of Wakefield's study involving Ted Ray, Kenneth Connor, Hattie Jacques, Charles Hawtrey, Kenneth Williams, Joan Sims and a young Richard O'Sullivan, of *Man About the House* fame, as one of the ringleaders among the schoolchildren. Location shooting at the school, which was actually Drayton Secondary School, West Ealing, London, was wrapped up by 10 April. While local children were recruited to make up the playground numbers in non-speaking roles, more substantial parts were offered to children from London's Corona Academy School, including George Howell and Larry Dann, who played Billy Haig and, simply, Boy, respectively. 'We were chosen for type – spotty-faced, bespectacled, long-haired idiots – which is why I think I got it,' recalls George Howell, laughing. 'Naturally, I had my teeth straightened, got contact lenses, shortened my hair and started working for a long time! Interestingly, all the pupils who played in the orchestra could actually play their instrument. Richard [O'Sullivan] was an excellent pianist.'

Howell enjoyed working on the film and recalls the many pranks that were played. 'Everybody got involved in them, including Gerry

Thomas and the stage crew who, for example, prevented us getting off the stage when the sprinklers started. It was a complete surprise for us because we didn't know they were coming on. It was a laugh from beginning to end.'

Even camera operator Alan Hume recalls being involved in a prank, with Kenneth Connor, as nervous science master Gregory Adams, the target. 'One scene saw him walk around and sniff in a big pot. Just as the scene was about to start we dropped a stink bomb in it. He put his nose in and you should have seen the look on his face. There was a big laugh, although Kenny [Connor] didn't see the funny side of it until later,' says Hume, who admits he often operated the camera with a hankie stuffed in his mouth to stop him laughing.

George Howell got on well with Kenneth Williams, whom he met again at a function organised in connection with the West End revue *Pieces of Eight*. At the time, he supplemented his acting income by working as an electrician at the Apollo Theatre in between jobs. Williams invited Howell to his dressing room during the interval. 'He asked how I was doing, so I told him I was out of work but that I was meeting someone in a couple of weeks. Saddened to hear of my situation, he asked me to come and see him at the end of the show.' Howell returned once the curtain had come down and engaged in more lengthy conversation with Williams. 'As I was leaving, he said: "This is for you." He gave me £2. I didn't want to take it but he said: "Take it, you don't have any money, you might need it." I thanked him. The following week, after we'd been paid, I went to see him with £2 in my hand but he wouldn't take it, saying: "I don't lend money to my friends, that was a gift."'

Larry Dann, who'd go on to appear in three other *Carry On*s, recalls a 'great time with all my mates', despite his best scene ending up on the cutting-room floor. 'For me, it was one of the best moments because I got a huge round of applause after finishing it. During the orchestra scene, the band did a jazz number and it became chaotic. I was on the drums, playing a stupid, dumb boy, and went bananas. It was terribly sad that the scene ended up being cut.'

The film received its first public screening in London on 11 August

1959. The response from critics was largely positive, with a journalist in the *Kinematograph Weekly* rating it 'slightly less exuberant and ribald than *Nurse*, but nevertheless packs belly laughs in plenty'[53] and while he classed Ted Ray as 'no more than adequate'[54] he termed the picture as a 'gilt-edged . . . infallible British moneyspinner.'[55] *The Daily Cinema* expected it to 'prove an even mightier box-office hit than its . . . predecessors'[56] while the London-based correspondent for *Variety* thought it would emulate the success of the two earlier entries with Hudis creating a 'slightly stronger story-line'[57] and making the characters 'more credible.'[58] But, as always, there were those who didn't rate it, and most of the grumbles came from the popular press rather than the industry publications. Derek Prouse in the *Sunday Times* felt that Hattie Jacques and Leslie Phillips were two actors who 'triumph over material so remorselessly juvenile that one is battered into a kind of fascinated admiration'[59] while a critic in *The Times*, again singling out Jacques, said the film seemed 'funnier or, to put it another way, less painfully unfunny when she is on the set.[60] The *Sunday Express*'s reviewer, meanwhile, thought the 'slapstick is rather thin, the laughs not very hearty, the scripts far weaker than the tolerable acting and some of the inevitable romantic interludes seem to be extra vulgar.'

The *Daily Mail* correspondent, meanwhile, questioned whether the film censors were 'either unexpectedly indulgent or very innocent'[61]; the censors did pick up on one sequence when Leslie Phillips's character, whose heart raced upon spotting PE teacher Miss Allcock [Joan Sims], uttered, slowly and provocatively, the teacher's name. In her autobiography, Sims recalled: 'Miss Allcock was a great role to play, but she was very nearly not Miss Allcock at all. When the screenplay was submitted to the Lord Chamberlain's office, concern was expressed about the name, and it was decreed that it could only be pronounced with equal stress on each of the two syllables.'[62] But, she says, Phillips's pronunciation was 'more heavily charged than anything the Lord Chamberlain could have dreamed of.'[63]

Assessing the success of *Teacher* today, Norman Hudis says: 'Once more unto the breach of age. Valiant and energetic though their performances were, the young actors in this most sentimental of the series were at least five years too old. The reason, I guess, was entirely practical. Laws governing the employment of child actors very properly require quite expensive supervision and tuition.

'Since the theme of *Teacher* was that a determined group of pupils concoct a spectacular sabotage plan to prevent a beloved headmaster moving to another school, the children, to my mind, should have been eleven or so. Such kids would still have had several years of schooling ahead of them and might have made the effort to compel the headmaster to stay with them. At ages 16–18, I felt they wouldn't have given a toss: they'd be too close to leaving school for their first jobs, university or whatever to worry about the head moving elsewhere.

'Perhaps I was too logical and it's possible that this didn't occur to anyone else. At any rate, in line with the *Carry Ons*' reputation for economical production methods, teenagers, unencumbered by pricey labour legalities, got the roles. And no one else, except the pernickety screenwriter, ever, to my knowledge, found the casting incongruous.'

Hudis may regard his actions as 'pernickety' but it was such attention to detail that did him credit, even if by the very nature of the *Carry On* vehicle he was afforded a latitude in authenticity that he could have exploited. The film contains what Hudis classes as 'hasty action, during production, misfiring in its intention.' He explains: 'The children's plan, during a fortuitous inspection of the school, is to engineer a series of catastrophes so that the headmaster, ultimately responsible, will appear incompetent and the new school will reverse its offer to hire him. When the inspectors arrive, a child's voice-over explains: "These are the ones we have to get rid of." This is a line I didn't write, simply because it completely reverses the children's intention: not to get rid of them but to *keep them there*, long enough to witness a few pupil-made catastrophes to decide that the head has no control over the school. Someone decided that this intention needed to be verbalised – and came up with totally the converse impression. This kind of thing causes press-show palpitations, when the writer, for the first time, hears such ineffectual and, in this instance, downright unhelpful and confusing interpolations.'

Compared to previous scripts, *Teacher* was heavy in terms of plot and, despite it being the most pleasant in spirit, Hudis doesn't consider it as successful as the others. He admits, however, having a sentimental attachment to the script, thanks to a teacher, Mr Jenkins, at the County School, Willesden who encouraged him to be a writer. 'I wanted to be a journalist at the time. I was a very bad student, though, and disliked anything that didn't pertain to English writing. Nevertheless, I had a very perceptive headmaster, Mr Wallace, who felt I merited a break, even though my scholastic record was abysmal. So it was he who wrote to the local newspaper and recommended me, and that's how I got started on the local paper in Hampstead.'

V

After cultivating the fecund soil of familiar institutions – the armed forces, the medical profession and the educational establishment – the *Carry On* focus turned to the police force for the next picture, a subject that had been flirted with previously, back in the autumn of 1958 when Peter Rogers commissioned writers John Antrobus and Brock Williams to deliver treatments under the title *Carry On Constable*. While Antrobus's effort became the premise for the 1965 comedy *The Big Job*, starring Sid James, it is unclear what happened to Williams's script for which he received £1,000, other than his idea being acknowledged in the credits of Hudis's *Constable*.

The first draft of the screenplay was delivered on 24 August 1959 and a revised version followed by the beginning of October. The script had taken more time than usual to complete. Peter Rogers recalls: 'I said to Norman [Hudis]: "You'd better go to Slough Police Station and absorb the subject." He went but was so upset by the stories he heard that he couldn't write anything. I told him to forget it for now and we'd return to it later. In the meantime, he got on with another script and when he eventually returned to *Constable* he'd forgotten about all the nasties and the upsets – Norman's a very sensitive man.'

Hudis recalls his depressing research visit. 'I was shown around with this reverence for even a minor character in the film industry. Everyone was charming and helpful, but the environment was solemn; it depressed me so much. They showed me the cells and then took me up this circular, narrow, confining staircase to the dock in the police court – it was oppressive and punitive. I told Peter how it depressed me and we waited a few weeks, by which time I'd heard about blue flu.' An outbreak of flu that forced police constabularies to call up specials and newly qualified constables to boost their depleted workforce presented Hudis with the building blocks for his story.

Utilising the 'blue flu' situation, the plot revolved around a group of novice policemen who, on leaving training college, were drafted in to help a local constabulary when staff numbers were decimated by the epidemic. Although some may argue the picture was critical of local police forces, the obvious comedy potential in the subject was unquestionable. Joining the now recognised regulars, Leslie Phillips was again recruited, this time as PC Potter, while Terence Longdon, Shirley Eaton and Eric Barker made welcome returns.

But it was the introduction of a new face, a heavily furrowed one at that, which would have the largest impact on the future of the *Carry On*s: making the first of nineteen appearances was South African-born Sid James, who would become the linchpin for many of the films. Despite being an extremely busy actor and never short of work he became synonymous with the *Carry On* films, such was his screen presence. Equally representative of the pictures was his trade-mark dirty laugh which would become prominent when the dawning of the Talbot Rothwell era marked a shift towards naughtier scripts. With his crumpled face and perfect timing, James was already a stalwart of the film industry before he joined the *Carry On* clan and the confidence he exuded showed in an array of deftly crafted characterisations.

The son of vaudeville artists, James was born in Johannesburg in 1913. He arrived on British soil in 1946, determined to become an actor. Although he'd trained as a hairdresser in his homeland, he'd been bitten by the acting bug while turning out for the Johannesburg Repertory Players, an amateur company, before enlisting in the South African Defence Force. Within months of arriving in England he'd not only secured an agent but a small part in the first of many movies. Not romantic-lead material, he exploited his craggy features to good effect and specialised in tough roles, quickly establishing himself as a trusty character actor. He brought a wealth of experience to the *Carry On* team and was appreciated by cast and crew alike. 'He was an anchorman, just as Ted Ray and Eric Barker were, the one everything seems to hang on,' explains Peter Rogers. More times than not, James simply played himself and never tried to be funny, believing that being the straight man would draw its own laughs – and he was right. The lecherous characters with which we associate the actor, epitomised by sex-mad Sid Boggle in *Camping*, would present themselves later; for now he was cast in more sympathetic, even altruistic roles such as the understanding Sergeant Wilkins in *Constable* and Bert Handy in *Regardless*. Whatever was asked of him, however, he'd deliver the goods in his usual unfussy way.

Much of the exterior filming for *Constable* took place in and around Ealing and caused quite a stir, thanks to Sid James, the highest earner on the film, receiving £2,500. Crowds thronged the streets and traffic, at one point, was at a standstill in Ealing's High Street. Vehicles queued behind the outstretched arm of a police sergeant as he ushered people across the road, annoying drivers until they noticed that actress Shirley Eaton was one of the pedestrians. Tempers cooled further when the mystery was resolved and motorists learnt that the policeman was actually Sid James who, in the interest of authenticity, was out gaining first-hand experience of traffic control in preparation for the film.

Although *Constable* trod new ground inasmuch as it contained the first *Carry On* nude scene, with the newly qualified bobbies seen scampering between the showers and revealing their backsides in the process, it attracted the expected response from critics on its release in February 1960. Opinions were divided between the broadsheet critics who regularly questioned the films' value, journalists from the tabloids who largely accepted the pulling power of the *Carry Ons* and writers for the trade publications who appreciated the films' popularity with the cinema-going public and their importance to the home-grown film industry. The mix of reviews ranged from a journalist in *Kinematograph Weekly* assuring its readers, 'Make no mistake, *Carry On Constable* will give exhibitors big houses'[64] to a correspondent in *The Times* stating that the film had 'little to recommend it . . . good ideas are few, and there is material here for little more than a modest series of television sketches farcically involving the police.'[65] Meanwhile Campbell Dixon, in the *Daily Telegraph*, acknowledged it would almost certainly be a hit with the public but wasn't so complimentary about its merits, writing: 'Here are all the tiresome clichés of British farce . . . There must, I suppose, be something in these stereotypes that appeals to the British public – though not, so far as I am aware, to any other – and I dare say some psychologist could explain it to me. On the whole, though, I'd rather he didn't.'[66] The *Daily Express*'s critic didn't need a psychologist to explain why the films had its audiences in fits of laughter because he was a fan, too. He wrote: 'There are lavatory jokes, there are puns, trousers fall down, there is a car chase . . . it is all predictable and I would not have it otherwise, for I have rather a liking for the *Carry On* series.'[67]

VI

Until now, Norman Hudis had written scripts about everyday situations to which people could relate: National Service, hospitals, schools and the police force. But with *Regardless*, his penultimate *Carry On* film, he began straying beyond day-to-day experience. Forthright about his screenplay, believing it lacked narrative strength, he admits: 'I thought it was rather a mess because I was beginning to strain a bit by then.'

Regardless introduced viewers to the world of Helping Hands, the well-meaning but inefficient agency run by Bert Handy (Sid James) whose employees were 'always ready to lend a hand'. No job was too small for the company, whether it was modelling a woman's wardrobe, walking a dog (or a chimp, for that matter), or helping keep someone's place at the outpatients department. Handy's company of incompetents was inspired by a real-life London-based organisation, Universal Aunts, which was actually run by reliable staff who were just a phone call away when would-be customers wanted someone to help – and nothing was too much trouble. It still isn't, because Universal Aunts continues to offer its services and expertise, something it has done successfully since opening its doors in 1921. 'I based the script on that concept, created Helping Hands and presented the characters with amusing situations to deal with,' says Hudis, who rates the screenplay as his least favourite. 'It was evidence that I was running out of easy targets and beginning to stretch a little to find something. At least we didn't need too much of a story and could string together a series of sketches.'

I happen to rate *Regardless* as one of my favourites – the lack of plot and sketch-like structure do not hamper my enjoyment of the film. But Norman Hudis, always honest when assessing his own work, doesn't agree, although he admits liking the sequence based on a misunderstanding. In it, Sam Twist (Kenneth Connor) races to the Forth Bridge, believing he is taking part in a scene from *The 39 Steps* when all that is required is a fourth at bridge. 'I was happy with that sequence, with the ever-reliable and inventive Kenneth Connor misunderstanding an assignment to the extent of believing it involved him in the Secret Service. Moreover, it put him on a train destined to cross the Forth Bridge, a clear link with the mysterious shenanigans of *The 39 Steps*.'

In the writer's view, it is scant compensation when the overall package is deemed 'bitty', and the Stanley Unwin interpolations 'unrealistic and eventually tedious'. Hudis recalls: 'He was a popular comic figure at the time so it was justified and it got a laugh. But, like most writers, I enjoy telling cohesive stories, even the slender ones which sprout complications in most comedies. But the thread – that they feared eviction from the agency's premises and were repeatedly visited by a gobbledegook-speaking landlord – was extremely slender and, in my troubled eyes, got more emaciated as the footage unreeled.'

Hudis wasn't fond of the closing scene, either, with the Helping Hands team working amid a cloud of dust as they frantically clean a dilapidated house only to see it collapse around them. 'It made me cringe,' he admits. 'It was real pantomime. *Sergeant* had a sentimental ending, which was almost mandatory because you had a hard atmosphere like army training so you needed a lump-in-the-throat ending. With *Nurse* we were lucky because my mother-in-law told me the joke about the daffodil and I adapted it and in *Teacher* the sentiment was clearly dictated by the theme.'

That wasn't the only comedic sequence to irk Hudis. 'When director Frank Capra realised, during a sleepless night, what was wrong with his cut of *Lost Horizon* – the entire opening sequence – he raced to Columbia Studios, retrieved the negative and burned the superfluous reel. That is what I'd like to do to the sequence wherein Kenneth Connor tries to give up smoking.' (His character's craving for a cigarette can't be assuaged by any other means and he gives in to his old habit.) The reasons for Hudis's intense dislike are, firstly, that he believes the sequence is evidence of hurried plotting and, secondly, that Connor's final line of dialogue – 'No drawers' – is 'not so much a punchline as a limp and soggy punline, feeble and furtive instead of heartily vulgar.' He adds: 'Once more, though, I have to report that no one else found it objectionable and, at all screenings I attended, it got a generous laugh. Nevertheless, I don't believe, as hit playwright Terence Rattigan once famously recommended, that one should never write anything which would offend one's Aunt Edna. But, while realising that "good taste" nowadays extends to an ever more distant boundary, there *is* a limit beyond which it is distasteful to stray. That line is the only one in all my scribblings of which I am actually penitently ashamed. You may say that I'm ashamed all the way to the bank. Fair enough. But truly ashamed I was and am.'

Hudis's assessment of *Regardless* is rather harsh, though, because the film contains plenty of amusing scenes, such as when Lily Duveen (Joan Sims) is hired to collect invitations at a wine tasting. With her job complete, she is invited to partake in some sampling but gets carried away and ends up tipsy and making a fool of herself. In the process, she pours wine over the head of a character called Wolf, the only appearance that Nicholas Parsons made in the series. Playing jokes on one another wasn't atypical; in fact, it happened regularly, another sign of a happy family having fun while getting on with the job at hand. So when some prankster decided to use neat gin instead of water to represent white wine it was all in a day's work for the team.

Nicholas Parsons had been asked to appear in a *Carry On* before

Regardless but theatre commitments prevented this happening. Recalling the scene with Sims, he soon learnt, to his regret, what was and wasn't expected on a *Carry On* film. He had worked with the Boulting Brothers, where retakes weren't uncommon. 'In a *Carry On* film, once they had a take that was good, they didn't say: "I think we can do better." There wasn't the time, it was a case of, "We have a good take – keep it."'

After filming the scene with Sims, Gerald Thomas asked Parsons how he felt. 'Being honest, I said the run-through of the scene in rehearsal had been better. He agreed, but said that he was satisfied. I should have been happy with that, but when he asked if I'd like to go again, being that it was my big moment in the film, I replied that I felt I could make the part funnier. We did another take and both agreed it was better. The following day, however, I heard through my agent that I'd been reported as being fussy. I never worked on another *Carry On*. I hadn't the faintest idea; it was just that I hadn't done a *Carry On* before and hadn't got to grips with the style in which they worked.'

Another incident which Parsons feels was misinterpreted was when he commented on the ill-fitting suit he was asked to wear. 'It was absolutely ghastly. I knew it was going to be ruined so it didn't really matter, but I was supposed to be terribly smart, so I mistakenly said: "Don't worry, I can wear my own clothes and get them cleaned afterwards." Because the clothes had been bought for me, I was misunderstood and was, I think, taken as being a bit fussy.'

Such successful scenes don't alter Hudis's evaluation, though, and as well as regretting selected lines and scenes in the finished product, he also rues losing a sequence rich in double meanings. Rejected by the censor, it saw Charles Hawtrey clamber into a woman's wardrobe to hear and report on her talking in her sleep. 'Pointless, I suppose, to recall that hearty and very popular stage farces, at the Aldwych Theatre and elsewhere, revelled for generations in far more suggestive situations without undermining public morality.'

Sid James's arrival on the *Carry On* scene had produced an instant impact in *Constable*, so it was no surprise when he was given the anchor role in *Regardless*, as the owner of Helping Hands. His value to the overall fabric of the films was discernible from the beginning and, as a journalist wrote in response to James's debut in the series, 'for the next and subsequent *Carry On*s, he should be able to write his own cheque.'[68]

While James stepped into the shoes of Bert Handy with ease, all the regular faces were back on the payroll, playing their parts in the same resourceful and skilled way. By now the *Carry On* momentum was such that any films deemed weaker than others in the series were carried along by the popularity of the gold mine that was the *Carry On* genre, although the critic in the *Monthly Film Bulletin* did detect that *Regardless* seemed 'staler'[69] than others in the series. And a contemporary, in the *Daily Cinema*, felt that the film lacked the 'zest of the early *Carry On* comedies and there's barely a pretence of a plot.'[70] But he also related to the strength of the brand itself, believing that the regular actors were so firmly established in the public's psyche that 'just putting them on the screen and letting them do what comes naturally is enough to raise the guffaws.'[71] The film received its share of positive reviews when it began entertaining the nation in March 1961. Penelope Gilliatt in the *Observer* stated that she wouldn't be surprised if the film was a 'colossal success,'[72] adding: 'Apart from having a completely undisturbing sense of humour, and apart from drawing off the best-loved stars of revue, TV screen and radio ... it also expresses many of our deepest popular assumptions.'[73] By the time such reviews were in the public domain, everyone's attention at the *Carry On* camp had turned to the next in the line – *Cruising*, which marked a milestone in two respects: it was the first *Carry On* to be made in colour and the last – the last that made it to the big screen – to be written by Norman Hudis.

VII

Peter Rogers registered the title *Cruising* with the British Film Producers' Association in March 1961, the same month as *Regardless's* release. By the summer he'd received a story treatment, titled *Carry On At Sea*, from Eric Barker, which cost him £750. Although Barker received a credit on the film titles when it joined the cinema circuit in April 1962, it was Hudis who, again, scripted the screenplay.

When the finished product was delivered to Rogers by Christmas 1961, Pinewood's publicity machine issued promotional material prior to the film's release, including a synopsis of the story: 'The SS *Happy Wanderer*, commanded by that intrepid mariner Captain Crowther (Sidney James) is due to cast off on a Mediterranean cruise, when he discovers that his regular key personnel of officers have, for one reason or another, been replaced by a bunch of raw but well-intentioned strangers.'[74]

During the pre-production meeting on 4 January 1962, it was mentioned that a shot of a liner entering and leaving port – which would be used as a scene-setter – would probably be filmed in Gibraltar but, just as with all the other *Carry On*s, no one set foot outside Britain. For scenes set aboard the *Happy Wanderer*, no one rode the ocean wave because the ship was designed by art director Carmen Dillon and constructed at Pinewood Studios. The full-scale replica of the liner included a games deck, a bar, cabins and a swimming pool, in which diminutive actress Esma Cannon, playing nervy eccentric Bridget Madderley, took a dip, despite being a four-feet-nine non-swimmer. Donning an antiquated bathing dress, Cannon, a gallant trouper, emerged from the pool to a round of applause from the cast and crew, as well as from the proficient swimmer whom director Gerald Thomas had hired, just in case. While the various pool scenes were shot under the glare of the studio lighting representing Mediterranean sunshine, the grounds of Pinewood and surrounding countryside lay under several inches of snow as winter set in with a vengeance.

Surprisingly, Sid James, who earned £4,000 on the film, wasn't the highest earner, with Kenneth Williams pocketing £5,000 and Kenneth Connor £4,500. A new face in the team, in what would be his only *Carry On* appearance, was Lance Percival, who received £600 when he stepped in as a last-minute replacement for Charles Hawtrey, who was dropped after demanding more money. Peter Rogers explains how an article in *Cinema Today* led to the artist's request for more cash. 'The article said there was another *Carry On* coming and if it didn't have Charles Hawtrey in it, it wouldn't be worth seeing. The remark went to Hawtrey's head and he wanted three times the money, to be above the title and to have a star on his dressing-room door. So we didn't have him: we chose Lance Percival instead.' Rogers wasn't going to be held to ransom by an actor with inflated ideas of his importance in the project as a whole. His personal standing was something which played on Hawtrey's mind. Even when he returned to the fold, he was keen to push his name up the cast list: on returning the contract for *Cleo*, for example, a note from his agent stated that his credit should be not less than fourth co-star.

Born in Sevenoaks, Kent, in 1933, Percival formed a calypso group while living in Canada. He toured the country and America before returning to the UK where he joined the cast of *Here is The News*, a satirical revue touring the country, followed by *One Over the Eight* with Kenneth Williams. He'd already worked for Peter Rogers in two films, including *Twice Round the Daffodils*, when he joined *Cruising*. 'The reason I got those small parts was because of the revue with Kenneth Williams; I was his feed for a year and everyone came to watch Kenneth, so that got my face into the Peter Rogers domain. I was put up for the barman or drunk, I've forgotten which, in *Cruising* but when Charles Hawtrey asked for too much money and didn't get the part they offered me the role of Wilfred Haines. It was never dull for a second making the film, especially with the two Kenneths [Williams and Connor] larking about all the time.'

It's rare that filming knits together perfectly in just one take, and Percival recalls the scene when he prepares Captain Crowther's birthday cake, only to see it explode. 'It was supposed to blow up in my face but we had to do it five times.' In reality, a pipe from which the contents would explode was hidden inside the cake but it wasn't always a success. 'Sometimes the mixture didn't hit my face properly, other times – because I knew what was going to happen – I blinked just before the stuff hit me. It took ages to complete the shot because every time we had to go again, I had to visit the changing room, put on a new outfit and wash it all off!'

Another notable absentee from the cast was Joan Sims, who needed a rest after the rigours of a long run in the play *The Lord Chamberlain Regrets!*. Replacing her at four days' notice was Dilys

Laye, who enjoyed every minute playing Flo Castle, apart from the strenuous scenes in the gym where her character tried her utmost to impress Jenkins, the gym instructor, portrayed by Vincent Ball. 'They weren't the most comfortable, I have to be honest,' laughs Laye, reflecting on the first of her four *Carry On* run-outs. 'Sliding down the rope, which happens terribly fast when you see it, took a long time to do and I ended up bruised and tired with burns on my hands. But it was lovely playing the part; I don't usually play the man-hunter, I'm not the man-hunting type to look at.'

Normally a brunette, Laye arrived at the studio with her hair dyed blonde for a previous show. 'I'm very dark naturally, and still am, but I had a very bad hair dye. At the beginning of filming, a piece of hair actually broke off, so Biddy Chrystal [hairdresser on the film] sewed a false curl onto a little slide comb and slid it under my hair to cover the gap. By the time I'd finished, I had about five false pieces in – so much of the hair was artificial because mine was so badly damaged. The minute the film finished, I had the whole lot cut off – a bit like Joan of Arc – and let it grow again.'

Cruising, which was made between January and February 1962, was released in April with *Monthly Film Bulletin*'s critic welcoming the first *Carry On* in colour, noting that the style was even more easygoing than the previous pictures, with everyone 'achieving a kind of comedy shorthand which often relies on the familiar screen eccentricities of the regulars . . . to raise a laugh without the strain of developing a given situation to its illogical conclusion.'[75] Most other reviewers held the same belief: that the film would provide its normal dose of laughs, comic situations and cosy predictability. And such familiarity paid dividends. Concerning the films' basic similarity, Gerald Thomas once commented: 'We came to the conclusion that this is what the audience wanted and expected: they expected the characters to play certain parts in a certain formula. But each film is quite different and this is the only reason one can keep this terrific enthusiasm for them. Each one in its own way is a challenge. We try to balance them so that we have, probably, one period subject and two moderns and so on. We approach each as a separate picture but we do try to keep faith with the public, inasmuch as we make our team behave in the predictable and expected way.'[76]

Meanwhile, across the Atlantic, a reviewer was treading more cautiously: although he suggested it would be another box-office success, he questioned whether *Cruising*, despite sticking to the proven formula on which the *Carry Ons*' success was built, was 'beginning to wear very thin'.[77] He added: 'Maybe Norman Hudis, who has so skilfully scribed this run of comedy hits, should have a sabbatical. Perhaps a new writer might infuse new angles into predictable situations, gags and characters.'[78]

While writing the script, Hudis tried revisiting the format which had served him well, particularly in *Sergeant*, which was why Sid James's character, a veteran of the seas, had been landed with a group of potentially incompetent crew members on this, his final cruise. 'Most of the regulars were there, although I would have preferred Joan [Sims] to have been in the cast. Dilys Laye is a nice girl but she couldn't play a drunk like Joan Sims could. But there wasn't much I could do in terms of the material, other than turn it into slapstick afloat,' admits Hudis. 'Because people were on holiday, it opened up the possibility of a little fun and flirtatiousness.'

As well as losing Sims, the film missed the feyness of Hawtrey; the void they each left reduced the familiarity within the team dynamics. 'All cheers for Dilys Laye and Lance Percival, but they just weren't Joan or Charlie. For me, it made a touching difference,' stresses Hudis, who points out that one of the biggest laughs he ever received was in response to a line in the *Cruising* script, although he classes it as one of the 'silliest'. 'Kenneth Connor comes up on deck and talks to someone, asking: "What's afoot?". The other person replies: "That funny thing at the end of your leg." It received the biggest laugh in the whole film and shows that you can exercise wit, satire, wordplay, incongruity and all the other elements, and a silly one like that has people falling about; throw it away and it works.'

As with *Regardless*, Hudis regretted having to step beyond the realms of everyday experiences. Even though journeying to far-flung corners of the globe had increased post-war, cruising was still a luxury reserved for the lucky few. Hudis admits: 'Though it had plot coherence and comedy chances of the *Sergeant* kind – eager people thrust into an unfamiliar atmosphere and having to succeed in it – it was not on as general or public a theme as the first four films.'

But big changes were afoot in the *Carry On* world as Norman Hudis prepared to move on to pastures new.

Part 2

The Rothwell Era:
A profusion of innuendoes

I

The release of *Cabby* in 1963 marked the dawning of a new era for the *Carry On* films. After writing the first six pictures, scriptwriter Norman Hudis waved goodbye to the series and Talbot Rothwell, who'd made a name for himself penning material for *The Crazy Gang*, took up the mantle for the next twenty films.

When Hudis delivered his *Carry On* swansong in the shape of *Cruising*, he knew deep down that the end of his tenure as the films' writer was nigh. 'All the staple topics and situations had been used up, so that's why they needed someone like Talbot Rothwell – wonderful, inexhaustible, creative – a true professional.'

Hudis believes that what finally signalled the end was a script that he penned for *Carry On Spying*. Rothwell's effort reached the screen in June 1964 but Hudis had submitted his version a year earlier, although it hadn't been to Peter Rogers's liking. The first of the *Carry On* parodies came hot on the heels of the successful spy movies, most notably the James Bond pictures. Wanting to strike while the iron was hot, Rogers dispatched Hudis to write the script, but his initial treatment was rejected. 'My idea involved a group of incompetents, working as secret agents, getting involved with the atomic bomb.'

At a certain point in a comedy series, when you have an audience indulgent towards you, Hudis believes, you can 'legitimately and confidently introduce for a moment or two – or even thematically for a while – a serious topic.' Hudis cites *All in the Family*, the American version of *Till Death Us Do Part*, as a prime example. 'They were able to discuss themes like cancer, abortion and racial relations. I wanted spies to try and get into an atomic energy station but there was a CND demonstration taking place with people lying down.' Protecting the station were security guards, among them a middle-aged man sporting a chest bedecked with ribbons from World War Two. 'He watched the demonstration and there was a scene, just a few seconds long, where he turned to his mates and said: "They're right, you know, this is a filthy weapon." Then he went out, took his cap off and lay down with them.' Hudis is convinced that scene marked the beginning of his separation from the series. 'Yes, I think it cost me my place on the *Carry Ons*. Peter and Gerald probably thought: "This has no place in the films." I think that's what happened, or perhaps they just decided I was all written out in terms of subjects, and they were probably correct: I was obviously most at home with schools, the army, the police force. So it was time to go.'

Before parting company with Rogers and Thomas, Hudis revised his treatment for *Spying* in the vain hope that he could provide a suitable piece of work. Delivering it on 20 February 1963, the script saw Joan Sims, Kenneth Connor, Hattie Jacques, Charles Hawtrey and Sid James playing five eager recruits involved in Operation Smith. Objective: capture the head of the most successful spy ring in the country, who's stolen a top-secret file from the Department of Obsolete Missiles. Their target is wanted alive so the agents are ordered not to use guns, but their task is made increasingly difficult when, among other things, the spies are sent on wild-goose chases and Jacques's character, Dauntless, is drugged and temporarily brainwashed.

Unhappy with their lack of progress, the director of British Operations Security recalls them to HQ. While they are fumbling in the dark, the master spy, Smith, whips another secret: the strastospheric air mask, which aids respiration in outer space. Sent off again to capture Smith, they head for the Ministry of Supply General Research Centre and a long chase ensues. Meanwhile, Smith's accomplice Stamp heads for Docklands Café where he tries to escape on a boat with the café owner but is captured by the five agents. They return triumphant to Operations HQ, only to discover that their escapades have been just part of their training.

But Hudis's revised attempt didn't interest Rogers and Thomas. 'The way I handled it obviously didn't appeal to them,' he admits, reluctantly. 'What they needed, now that we'd more or less run out of easy targets, was what they found in the untiring and hugely gifted Talbot Rothwell – a comedy style lending itself to broader, freer treatment.' Hudis remarks that if the material in the revised script wasn't enough to send him packing, the earlier CND protest scene sealed his fate. 'I don't presume to know what Peter and Gerry's views were – that was immaterial; that they clearly didn't want any such views, pro- or anti-, to be portrayed in a *Carry On* was their absolute right and they exercised it.'

During research for this book, Norman Hudis was afforded the opportunity of reading his *Spying* script for the first time in over 40 years and admits, candidly, that it didn't make pleasant reading. 'It was an abominably inept screenplay shrieking of a tired mind, running on empty, limping along on autopilot. Some routine wordplay crosstalk at the beginning isn't all that bad, but it doesn't get beyond that in ideas or characterisation or, God help us, humour. After six *Carry On*s, I was ready to be carried out.' Hudis couldn't even finish reading it, such was his embarrassment at what he'd produced all those years ago. 'I recall that Hawtrey was characterised as a secret agent whose front was as a jazz pianist, and that he was washed down a sewer at one point; you'll note that I was dealing in high-comedy concepts at the time as exemplified by another scene where he fell down a chimney and landed in the grate, sooty and black-faced, complaining. All in all, this deeply embarrassing piece amply endorses Peter and Gerry's view that, with the switch to "unrealistic" themes imminent for the *Carry On*s, our Normie was no longer suited to be Writer in Residence. I didn't have the right anarchic touch and still don't. If it isn't real, I don't have the feel. That doesn't make me a superior writer, just a limited one. It's a limitation that I accept with relief.'

Hudis suggests, though, that other institutions could have been lampooned, like Fleet Street, the pop-music world, 'even perhaps, as typically healthy and British social irreverence developed, royalty.' He adds: 'Rothwell came in fresh and fertile and on an exhilaratingly different tack, which must have been a huge relief to Rogers and Thomas. I only met Talbot once and fleetingly; no one appreciated and admired his facility and inventiveness more than I did.'

Peter Rogers paid off the remaining year of Norman Hudis's

contract, leaving him idle until the opportunity of emigrating to America arose one sunny morning via a phone call. The success of *Nurse* Stateside had prompted Lee Rosenberg, from the newly-formed Adams, Ray and Rosenberg literary agency, to approach Hudis. Initially Hudis believed it was an old chum winding him up but, realising that the offer was genuine, he agreed. For the next twelve months – during which time Hudis scripted *Mr Ten Per Cent* for comic Charlie Drake – Rosenberg found that while Hollywood knew *Nurse*, the scribe's name was unfamiliar. Needing to raise his profile, Hudis made two trips to America and before long assignments started trickling his way, including *Oh, Nurse!*, an attempt to create an American small-screen version of *Carry On*. Hudis was later flown back to the States to complete rewrites, such was CBS's interest in the project, but a series never materialised. Another assignment enabled him to reimburse Rogers, not that it was necessary. 'It was sheer pride, I guess,' admits Hudis. 'It was the biggest cheque I've ever written.' It was also an example of his loyalty, exemplified previously by his reaction when film companies had clamoured for his services upon the earlier success of *Sergeant*. That film's popularity had taken everyone by surprise and had led to a flood of offers from a raft of British production companies. 'When the contract was put in front of me, all I had to do was fill in the amount and sign it. The business is like that: if you have one success they'll give you anything; if you have a flop, they'll cut you off at the knees. It's business – and showbusiness at that. There's no mercy.' While Rita Hudis had felt the time was right to move on and capitalise on *Sergeant*'s success, Norman had thought it would have been 'disloyal' and had chosen to stay with Rogers and Thomas. As he later discovered, the producer and director would have understood if he'd upped anchor in search of new adventures. When Hudis had signed up for another year after *Sergeant*, Gerald Thomas had told him that, with the world now at his feet, he and Rogers had expected him to depart. By 1966, though, with the American agency securing work and with one of his first major jobs being *The Man from U.N.C.L.E.*, Hudis's future in America was firmly established.

II

While Hudis was adept at writing tear-jerking moments as well as straight comedy sequences, Talbot Rothwell's fortes were innuendo, double entendre and good old slapstick. His was a bawdy humour: cheeky and titillating but never rude or offensive. If Hudis's scripts boasted meaningful moments and subtle humour, Rothwell's were the antithesis of his predecessor's: blatant, unabashed in-your-face wit and he was to play an indispensable part in developing the *Carry On* style and endearing it to a growing number of people over the coming years.

Born in Bromley, Kent in 1916, Rothwell studied at art school before gaining employment as a clerk at Brighton Town Hall. Three months later he moved on and joined, in 1936, the Palestine Police for eighteen months before returning home. At the outbreak of war, he was commissioned into the Royal Air Force as a pilot, based in Scotland; unfortunately, his plane was shot down over Norway and he spent the next five years as a prisoner of war. During his days at Stalag Luft 3 Air Force Prisoners' Camp, Rothwell started nurturing his talent for writing by supplying sketches for camp concerts; it was at the camp that he also met Peter Butterworth, a fellow prisoner, with whom he would work on the *Carry Ons*, beginning with *Cowboy*.

After the war he resigned from the forces and pursued his ambition of becoming a professional writer. Soon he was supplying material to the Crazy Gang and Arthur Askey. His first play, *Queen Elizabeth Slept Here*, was staged in 1948, with a second, *Once Upon A Crime*, following quickly, by which point he was also writing for Terry-Thomas's radio shows. Later, he found himself writing for Thomas again, this time for his television programme *How Do You View?* as well as for a host of other productions, including *The Ted Ray Show*, *Dear Dotty* and, notably, Frankie Howerd's *Up Pompeii!*.

In engaging Talbot Rothwell, Peter Rogers realised that his films would be moving in a different direction. 'His writing was entirely different from Norman's,' says Rogers. 'Norman Hudis was more sentimental, in terms of writing, than Talbot Rothwell could ever be. Talbot couldn't do tear-jerkers and was the first to admit it. He said: "No, I can only do Crazy Gang sort of material." It stood us in very good stead, of course, but was an entirely different way of working.'

The new direction for the *Carry Ons* might have been determined by the first script that Rothwell sent to Peter Rogers. In June 1962 his agent Kevin Kavanagh posted Rogers a comedy storyline. Hoping that the props for *HMS Defiant*, the Lewis Gilbert-directed naval adventure starring Alec Guinness and Dirk Bogarde, were still 'lying around'[1], Kavanagh suggested his client's storyline might provide a 'completely new look'[2] for the team. He hoped the material would amuse Rogers – and it did.

He took out an option on Rothwell's naval treatment, *Up the Armada*, which the censor ultimately refused to allow as a title. But Rogers had an alternative script that he wanted the writer to concentrate on. Writers R. M. Hills and S. C. Green had submitted a treatment titled *Call Me A Cab*, and on 1 June 1961 Rogers initiated an agreement for the writers, for the sum of £3,000, but asked Rothwell to undertake the project of penning a full-blown script for a fee of £1,750, which included payment for the final 'chase' sequence, written by fellow writer Sid Colin for a script titled *The Streets of Town*.

Rothwell submitted the final draft of his script in January 1963; it still carried the title *Call Me A Cab*, with initial publicity material stressing that it was the return of familiar faces but wasn't a *Carry On*. This stance remained until, at the eleventh hour, it was renamed *Carry On Cabby* to capitalise on the series's growing popularity.

Bringing a new scriptwriter into the fray wasn't the only change at this stage in the film series's history. The upbeat, jolly musical scores that would become another trademark would now be composed and conducted by Eric Rogers, usurping Bruce Montgomery. Upon being demobbed from the Air Force after the war, Rogers spent his gratuity on forming a small orchestra to play at various London venues. His musical talents were soon spotted and he was employed as an accompanist/arranger for artists like Fred Emney and Julie Wilson before he became a musical director and, ultimately, a composer of background music for small and big screen productions.

Leading the orchestra for the *Carry On* scores, which normally took two days to record, was Pat Halling, who reminisces about days spent recording the music at Anvil Studios, part of Denham Film Studios. The morning session always began with a tot of Scotch, a ritual enjoyed by Eric Rogers. He'd arrive at the studio carrying his violin case, specially adapted to transport two bottles of Scotch and a supply of glasses. 'He referred to it, jokingly, as "Taking an 'A'" – because before the start of the recording we'd all tune up together, usually taking an "A" from the oboe or piano.' Everyone was invited to join Rogers for a snifter. 'On a cold morning, it wasn't a bad idea and set the tone for the day.'

Although Halling enjoyed working with Rogers's predecessor Bruce Montgomery, whom he described as a 'true professional' although 'a little undisciplined', he has nothing but respect for Eric Rogers. 'There was really no comparison. Eric was a genius, both in his writing and his command of fitting music to picture – he had no equal. Working with him was exciting; he had a razor-sharp musical mind and was always ahead of everyone in the orchestra.'

Behind the morning ritual and Rogers's propensity for sharing a joke or two lay a dedicated man who set consistently high working standards. 'Yes, he joked a lot,' recalls Halling, 'and if you were taken in by all the jokes you'd think he wasn't serious about his work, but of course he was. He was a total and natural musician. He could have done all sorts of things, he was so clever.'

Pat Halling regards the signature tune and incidental music as 'tremendous aspects of the films. Eric wrote some very nice gentle violin solos; they weren't meant to be taken seriously and were probably used for scenes where Hattie Jacques and Kenneth Williams did something silly. He also wrote some rather touching tunes. We covered plenty of music, a lot of it ending up on the cutting-room floor. But if you listen carefully, there are some beautifully cast pieces of music.'

Recording the tunes was a complex affair for Eric Rogers, who had a multitude of tasks to keep an eye on. The film being scored would be playing on a screen, affording Rogers the chance to check on timings. The orchestra, usually consisting of around thirty musicians, sat with their backs to the screen. 'Heaven help anyone who turned around to look at the screen when they were supposed to be working,' says Halling, laughing. 'That was the biggest crime you could commit. Eric was so organised, though, because he had to read the score, listen to the music, give cues to the orchestra, do lead times, watch his clock and the scene – all at the same time.'

Although *Cabby* was a Rothwell script – based on Hills and Green's treatment – in many respects it resembled a Hudis effort more than the style for which Rothwell would later become famous. Scripts bulging with naughtiness and innuendoes were to evolve over the next few pictures. *Cabby* was a taut production with finely tuned performances from cast and crew alike. The storyline concentrated on a battle of the sexes. Charlie Hawkins (Sid James), proud owner of Speedee Taxis, spends so much time running his business and grabbing every opportunity to climb behind the wheel of his cab that cracks begin showing in his marriage. At her wits' end, his long-suffering wife Peggy (Hattie Jacques) seeks revenge by hitting Charlie where it hurts – in his pocket. Adopting the name Mrs Glam, she launches her own taxi service, Glamcabs, with leggy lovelies driving plush Ford Cortinas, their comeliness enabling them to poach Speedee's business with ease. When Charlie discovers who is at the helm of the rival firm, divorce seems inevitable until Peggy and her friend Sally run into serious trouble. Hijacked by crooks while en route to the bank with their takings, it is Speedee Taxis who come to the rescue, with Charlie marshalling his cars to intercept the vehicle, saving his marriage in the process.

All the usual faces were back, except Joan Sims and Kenneth Williams. Williams declined to take part because he'd read the script and 'hated it'.[3] Fans were delighted to see the return of Charles Hawtrey after his absence from the previous film. Hawtrey, though, was worried when, reading the script, he discovered he'd not only have to ride a scooter but drive a cab, too – and he hadn't even learnt to drive. He joked: 'At least I knew that one part of the film would be easy enough, the part where I had to ram a taxi with my scooter!'[4] But in preparation Hawtrey stoically packed in as many driving lessons as possible and passed his test days before filming began.

His delight was short-lived because on the first day at Pinewood Studios, with the car park doubling up as Speedee Taxis' yard, he was involved in an unscripted incident. 'While driving my scooter, Charlie banged into my car in the car park and made a dent. He'd put the scooter in gear and let the clutch out so, of course, it lurched forward. There were a few dents in the scooter, too. He was hopeless at driving, a real danger,' recalls Director of Photography Alan Hume, for whom *Cabby* presented a technical challenge. 'There were lots of close-ups in taxi cabs. When travelling along, I was often hanging outside the taxi with the camera, or fixing cameras on the bonnet or inside facing forward. It was difficult lining the shot up and getting the actors to look as if they were driving. I also remember going round and round a roundabout while lying across the front of the cab.'

The film was released during the first days of summer 1963 with several critics noticing a sturdier storyline than those of its predecessors. A journalist in the *Daily Cinema* wrote: 'More merry *Carry On* larks, brightly plotted and smartly handled, with a full quota of typical jokes . . . In nearly every essential the formula's much as before . . . But the plot's more enterprising – and more in evidence – than in many of the *Carry On* capers.'[5]

Two sequences highlighted as being overdone were the 'Expectant Father' scenes with Jim Dale (making his debut) and the final car chase, but most regarded *Cabby* as a noteworthy entry in the series, full of the usual quips. Meanwhile, a critic in *Variety* noted the early signs of Rothwell's style of *Carry On* scripting emerging. He wrote: 'Slapstick and audacious dialogue of vulgar but honest type of innuendo, especially along sexy lines is generously laced throughout the film.'[6]

III

While the well-played and finely scripted *Cabby* had provided a welcome addition to the *Carry On* list, the same can't be said of the subsequent film, *Jack*, which also began as a non-*Carry On*. Talbot Rothwell returned to the draft script that his agent had sent Peter Rogers prior to *Cabby*. Beginning life as *Poopdecker, R N*, it was also titled, at various moments, *Up the Armada, Carry On Mate* and *Carry On Sailor* before being christened *Jack*. Changing titles repeatedly meant, perhaps, that it suffered an identity crisis, explaining why this limp film lacked fire in its belly. Having Hattie Jacques, Joan Sims and Sid James missing from the line-up didn't help its cause; even Kenneth Williams disliked the final product. After watching it one Friday evening in February 1964, he recorded in his diary: 'It was a lousy, badly made film. Really badly made. The editing was all wrong for comedy.'[7]

The *Carry Ons*' first period piece featured many new faces, with Juliet Mills, Percy Herbert, Donald Houston and Cecil Parker making their only appearances in the series. Set in the days of Nelson, the nation is at loggerheads with Spain and with a bigger navy required to prevent defeat, new recruits, and some who haven't even graduated from naval academy, including Albert Poop-Decker, who's been trying for eight and a half years to make the grade, are roped in to defend Britain.

The team's first foray into period costume wasn't universally welcomed by the press, with a reviewer in *The Times* thinking 'the series should return to form when it returns to the twentieth century.'[8] The dearth of regular faces, as well as a scarcity of females, limiting the scope for sexual innuendoes, was noted by David Robinson in the *Financial Times*.[9] But there was the exception, with a journalist in the *Daily Cinema* suggesting that the 'tried and true humour which latterly tended to lose its lustre through overwork in modern surroundings, here takes on a freshly funny impact in Nelson's navy.'[10] Still, Patrick Gibbs in the *Daily Telegraph* regarded the film as 'a good deal less exuberant than its predecessors.[11] Although some applauded the film, it was hardly the best to date, and it was the most expensive, with production costs reaching nearly £170,000.

Before tackling period costume in earnest with *Cleo*, the spy spoof *Carry On Spying* saw the team delight *The Times*'s critic by returning to the modern day. With a working title of *Come Spy With Me*, an early version of the script – before casting – had character names of Philip Bull for Kenneth Williams, Janie May for Joan Sims, Art Accleston for Kenneth Connor, Fingers Allen for Charles Hawtrey, Lucky Dexter for Sid James and Amelia Barley for Esma Cannon.

Some of the actors weren't available for the film and, ultimately, none of the character names survived the various drafts.

The film did, however, launch Barbara Windsor's *Carry On* career. Strolling into the ninth film with ample supplies of cheekiness and charm, her personality soon endeared her to everyone associated with the films. Born in East London in 1937, Windsor, the daughter of a bus conductor and a dressmaker, knew from childhood that she wanted to make a living from the world of entertainment. As a teenager she enrolled at the Aida Foster Stage School and at fifteen made her West End debut in the chorus of *Love from Judy*. Subsequent stage work took her around the world, while her film debut was as a schoolgirl in 1954's *The Belles of St Trinian's*. But it was an appearance in 1963's *Sparrows Can't Sing* that led to her being cast in *Spying*.

Windsor played Daphne Honeybutt, the secret agent with a photographic memory who's part of the team headed by inept Desmond Simkins (Kenneth Williams). They are sent to retrieve a top-secret formula stolen from a research unit at Bilkington by the infamous Milchmann, who works for the abhorrent Dr Crow and her subversive organisation S.T.E.N.C.H. Windsor's appearance complemented the film, with one critic describing her arrival as 'decidedly an asset',[12] while even Kenneth Williams was impressed, telling his diary, 'I must say I like this Barbara Windsor. She is a charming little girl.'[13]

Spying became the last *Carry On* instalment in black and white. Standards in film-making were improving all the time and the use of colour was becoming the norm, so it was inevitable the *Carry Ons* would eventually adopt the mode full-time, adding to *Cruising* in terms of colour. For period pieces like *Cleo*, *Henry* and *Don't Lose Your Head*, colour undoubtedly enhanced the product, providing a richness that black and white lacked; and for technicians like Alan Hume, it was a simpler medium to work with. Despite the obvious advantages of colour for contemporary subjects, black and white cinematography engendered a unique atmosphere. For example, observe the scenes set in Vienna in *Spying*, where the agents are spotted scampering around dimly lit streets and alleyways, dodging puddles in the dark evenings. This almost resembles the visual style associated with classic *film noir*.

As well as regulars Hawtrey and Williams – who swapped his hitherto 'uppish' characterisations for an amusing portrayal laced with all the hallmarks of the famous 'Snide' character used to such good effect in *Hancock's Half-Hour* – Bernard Cribbins provided solid support as a fellow agent together with other reliable performers, including Richard Wattis, Eric Barker and Dilys Laye – donning a fur coat supplied by Peter Rogers's late wife, film producer Betty Box. Jim Dale, meanwhile, appeared in his biggest role to date as Carstairs, 'Our Man in Vienna', which necessitated him dressing as six different characters – a challenge he relished. 'The difficulty was in projecting my main character through the disguises. On at least two occasions I am, facially, totally unrecognisable but to keep to the storyline it was important that the audience wouldn't think an entirely new character had been introduced into the plot – I only hope that I succeeded.'[14] Of the various disguises he used, he enjoyed them all 'except the pick-up girl. The padding I didn't mind, but wearing those high-heeled shoes . . . my feet were killing me!'[15]

Spying met with approval from the critics, with a *Times'* journalist welcoming its return to form after the 'unfortunate tangle with the costume extravaganza'[16] while Ian Cameron in the *Spectator* rated it the 'funniest'[17] to date. Other broadsheets, unlike their reviews for earlier films in the series, were equally complimentary, with Dilys Powell in the *Sunday Times* rating the standard of farcical acting 'pretty good'[18] and singling out Bernard Cribbins for praise. Of course, you can't please everyone, and a journalist at the *Daily Telegraph* thought the series was beginning to 'look and sound remarkably tired'[19] but a contemporary's assessment in the *Guardian* typified the essence of the films, stating: 'It is pretty funny if you're in a really undemanding mood.'[20]

The final production cost for *Spying* was just over £142,000, an overspend of more than £11,000 against the modest budget. An astute businessman as well as a skilful producer and writer, Peter Rogers had a reputation, of course, for turning out films on time and under budget. Although the overrun wasn't significant in retrospect, Rogers explained the reasons to Stuart Levy at Anglo-Amalgamated. Several unexpected incidents had contributed. On 29 April 1964,

Rogers wrote: 'Due to a chapter of accidents in which (a) Charles Hawtrey collapsed on the set owing to being held upside down too long (b) Kenneth Williams injured himself falling from a piece of angle iron in the roof [and] (c) an iron girder split because of unsuspected metal fatigue and had to be renewed; thus holding up production during the intricate automation sequence at the end of the film, artistes' contracts went over their specified period resulting in a certain amount of daily-rate overage.'[21]

Completing films in six weeks was the norm, with a momentum beginning from day one on the set: everyone associated with the *Carry Ons* knew exactly what was expected of them. Peter Rogers says: 'The director David Lean used to say to me: "Peter, I don't know how you can make those films as quickly as you do. You must have weeks and weeks of rehearsals before you shoot." I replied: "No, we just rehearse and shoot."'

Just as Rogers and Thomas retained a cluster of actors who would move from one film to the next, they also tried to hire the same production team each time; that way, not only did the producer and director know what to expect from their crew but the cameramen, make-up designer and other members of the team were aware of the high expectations required of them if they were to hack it on the *Carry Ons*. 'I was independent so helped myself to whoever was going, if available,' states Rogers. 'We were released through ABC who couldn't understand why I wouldn't make the films at Elstree, where their studios were. I told them I was staying at Pinewood and that if they didn't like me making them there, I wouldn't make them at all. I knew the cast there, the workmen, the sparks, the chippies – everybody. I wasn't going to start working at a studio where I'd never worked before.'

Director of Photography Alan Hume recalls: 'The films got a reputation for being low-budget and a bit "hurry, hurry, hurry". The schedule, no matter what, was six weeks. The preparation was about two days, during which time you had to get all the equipment ready and pre-light the first set. We then had six weeks, which included the end-of-picture party. There weren't many films that actually finished bang on schedule, but the *Carry Ons* usually did.' Hume admits that, at times, the pressure intensified. 'Sometimes it wasn't easy keeping up, especially on location because you had no control over the weather. You could go out and start shooting a scene and it would be lovely but before you knew it, it was raining. In the studio, of course, you had total control and it was simply a question of getting on with it.' He admits that it would have been better without the pressure, but understands the reasons for the tight schedules. 'Peter and Gerald were there to make money and time *is* money in the film business.'

The pressure was equally intense for the actors, especially those who joined the team later on and weren't used to the methods of working. Berlin-born actress Elke Sommer, for example, appeared in just one film, *Behind*, as sexy Russian archaeologist Professor Vooshka. When interviewed, she said: 'If it rains or snows they don't care – they shoot it, which is okay because they are really moving along. They're shooting incredibly fast, so you have to know your lines because there's no such thing as shooting a scene five times in this picture.'[22]

The work ethos didn't change, even as the series developed and the films became mainstays of the British film industry. 'Peter and Gerald didn't start saying: "Oh well, we're making money now . . ." No, everything remained the same, with a tightly controlled schedule and budget,' says Hume. 'No overtime was worked – in fact, the studios were locked at lunchtimes. When we finished work it was 5.30 or 5.40, bang on the dot – finished! I can't remember ever working overtime on a *Carry On.*'

Shooting began at 8.30 a.m. but Alan Hume usually reached the studio for 8 a.m. He'd meet with the chief electrician and set to work lighting the first shot of the day, by which time Gerald Thomas would have arrived. 'Everybody was on time; it's bad news to be late on a film set because you're holding everybody else up. By 8.40 at the latest, we'd be ready to shoot the first scene of the day.' The actors would appear on the set and rehearse. 'It wouldn't take them long – they were so professional and knew their lines. For the other shots, while we were setting up the lighting and so on, their stand-ins would come in and the actors would sit in a group, rehearsing the scene. Sometimes they'd be laughing their heads off; there was always a lovely atmosphere on the stage. Everyone enjoyed working on the *Carry Ons.*'

Bob Monkhouse and his wife, Elizabeth, during a break in the filming of *Sergeant*.

Amanda Barrie made her second and final appearance in *Cleo*, playing the sultry Cleopatra.

Hengist Pod (Kenneth Connor) became an unexpected hero in *Cleo*.

Secret agent Daphne Honeybutt (Barbara Windsor) finds herself being interrogated in *Spying*.

Gun-slinging Annie Oakley (Angela Douglas) sought revenge in *Cowboy*.

Harry H. Corbett, alias Harold Steptoe, made his one and only appearance in *Screaming!*, regularly filming alongside Fenella Fielding.

Peter Butterworth (back right) and Bernard Bresslaw (gritting his teeth) headed for Camber Sands, East Sussex, for *Follow That Camel*.

Angela Douglas (front left) relaxes with her husband, actor Kenneth More, and Kenneth Williams while filming *Follow That Camel*.

Mr and Mrs Eyer, who managed The Royal Goat Hotel, where the cast stayed in Snowdonia while filming *Up the Khyber*, met Kenneth Williams at Pinewood.

Terry Scott reveals his tummy while filming *Up the Khyber* in Snowdonia.

Anita Harris, as Nurse Clarke in *Doctor*, stands outside Maidenhead Town Hall, used to represent the Borough County Hospital.

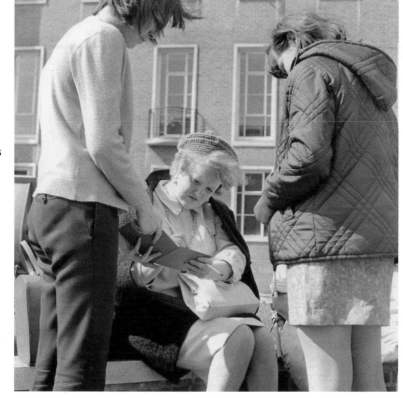

Patsy Rowlands signs autographs while taking a break from filming *Again Doctor*.

Jim Dale entertains some admirers.

Dr Carver (Kenneth Williams) returns from a tropical nightmare in *Again Doctor* to discover it's all change.

Accident-prone Dr Nookey (Jim Dale)
was soon sent packing in *Again Doctor*.

It's all smiles as some of the *Carry On* regulars pose.
(Left to right) Charles Hawtrey, Kenneth Williams, Hattie Jacques,
Sid James, Joan Sims, Jim Dale and Barbara Windsor.

One of the most famous *Carry On* scenes saw Babs (Barbara Windsor) lose her bikini top during an early morning PT lesson in *Camping*.

Certainly not camping weather, the mud in Pinewood's orchard, used to represent the Paradise Camp Site, was sprayed green to represent grass.

Peter Rogers explains that everybody got on famously and some even popped along to the studio to be with their pals, even when they weren't on call. 'There were retired technicians and crew members who asked to come back when they knew another *Carry On* was being made. There was no nonsense about the shooting, it was professional. The sparks, chippies, plasterers, everyone knew what we were doing, that's how we managed to keep to our schedules. Soon, we had American pictures at Pinewood and technicians would say to me: "I wish you were producing this film, they don't know what they're doing."'[23]

Tight deadlines might have been the name of the game but sometimes actors would have welcomed a little more rehearsal time. Rosalind Knight, who played bespectacled young Nurse Nightingale in *Nurse* and stern-faced school inspector Felicity Wheeler in *Teacher*, says: 'To rehearse some of the major sequences, like the scene in the staffroom with the itching powder in *Teacher*, Gerald Thomas told us to "itch slowly at first", then more frantically and then to "go round the table scratching each other". That was the direction. I also had to film the love scene with Kenneth Connor on the very first day of shooting – I didn't even know him. We'd got through that day's schedule so quickly it was suddenly time for the love scene. I said: "I don't know him, this is the first day!" I was told not to worry, just to get on with it. It went very, very well, though.' That was the case with most scenes: yes, there are production bloopers throughout the films, but at the time it wasn't felt worthwhile, economically or practically, to reshoot: now, decades later, such continuity slip-ups have become part of the *Carry Ons*' appeal.

Alan Hume enjoyed working with all the regulars. 'Kenneth Connor was very funny and used to make me roar with laughter, a great character. Kenneth Williams was the top dog, I'd say. He was very clever and had a wonderful "I'm better than you" personality. Hattie Jacques was a charming person, Joan Sims was lovely and Barbara Windsor was great company on the set. Charles Hawtrey was slightly oddball, though; latterly, he was fond of a tipple at lunchtimes. His mother used to come to the studio to try and look after him. He was very good and seldom fluffed a line but sometimes people were worried about him, and his mother would almost hold his hand.' Concurring with Hume, Rogers recalls Hawtrey's mother getting drunk, too, and throwing toilet rolls along the studio corridor.

IV

A key reason why the films were completed on time and within budget was director Gerald Thomas. His experience as a film editor paid dividends when working swiftly because he could deconstruct a scene in his head, knowing exactly the shots required to keep editing to a minimum. 'He was the leader of the team,' says Hume.

His competency bred confidence among crew and cast, which they needed when filming *Cleo* and the subsequent historical yarns *Don't Lose Your Head, Henry* and *Dick*. For such non-contemporary settings, more research was required; although no eagle-eyed members of the public were out to spot mistakes of authenticity – after all, it was a *Carry On*, not a historical biopic – accuracy remained important. The use of colour came into its own for these lavish – well, by *Carry On* standards, anyway – productions. It helped, of course, that for *Cleo* Richard Burton, Elizabeth Taylor and Rex Harrison had just finished filming 20th Century Fox's 1963 Oscar-winning blockbuster, *Cleopatra*. Sets and costumes from this production were deposited in the stores and quickly requisitioned for use on *Cleo*. Often, such historical romps contained larger than normal casts, with plenty of extras required for various scenes, and the costume designers had their work cut out sourcing sufficient costumes within their modest budgets, as Julie Harris, designer on *Cleo*, explains. 'There was a terrible lack of money, a very tight budget. When it's like that, you have to rely on goodwill with the costumier: getting them to put an additional yard of material in or making an extra little bodice that's not in the budget.' As for the amount of research invested, Harris says: 'I can't say one did as much as one might have done on something as serious as, say, *Cleopatra*. But one always kept the period in mind, although there was some invention.' Even though *Cleopatra* had one thing in common with the *Carry On*s, – namely, that some critics weren't enamoured of the end product – there were few other similarities, particularly in terms of expenditure. While the Taylor-Burton production was allocated a budget in excess of $30 million, *Cleo*'s was £194,000. But when 20th Century Fox decided that costs had to be slashed, many sumptuous sets were discarded. So *Cleopatra*'s loss was *Cleo*'s gain.

Producer Peter Rogers and director Gerald Thomas, however, nearly came unstuck when retailing giant Marks and Spencer considered suing the film-makers on seeing the name 'Marcus et Spencius' used for the brothers specialising in buying and selling slaves in the film; apparently, it was using the firm's trade-mark green and gold colours – an unintentional action – which annoyed the company most. Fortunately, matters were resolved before any legal action was deemed necessary. But an incident involving the advertising poster for *Cleo* went further: the film company, 20th Century Fox, owned the copyright of a painting by artist Howard Terpning which they'd adapted for *Cleopatra*'s publicity campaign. The poster design was adopted for *Cleo*, too, with minor changes involving the actors' faces; 20th Century Fox weren't amused by Anglo-Amalgamated's tongue-in-cheek act and took the distributors to court. Issues were finalised with Anglo-Amalgamated agreeing to make minor alterations to the *Carry On* design. Meanwhile, away from the law courts, *Cleo* – which saw Amanda Barrie recruited as sultry Cleopatra – was released to much acclaim.

The first public screening was on 17 December 1964, and by February 1965 the managing director of Associated British Cinemas was writing to Peter Rogers stating that *Cleo*'s run in London alone, which had pocketed around £100,000, had only been bettered within the last twelve months by the epic *Zulu*. The film's success wasn't confined to this country, with Philip Jacobs, Anglo-Amalgamated's overseas sales manager, announcing that the film had broken all records in Australia, beating such prestigious productions as *Lawrence of Arabia* and *El Cid*.

The use of the lavish *Cleopatra* sets was noticed by the critics, with a scribe in the *Daily Express* commenting: 'It is all done with enormous gusto, every joke is bludgeoned home with a leer or a nudge in elaborately splendid Roman and Alexandrine settings.'[24]

And while some felt that the script could have been funnier, Ian Wright in the *Guardian* regarded it as a social document in 'its own right with "Made in Britain" stamped on every frame.'[25] Cecil Wilson in the *Daily Mail* poured scorn on Burton and Taylor's production, classing Rogers and Thomas's release as the definitive film about Cleopatra. Wilson, who'd often been a lone voice among his contemporaries by publicly supporting the *Carry On*s, went further with his compliments: 'It is the most sumptuous of all the ten *Carry On* comedies. Not the funniest but still very funny in parts and a far bigger laugh than the more ambitious efforts of the Taylor-Burton-Harrison team.'[26]

In *Carry On* circles it seemed that 'spoofs' was the in-word: after parodying spy films and historical blockbusters, the last two films to be distributed by Anglo-Amalgamated were in the same vein – this time concentrating on westerns and horror flicks with *Cowboy* and *Screaming!*, released in 1965 and 1966 respectively. The former marked the debuts for two actors who would join the club of regulars: Bernard Bresslaw, the gentle giant who would usually portray good-hearted but rather obtuse characterisations, and Peter Butterworth, who instilled a diffidence and a dithering quality to his sixteen character portrayals, ranging from Josh Fiddler in *Camping* to Tom in *Dick*.

Born in London in 1934, Bresslaw studied at RADA where he was awarded the Emile Littler Award for 'Most Promising Actor'. Soon after graduating, he appeared in the Laurence Olivier-staged *MacRoary Whirl*, playing an Irish wrestler; so impressed was Olivier with the performance that he later asked Bresslaw to replace him in *Home and Beauty* while he took a well-earned rest. Before long, Bresslaw was appearing on the big and small screens, with film credits including *Men of Sherwood Forest*, *Up in the World* and *Too Many Crooks*; his early television work, meanwhile, included appearances in, among others, *The Vise*, *Danger Man* and the long-running sitcom *The Army Game*, in which he played Private Popplewell, the most prominent of his small-screen roles. Thanks to Popplewell, he became a recognised face although on the screen thereafter he was largely restricted to goofy roles and, sadly, screen audiences rarely had the opportunity to see Bresslaw turning his hand to more serious parts, something he was more than capable of doing. But while his range was limited on screen, he continued exploiting his classical training with wonderful aplomb on stage, his preferred medium, appearing in, for example, Shakespeare's *Two Gentlemen of Verona* and *Much Ado About Nothing*.

The other newcomer was equally experienced. Peter Butterworth, born in Bramhall, Greater Manchester, in 1919, was nearing thirty when he decided to tread the boards professionally. Prior to acting, it seemed as if he was destined for a military career; he enlisted in the Fleet Air Arm when the Second World War began in 1939, but when, two years later, his plane was shot down over the Dutch coastline, he spent the rest of the war years in a POW camp, where he met writer Talbot Rothwell and performed in camp concerts.

Bitten by the acting bug, Butterworth returned to civvy street determined to become a professional actor and before long had secured work in repertory theatre, revues and summer shows. Television work followed, starting with children's productions before he branched out and appeared in, among others, *Emergency – Ward 10*, *Danger Man* and *Public Eye*. Prior to making his *Carry On* debut, he'd gained experience in films, too – his credits included *Murder at the Windmill* and *Murder She Said*.

As always, there was much jollity on the set of *Cowboy*. Before long, Bresslaw realised there was going to be a lot of hanging around – literally, much to the merriment of Gerald Thomas and the gang because Bresslaw was subjected to a prank, as his widow Liz Bresslaw recalls. 'Bernie was scared of heights. He'd always joke: "Considering I'm so tall, it's a ridiculous thing to admit, but I do hate heights."' In *Cowboy* he played an Indian and had to go up a tree. Apparently it took quite a time to coax him up. He said to Gerald Thomas: "You're not going to leave me up there long, are you?" Gerald reassured him that they'd get him down as quickly as possible. He eventually perched himself on a high branch, at which point Gerald said: "OK, everybody, break for lunch."' But the director wasn't joking, and Bresslaw found himself stranded in his eyrie, on a wooden platform, with his snack winched up to him.

For this, the eleventh film, we head west to Stodge City, where the Rumpo Kid, alias Sid James, causes mayhem in the once-sleepy town. The Kid is trigger-happy and turns to his pistol whenever he feels the need; sadly, no one has the guts to stand up to the gunslinging bully, until Annie Oakley and Marshall P. Knutt, played by Angela Douglas and Jim Dale, arrive on the scene.

As always, location shooting was kept local, with Chobham Common and Buckinghamshire's Black Park replicating the American Wild West, while the masterly crafted streets of Stodge City were constructed on Pinewood's back lot. It was the responsibility of art director Bert Davey to create Stodge from the thoughts of scriptwriter Talbot Rothwell. Studying myriad books on the Wild West, he designed the façades of housing, offices, a jail, a bank, a gunsmith, a saloon and much more – all within six weeks.

Suitable outdoor locations to represent the windswept landscapes of the West took some finding, particularly a piece of land large enough for filming a scene where Indians attack the stagecoach transporting Annie Oakley and Marshall Knutt to Stodge. Rogers thought some of the humour would be lost if the landscape didn't look right, but within days he had found his spot: with the addition of a few dummy cacti and plaster rocks, Surrey's Chobham Common was transformed into the plains of Arizona.

Talbot Rothwell submitted the final draft of the screenplay on 11 May for his usual fee of £5,000, although his agent Kevin Kavanagh had tried, unsuccessfully, to secure Rothwell a slice of any subsequent profits. When Kavanagh reported back to his client, Rothwell wrote to Rogers expressing his disappointment: 'I have instructed Kevin to forget the whole thing, and would be pleased if you would do likewise. It just doesn't matter. Life's too short as it is. The only important thing is that I'm doing something I want to do, and am grateful to you for giving me the chance to do it.'[27] Rothwell, feeling deflated, also wrote that 'it's quite obvious that both he [Kavanagh] and I have seriously overestimated my worth.'[28] Rogers replied, informing Rothwell that no discussion had taken place with the agent and that such talk had originated from a throwaway remark some time ago, with Rogers stating that he *might* consider it. The producer, however, valued Rothwell's work and wanted him to know. Rogers's explanation helped and a week later Rothwell closed the matter with another missive, joking: 'Believe me, I couldn't care less about the percentage. As you well know, where money is concerned I'm about as ambitious as a eunuch at an orgy.'[29]

As the cast and crew gathered for the first day's filming on Chobham Common on 12 July 1965, the British summer was up to its old tricks and incessant rain meant the first day was wiped out, not the kind of start Rogers and Thomas wanted. Eventually, the scenes depicting Indians attacking the stagecoach were securely in the can, but it had been a challenging sequence for Director of Photography Alan Hume. 'We needed a good stretch to get the stagecoach going – there was lots to do. We also had to film the Indians going round and round, shooting arrows towards the stage-coach, film the driver, the horses, the wagon wheels, and then repeat these scenes over and over a few times. We shot a lot of repetitive material which the director put together in the cutting room, making it look like continuous action.'

The capricious weather continued to affect filming over the following days, but it didn't dampen the spirits of the principal actors. Although he had, as always, been rather critical of the films while completing his diaries, Kenneth Williams wrote in his auto-biography that he regarded *Cowboy* as the best in the series, although not the most comfortable physically. He adopted a distinctive voice for his character, Judge Burke, and paid the price. 'By the end of the first week one side of my face had become very painful and I realised that my American voice, spoken out of one side of the mouth, had taken my jaw out of alignment. I was stuck with it.'[30] Deciding to portray the character in this way on day one meant that he was lumbered with it for the entire shooting period.

Sid James enjoyed himself, too. His widow Valerie confirms that *Cowboy* was also her late husband's favourite. 'Sid loved doing the *Carry On*s, partly because he knew it was a guarantee that he'd do two a year. He was the rock and everyone else bounced off him. He loved *Cowboy* and even took lessons in how to ride a horse at the riding stables at Pinewood. He had a basic idea but was quite nervous about getting on a horse.'

Angela Douglas was another performer making her *Carry On* debut, and she too regards *Cowboy* as her personal favourite. Born in Gerrards Cross, Buckinghamshire in 1940, Douglas – who was married to actor

Kenneth More – recalls a phone call from her agent advising her that Rogers and Thomas wanted to meet her at London's Dorchester Hotel. 'I had a big spot on my chin at the time, probably because I was very young in those days – about twenty-six – and used to get stressed. So I had to hide it before going over to meet them. They offered me the role of Annie Oakley, which was great fun and my favourite part in the series.' Douglas recalls being shy when it came to her singing number in the film. 'I'm not a singer and was never very confident being glamorously dressed, showing my bosoms. My costume was fantastic, though, specially made and beautifully tailored. There I was in my diamanté and my tights. I was so nervous I think I was given a double brandy and pushed on.'

The farcical burlesque was executed perfectly by the actors, whose efforts were largely recognised in the press, with a correspondent in *The Times* classing the film as 'easily the best of their parodies.'[31] But the *Guardian*'s critic felt the film stood out because it contained the most 'obscene double entendres that have ever, I believe, graced the cinema.'[32] Ian Christie, at the *Daily Express*, classed the film 'Good simple, dirty fun'[33] and had nothing but praise for, in particular, Sid James who he felt had made 'a permanent dent in the image of the Western bad-man.' Even the assessments of the broadsheets' critics seemed to be mellowing, with more and more speaking in favour of the films, such as the *Sunday Times*'s correspondent, who regarded it as 'not only the best of the bunch but a corker of a comedy by any standards.'[35]

V

Such high standards flowed over into the next entry, *Screaming!*. A sublime piece of cinematic comedy and a highly amusing spoof on the Hammer horrors, it marked a welcome return for Fenella Fielding as vampish Virula Watt, who purred seductively in her figure-hugging maroon full-length dress. Apart from her role as a lonely housewife in *Regardless*, Virula provided Fielding with her only other excursion into the *Carry On* world – and what a splendid job she did, too.

Looking back on her career, Fielding explains that her big break was in the musical *Valmouth*. When the production's main player had to leave days before going into rehearsal, Fielding was offered the part, despite – under normal circumstances – being too young for it. The exposure, however, catapulted her along the career path and led to a revue, *Pieces of Eight*, with Kenneth Williams. Before long, she was cast in *Carry On Regardless*. Primarily a theatre actress, Fielding nonetheless enjoyed playing the vamp in *Screaming!* and has a story to tell about her revealing costume. 'Before we started shooting, the costume designer decided to try cutting out a diamond shape in the midriff of my dress, filling it with black elastic fishnet. But when shooting began, it was regarded as too distracting with all the cleavage. So the removed piece was put back.' Unfortunately, it resulted in the most uncomfortable costume for Fielding. 'When you sew something back without adding extra material, you make it much smaller; so the whole thing lifted up and moved further up my ribs, meaning that the waist was no longer in the right place. I couldn't sit down without creasing it, so ended up with a leaning board. I didn't sit down for six weeks, except for a scene with Harry H. Corbett, which was so difficult!'

Equally impressive in their roles were Kenneth Williams as Virula's dead brother, Doctor Olando Watt; Jim Dale as Albert Potter, who sets off on a danger-strewn hunt when his girlfriend Doris goes missing in Hocombe Woods; Peter Butterworth as the inept Detective Constable Slobotham who attempts to find the missing girl and Joan Sims as cantankerous, henpecking Emily Bung, wife of Detective Sergeant Sidney Bung. The role of the Detective Sergeant was almost inevitably drawn for Sid James, but when it was discovered that the craggy-faced actor was tied up with the Vince Powell-scripted ATV sitcom *George and the Dragon*, Harry H. Corbett, better known to audiences as Harold Steptoe in the long-running sitcom *Steptoe and Son*, was offered the role, earning him the princely sum of £12,000.

A latecomer to the film was Charles Hawtrey; the wiry actor replaced Sydney Bromley as Dan Dann, the toilet attendant. But whereas Bromley was going to pocket £125 for the one-off scene, Hawtrey collected £400. On hearing a rumour that Hawtrey, an ever-popular performer in fans' eyes, wasn't going to be cast, a critic mused about whether his absence would have a detrimental affect on *Screaming!*'s success. Worried that there could be some truth in the journalist's prediction, Anglo-Amalgamated's Stuart Levy contacted Peter Rogers, resulting in Hawtrey's casting as the toilet cleaner.

Due to a plot which called for the petrification of the characters so that they could be sold as shop-window dummies – Joan Sims, Angela Douglas as the kidnapped Doris Mann, and Sally Douglas, who played a girl snatched by the Watts and their monster, Odbodd, – all needed body casts made. The actresses had to endure the laborious business of having casts made from head to toe; the two-day task was organised by Bill Bain, head of the plasterers' shop at Pinewood Studios. The most uncomfortable part of the process was producing facial casts, when every inch of the face was covered, with two straws inserted in the nostrils to allow breathing. Recalling the experience, Douglas points out that her cast was left on the floor for a few days. 'They didn't bother putting its clothes on, so you can imagine the scribbles and markings, with arrows in various directions.' Lying the cast down didn't bode well for its figure. 'It gave me a huge ball neck, but from the neck down it was terrific – I wouldn't mind looking like that now!' she admits, smiling.

Joan Sims said: 'At that stage, I felt like all three wise monkeys, neither seeing, hearing nor speaking any evil. Frankly, I was terrified.'[36] Over lunch one day at Pinewood, Sims was overheard explaining to all and sundry about her experience at the plasterers' shop. 'A dear little man came over, looked me up and down and said: "You'll have to take that off" – meaning my blouse. I thought, I don't mind, so off it came. He looked at me again. Eyeing my bra, he was. "No, you don't," I said. "You'll have to take it off," he said, "otherwise the plaster won't stick!" What do you do in a situation like that? I thought, "Oh heck, here goes" and flung it away. The man went off and came back with a great brush and a pail of sloppy-looking stuff. "Lift up your arms," he said. So I put my arms up and he dipped his whitewash brush in and slapped this stuff all over my chest. "Turn round," he said, and he did me at the back, too.'[37] Sims relived the moment in dramatic fashion while telling her story. She added: 'That's not the end. Then the man took some gauze and whacked that on – and great fistfuls of plaster, with him patting round the curves. You can imagine what a terrible mess I looked, quite apart from the embarrassment. Then he did each of my legs. I had to go back the following day to get my head done!'[38]

The film was released in August 1966 and cost just under £180,000 but, surprisingly, met with more than its fair share of criticism – even the trade press, hitherto staunch supporters in most cases, found aspects that they disliked. A scribe in the *Monthly Film Bulletin* wrote that it was 'glum stuff even by *Carry On* standards. The regulars, Kenneth Williams in particular, seem too bored to care; Harry H. Corbett overdoes every line.'[39] Corbett came in for stick from other reviewers, too, with the *Daily Cinema*'s critic stating he 'mugs away as if the film depended on it'[40] while a journalist in *Kine Weekly* felt he still had 'the ghost of Steptoe about his personality'.[41] Michael Thornton in the *Sunday Express*, meanwhile, slated Corbett's performance. Acknowledging that the actor was usually an extremely funny man, here he was 'miserably unfunny in one of the most laboriously self-conscious performances I have seen.'[42] But it wasn't all doom and gloom, with one reviewer applauding the film's presentation, stating that it was 'put over with imagination, some clever trick photography and unbounded enthusiasm on the part of the cast.'[43] But the lion's share of the reviewers, after enjoying a high with *Cowboy*, felt deflated and disappointed by *Screaming!* Many regarded the film as among the dullest and least spirited with even *The Sun* classing it 'as flat as a badly drawn pint.'[44] Perhaps a better description would be wine because it's certainly matured with age and the film, in my view, scores in most departments. Yes, Corbett's style and delivery have all the *Steptoe* trade marks but his overall performance and those of the actors around him, including the far from subdued Williams, as one critic described him, and the seductive Fenella Fielding, as well as a brilliant display from Peter Butterworth, one of the unsung heroes of *Carry On*, are complemented by some credible visual effects, à la Hammer Horror, tight direction and a fitting signature tune. Some of the *Carry On* servings have warranted particular criticism but *Screaming!* deserved a less hostile reception when it entered the arena in summer 1966, just days after the country was enveloped in euphoria after footballer Bobby Moore had lifted the World Cup at Wembley.

Thirteen may be unlucky for some and, initially, it was for the thirteenth film, *Don't Lose Your Head*, the first to be distributed by the Rank Organisation. The change of distributors, as Peter Rogers explains, was not of his choosing. 'Anglo-Amalgamated's Nat Cohen didn't want to do any more. I used to say he got culture up his backside because he went into productions like *Far From the Madding Crowd* and that kind of thing. He didn't want any further *Carry Ons*, so I just crossed the road and went to Rank.'

Rank, however, were conscious of releasing future films under the brand of a competitor and so proceeded to release *Don't Lose Your Head* without the now famous and well-respected *Carry On* title. During the first Rank pre-production publicity meeting, held at Pinewood on 1 September 1966, Rogers appeared to alleviate any concerns about not using the prefix. In the minutes, he's recorded as wondering 'whether the words "Carry On" need be used in the picture . . . he thought that as the film was more visual than previous "Carry On" productions it could stand on its own without any reference to "Carry On".'[45]

The decision, though, was swiftly reversed when early takings at the box office were disappointing. After filming during the autumn of 1966, the picture, concerning two aristocrats who rescue their French counterparts from the guillotine during the country's late-18th century revolution, was released in time for Christmas. It had been another busy schedule for all concerned, especially for Sid James. As well as being cast as Sir Rodney Ffing, he was appearing on stage in Bournemouth for the first four weeks of filming. After a busy day at Pinewood, he was whisked down to the Dorset seaside town for the evening performance before being taken back to his home in Iver, Buckinghamshire for a few hours' sleep until starting the cycle again.

Although initial reaction from fans was slow, critics welcomed *Don't Lose Your Head*. The film's appeal was summed up proficiently by critic Penelope Gilliat, who wrote: 'The film techniques . . . have got better in their new film and the jokes, thank heaven, worse. There is probably no way of passing on to anyone born outside this country the English satisfaction in rotten puns, schoolboy squelches and blue innuendoes.'[46] She complimented the film, classing the photography as 'rather good'[47] and the double meanings 'dazzingly dirty'.[48]

There is no doubting the quality of this production. From top to bottom, there is a vitality which was complemented by a top-notch script from Talbot Rothwell, embracing all the usual prerequisites: period-costume extravagance; lean directing and fine cinematographic elements. But despite appreciating the film's attributes, it isn't one of my favourites – nor is the next, *Follow That Camel*, the second film distributed by Rank, and which, again, began life without the *Carry On* moniker. I haven't seen any guest star in a *Carry On* appear more incongruous than Phil Silvers in this Foreign Legion adventure, which saw Bertram West (Jim Dale) join the Legion after thinking he'd lost his sweetheart to another suitor, only for her to come running after him.

Silvers, who'll forever be remembered as Sergeant Bilko in the long-running American military sitcom, was paid £30,000, a colossal amount in *Carry On* terms, for giving up ten weeks, beginning 1 May 1967. The contract also included a thousand dollars per week expenses, first-class travel between Los Angeles and London, a separate limo and chauffeur for taking him to and from the studios and locations, and reimbursement for any reasonable excess baggage charges at the airport.

Location filming took place in the dunes at Camber Sands, Rye, to represent the desert. Silvers was the 'new boy', a position appreciated by singer Anita Harris, who regarded herself as the 'new girl' because she was making the first of her two *Carry On* appearances, playing Corktip, a belly dancer-cum-fortune teller. She was able to identify with the New York-born comedy actor. 'We hit it off as the "new guys". He realised he was in a different medium but he was bringing to it the extraordinary experience of what he had created so there was an element of great cultures coming together with great respect for each other, and I think it worked wonderfully. I don't think it was one of the most successful but it has grown over the years.'

Not everyone was complimentary about Silvers's performance and many of the regulars were guilty of sending him up at times. 'I saw it happening one evening when we were all in the hotel,'[49] admits Peter Rogers. 'I'm afraid I had to take the cast aside and say: "He is a guest, you must treat him properly – not as a star, just manners. Don't go out of your way to send him up."'[50]

The idea to suggest Silvers to play the token American in the film appears to have originated from scriptwriter Talbot Rothwell who, in a letter to Peter Rogers dated January 1967, admitted he was halfway through the script and everything was moving along smoothly; however, he wasn't so sure about the American character which, he wrote, 'simply yells for Phil Silvers all the way along. I just can't get this Bilko image out of my mind; it would fit this situation so well. And it would be wonderful if you could get him.'[51]

Kenneth Williams, in his diaries, said there 'seems to be no respite from this kind of man. Refuses to relax and shut up.'[52] Meanwhile, Angela Douglas, who was cast as Lady Jane Ponsonby, remembers being introduced to Silvers – and they didn't exchange the normal pleasantries one normally associates with meeting someone for the first time. 'I found him very lonely, very strange. I shook hands and said, "Hello, how do you do." He replied: "Angela, have you ever been constipated?" That was a chat-up line and a half!' she laughs.

The role of Sergeant Nocker was originally earmarked for Sid James until a heart attack put paid to any chance of him appearing in the film, which was loosely based on Percival Christopher Wren's novel *Beau Geste*. With Rank wanting an American recruited to help boost sales and distribution across the Atlantic, Silvers, much to Rothwell's delight, was offered the part. A veteran of American television he may have been, but he was hardly an A-list celebrity who'd guarantee audiences flocking to cinemas to watch him appearing in a low-budget British comedy, especially as his most recent US television show had failed; ultimately, he did little to improve the film's success in the States, while his style and vaudeville background were not compatible with the traditional *Carry On* style.

Follow That Camel, which took the cast beyond the normal environs for the first time, was released in September 1967 and, as expected, many critics discussed Phil Silvers's performance. Marjorie Bilbow in the *Daily Cinema* believed that he failed to reach the 'degree of solemnity'[53] enjoyed by others and that his performance was 'very slightly at odds with the rest of the cast.'[54] David Robinson in the *Financial Times* deemed him 'significantly off-form in the hands of . . . Gerald Thomas,'[55] while *The Sun*'s Ann Pacey felt that a fatal mistake had been made in casting Silvers whose 'American face, manner and sense of comedy are out of place in this very English desert. Out of place, in mood and understanding.'[56] Oh, how the cast missed Sid James, who would fortunately be back for the next film.

One of the most widely circulated stories about *Follow That Camel* is still worth another outing. It's the tale of the camel hired from Chessington Zoo in Surrey to add a little authenticity to the setting. The animal was transported in an oversized pantechnicon and en route was stopped by police because its head was poking through the top and causing traffic jams. But the real trouble began the following day when the camel's keeper tried walking it on the sand. The animal was having none of it. Having been born in captivity, he'd never experienced sand, only concrete. So while the camel was trained and encouraged to walk on sand, other scenes were shot.

VI

The obvious difficulties in trying to integrate Phil Silvers into the cast weren't typical of the normal goings-on during the making of a *Carry On* film. For cast and crew alike, getting together on the set was a happy occasion. Alan Hume, director of photography, says: 'By Sunday afternoon I was looking forward to going to work in the morning – it was always fun and always a laugh. I remember we were filming the scene in *Spying* where Kenneth Williams was rushing all over the place, treading on balloons. I had to leave the camera and go and find a quiet corner because I couldn't stop laughing. Next minute, Gerald Thomas came over because he couldn't stop himself laughing, either.'

Everyone on the set respected the skills and style of Thomas. When ready to shoot the next scene, he informed the actors accordingly; being true professionals they jumped to attention and prepared themselves for the shot. Thomas once described himself as much a ringmaster as a director. 'Everyone is enthusiastic because we like each other. My challenge is to keep the enthusiasm within the artists who've done the same thing time and time again – to infuse into them the same enthusiasm that I have for the subject.'[57]

When the actors weren't in front of the camera, they intermingled and chatted like a family or a group of intimate friends. Gerald Thomas once explained what it was like. 'Everyone would be fooling around. Kenny [Williams] was the most terrible practical joker. There would always be rows going on between him and Charlie [Hawtrey] because Charlie used to come onto the set with a plastic bag containing his newspaper, packet of Woodbines, sandwiches and bottle of Coke or Tizer. Every single day Kenny would hide it and when he [Hawtrey] wanted to sit quietly in a corner and do his crossword and eat his sandwich, it was gone. There would be this terrible eruption. But the First Assistant would come on the floor, clap, and say "Right, chaps, be loyal." As soon as he said that, all the fooling about stopped and everyone was ready for the job.'[58]

Once, while discussing the secret behind the *Carry Ons*' success, Sid James said: 'I always enjoy working with Peter and Gerald – they have a great flair for comedy. I think the secret lies in the way you're made to feel part of the team and the film is made without any apparent effort. Of course I know that a great deal of work and planning has been done, but there is never any fuss on the floor. That's the way I like to work.'[59] Charles Hawtrey stated: 'I think the enjoyment stems from the continuity. Unlike other films, where you give a performance and that's the end of it, in *Carry Ons* each performance is an extension of the previous one. You get to know the people you work with and the atmosphere is so much more friendly.'[60] Kenneth Williams, contrary to what he might have written in his diary, felt there must be a 'magic formula'.[61] He added: 'I think one of the greatest enjoyments is that producer, director, crew and artistes are such nice people.'[62] Joan Sims agreed. 'I'm one of the gang, they accept me and, brother, do I like to be accepted!

Sometimes, not very often, I'm down in the dumps, but if I'm working on a *Carry On* I know it won't be for long. They're an incorrigible lot and whether it be producer or tea boy they care about you. It's not just the merry japes or practical jokes, it's a simple and heart-warming fact that you belong.'[63]

Teamwork was one of the keys behind the *Carry Ons*' phenomenal success. Gerald Thomas once admitted: 'It's a kind of ensemble playing with cast and crew all working in the closest harmony. We all know each other's styles by now and can play to each other for effect.'[64] Jacki Piper, who appeared in four *Carry Ons*, says: 'Nobody got paid very much and nobody got star treatment, so you were very much a team. Because of this, no one pulled rank.'

Soon to become a regular face in the series, Jack Douglas adds: 'It really was a team. If Sid or Kenneth, for example, had to say a line or joke that they thought would best be said by me, they'd say so. I remember this happening in *Dick* and Kenneth passing the funny line to me. It got one of the biggest laughs in the picture but he was as pleased as I was that I'd got the accolade.' Douglas rates director Gerald Thomas highly. 'He was one the greatest comedy directors I worked with; he realised there was a lot of humour in the team itself and brought that out into the film.' The director always remained calm and in control and Douglas never saw him lose his temper. 'That's most unusual for a director. He clapped his hands, we stopped laughing and joking and got on with the work.' Peter Rogers, meanwhile, was seen less on the floor. 'He was in his office controlling the finances, making all the arrangements. He handled everything beautifully. He knew exactly what he was doing, where he was going. You couldn't make a suggestion to Peter because he'd already thought about it. They made a wonderful team and that's why they were so successful.'

Sid James said: 'We have an absolute ball. There's never a discordant note. It all stems from our director Gerry Thomas. He's so kind, gentle and understanding. If he was a sod, tempers would fly. If somebody now came on the set and started asking, "Where's my chair?" or complained about a crappy dressing room, the rest of us would be down on him like a ton of bricks.'[65]

Even the occasional *Carry On* players appreciated the convivial atmosphere on the *Carry On* sets, and unlike with other movies they were always welcomed into the 'family'. Alexandra Dane, who had cameo roles in five films, says: 'Working on the *Carry On*s was the happiest, happiest experience. Even when thinking about all the other bits and pieces I did in movies and on telly, I can't remember being happier because everyone was so sweet to you. I adored them all, it was like being part of a big family. They were lovely films to work on.'

Such enjoyment while making the films was evident in the next picture. It was a return, after a gap of twelve films, to the medical wards when *Carry On Doctor* went into production in September 1967, just as the year's other entry, *Follow That Camel*, was released. After clearing the use of *Doctor* in the title with his wife, fellow producer Betty Box, and director Ralph Thomas, who were responsible for the famous *Doctor* movies that starred Dirk Bogarde and others, Peter Rogers set to work. The conveyor-belt approach meant adventures at the Borough County Hospital were on screen by Christmas with Frankie Howerd making the first of his two *Carry On* appearances, playing Francis Bigger, the charlatan spiritualist who travelled around spouting his views on positive thinking being the way to health and happiness – not that his beliefs did him any good when he slipped off a stage and ended up at the Borough.

It was a welcome return for Sid James, albeit in a less prominent role, as bed-bound patient Charlie Roper who hadn't done a stroke of work for years. James was recovering from his earlier heart attack, which had forced his absence from the previous film, but it was a relief to see him back as one of the many patients in Fosdick Ward, where malingerers stayed as long as they liked, nursing minor ailments. James was pleased to be back, appreciating the less arduous role at this stage of his recovery. He joked: 'This ward looks so real, I could easily imagine that I'm back to when I was ill. As long as somebody doesn't come along and present me with a bill at the end of the picture, it will be a lovely way of convalescing!'[66]

And it probably was with beauties like Nurse Parkin, played by Valerie Van Ost, taking care of him. Having already appeared in *Cabby* and *Don't Lose Your Head*, Van Ost enjoyed joining the cast for another *Carry On* outing. 'One of the most famous doctor-patient pictures was taken of me tucking Sid James in bed and telling him off because he's smoking. They blew the picture up to about ten feet by twenty and stuck it outside the Odeon in Leicester Square. It became an amazingly famous picture and has been used to advertise all manner of things.'

It was good to see that James hadn't lost his sense of humour, which was always essential while working on a *Carry On* film as Joan Sims and Frankie Howerd showed while filming a scene in which their characters, with Sims playing Francis Bigger's loyal but extremely deaf assistant, get married when the preacher thinks, incorrectly, that he's only got days to live. With the Chaplain (Peter Jones) hard of hearing, too, the unfolding scene was hilarious as they tried conducting the wedding ceremony. 'For some reason – probably the simple one that it was an extremely funny scene – every time Frankie and I acted the marriage ceremony we would disintegrate into fits of giggles, and our laughter was so infectious that it instantly spread to the crew, which caused such a racket that before we knew it the set was being invaded by actors and technicians shooting other films at Pinewood who wanted to know what was causing all this mirth,'[67] recalls Sims.

After the disappointment of *Follow That Camel* it was good to see a return to what worked best: stories that were rooted in home territory, preferably within familiar institutions or set within environments that we all had experienced or could, at least, recognise. *Doctor* satisfied many critics, including Cecil Wilson in the *Daily Mail* who felt it was an improvement on the preceding film, stating: 'This is more like it. An all-British *Carry On* comedy with Sidney James back in the team, Frankie Howerd reinforcing the fun and no American guest stars chasing alien jokes uphill. It is in a sense a return to Square One, exploring as it does much the same line of bedpan and bedroom humour as *Carry On Nurse*.'[68]

Doctor was well received but of all the *Carry On* scripts that Talbot Rothwell wrote, it is the 1968 classic *Up the Khyber* that is regarded by many as his finest hour. Although I would choose other offerings, like *Abroad, Camping* and, of course, the various medical-based screenplays, *Up the Khyber* is frequently afforded the supreme accolade by fans when grading the films. Many argue that it's the best of the entire series and it was the *Carry On* picture which collected most votes when, in 1999, the British Film Institute ran a poll of the hundred finest British films ever made, with *Up the Khyber* creeping in at ninety-nine.

Rothwell's script, which earnt him £5,000, spotlighted the Third Foot and Mouth regiment, guarding at altitude along the Khyber Pass. Set in 1895, British rule has remained steadfast for decades until the Khasi of Kalabar, alias Kenneth Williams, grasps an opportunity, along with Bunghit Din and the Burpas, to try and rid his country of the British army. The British soldiers' seemingly untouchable position, under ultimate leadership of the governor, Sir Sidney Ruff-Diamond (Sid James), takes a severe dent when their image as unbeatable and brave soldiers is severely threatened thanks to fey Private Widdle (Charles Hawtrey) who is unexpectedly photographed wearing underpants under his kilt. Thinking that the Brits are nothing but softies after all, the Khasi seizes the initiative and attempts to defeat the British army.

The film's life began in earnest in late 1967 when Peter Rogers informed ex-accountant John Davis, who became managing director of the Rank Organisation, that he'd halted production of his planned film *The Man in the Mirror*, due to casting problems. Grasping a moment of opportunity, Rogers wondered whether Davis would be keen on a comedy titled '*Up the Khyber* (or some *Carry On* title) with my usual team of goons plus, probably, Frankie Howerd or someone. It would be about the British "thin red line" antics in India and so on – with all locations in and around Pinewood.'[69] As it happened, Frankie Howerd was already contracted to a stage production so couldn't accept the role of Fakir, initially more prominent than the diluted final screen role suggests. With Howerd's name out of the frame, it's reported that comic Tommy Cooper was considered but when, again, Rogers failed to secure another key target, the role was watered down and offered to Cardew Robinson.

As for Rogers's initial plans of, as usual, utilising locations in and around Pinewood, *Up the Khyber* became one of those rarities in the series because it involved extensive – well, extensive by *Carry On* standards – location filming. For *Up the Khyber* the team travelled further afield than ever before and further than they did in subsequent productions. But when cast and crew started packing their bags, it wasn't to jet off to film on the high peaks of the Himalayas; in fact, the nearest the gang got to traversing the mountains were the lower slopes of Snowdonia, which substituted for the world's highest mountain range. The choice of location certainly had some people fooled: actor Bernard Bresslaw, who played Bunghit Din, leader of the Burpas based in the Afghan hill town of Jacksi, was asked by an Indian waiter in a Newcastle restaurant, convinced that the film had been shot in India, whether he had enjoyed filming in his homeland. And Peter Rogers (who regards *Up the Khyber* as his personal favourite because 'it looks expensive but wasn't' – the final production cost totalled nearly £234,000) received letters from old soldiers who'd served on the North-West Frontier claiming that they recognised the locations.

Sourcing such places was finalised when a party that included director Gerald Thomas and art director Alex Vetchinsky conducted a recce in March 1968. Happy that the sites were apposite, a local man who'd been employed in the same capacity by 20th Century Fox on another film was hired to recruit locals as extras. Meanwhile, finishing touches were applied to the cast list. Along with the familiar faces, Terry Scott returned after a long absence, having last appeared in the inaugral entry, *Sergeant.* This time he earned £2,500 playing the ear-bashing Sergeant Major MacNutt, while Roy Castle was drafted in for his one and only appearance, playing Captain Keene for a fee of £3,500, a role originally intended for Jim Dale until theatre commitments precluded his involvement. When the film was finally released in September 1968, both Scott and Castle were recipients of praise from some critics, one writing: 'Roy Castle is a distinct asset to the team as the fearless Captain Keene, and Terry Scott is ferociously raucous as Sgt-Major MacNutt.'[70]

The cameras began rolling on Monday, 8 April with interior scenes shot on Pinewood's 'F' and 'H' stages, before moving out to the studio lot; sequences, including the opening-scene cricket match, were finalised before everyone headed north-west to Snowdonia. It was a blustery April day when the team checked in at The Royal

Victoria Hotel, Llanberis, and The Royal Goat Hotel, Beddgelert, their bases until the end of May.

The Goat was run by Rita Eyer and her husband; their daughter Ann Koper remembers clearly the day when the *Carry On* team members arrived. 'I would have been 14 at the time and it was exciting to meet all the stars,' she recalls. 'At the initial meeting, I asked if I could have a part as an extra and they said they'd see what they could do. Sadly, I didn't get a part but they arranged for me to be collected from the hotel and driven up to Nant Gwynant. From there I was taken in a Land Rover up to the Watkin Path and spent some time sitting on the side of the hill watching the filming.' She remembers one scene in particular. 'Two of the actors were running away from some gunshots and jumped on the backs of Angela Douglas and Joan Sims – or that's who it was supposed to be. I recall seeing the two stuntmen, dressed as women, thinking they looked nothing like the actresses and wondering how it would look in the film.' Although Ann didn't get her wish to be an extra, the production team made use of local residents, with a group of lads donning military uniform to portray non-speaking soldiers in the Third Foot and Mouth, guarding the Khyber Pass. For one man, in particular, pretending to be a member of the forces wasn't hard – after all, he was a regular in the Royal Marines.

Eric Vasey made his uncredited screen debut in the early scenes when Private Widdle (Charles Hawtrey) feels the cold while guarding the draughty Pass so risks ruining the regiment's highly regarded reputation as 'Devils in Skirts' by surreptitiously wearing underpants. Vasey's parents lived on the headland in Borth-y-Gest, just across the water from Portmeirion, the setting for the 1960s cult series *The Prisoner*. Vasey was enjoying repatriation leave after 18 months in Singapore when his father, a shop manager in the nearby town of Porthmadog, was asked whether his 21-year-old son was interested in becoming an extra. As well as being 'a bit of fun', it would provide 'some extra money' so he accepted the invitation.

'We were picked up by coach in Porthmadog and taken to the bottom of Nant Gwynant. The scenes were filmed on the Watkin Path [leading to the summit of Snowdon] so a local farmer took us up in his Land Rover,' recalls Vasey, whose Singaporean suntan caused a few headaches. 'I'd been there eighteen months so was as brown as a berry. What was noticeable was that when I wore a kilt my legs were brown and everyone else's were white. The production team had to decide whether to white out my legs, brown everyone else's or leave it alone. They decided on the latter.'

Vasey also swapped sides and played a Burpa, with one scene taking inordinate amounts of time to perfect. 'We were led by Bernard Bresslaw, as Bunghit Din, and completed a scene where we were coming down the side of a hill; every few yards there were boulders, and whenever Bernard took his glasses off he couldn't see a thing and would fall flat on his face.'

Meanwhile, a piece involving Kenneth Williams, as the anti-British Khasi of Kalabar, wasn't completed in one take, either, thanks to the actor's mischievous antics. 'All the extras had to walk down a path, with Williams leading us. We were dressed up as Burpas and tribesmen, rushing down the path,' says Vasey, smiling as he recalls the incident. 'We were supposed to be very angry, but Kenneth kept saying this monologue under his breath; we could all hear it except the director, which was just as well because it was as blue as blue could be! It was hilarious, too. He had us in stitches and the director [Gerald Thomas] said: "You're supposed to be annoyed, not laughing!" We had to shoot it a couple of times because we couldn't stop laughing, thanks to Kenneth Williams.'

But the principal actors weren't the only ones grasping any opportunity to fool around. Unbeknown to the *Carry On* crew, Vasey initiated a prank causing confusion. Having worked as a radio operator in Singapore, he couldn't resist the chance to lark about when he realised that the production team were using two-way radio between the bus ferrying people back and forth and the mountain location. 'We were waiting on the bus one day when I noticed the radio on the front seat. Deciding to show off, I pretended to be two different military stations talking to each other. Because I knew all the call signs, I was convincing. I kept the crew off-air for about fifteen minutes before someone finally said something, to which I replied: "Who's that? This is military radio." They went very quiet and started worrying that they were using military air bands. It was only after making the communications increasingly silly, like saying there was a danger of low-flying tanks, that they finally cottoned on to the fact someone was messing around.'

Eric Vasey found most of the cast and crew affable, with one exception: Charles Hawtrey. 'He didn't speak a word to anybody. He had a blanket to keep him warm and sat on his chair with a grim expression on his face. He didn't speak or make eye contact with anyone until it was time to film one of his scenes; then he'd spring to life and do his bit before reverting to the chair again, saying nothing.'

Reflecting on his brief moment of fame playing a 19th-century soldier, Vasey has nothing but happy memories, views shared by other surviving members. But there was a moment, just a brief moment, when it seemed that mutiny was brewing among the ranks. Along with Vasey, farmer John Pritchard, from Beddgelert, was involved in a dispute over money. He explained: 'The strike didn't last long, just a day or two, and they paid us more. They were okay with us and we all shook hands afterwards. It paid a lot better than farming.'[71]

Before filming was complete, a royal visitor arrived on set. Princess Margaret watched some scenes being shot but wasn't too pleased, allegedly, when shown a clip where Sir Sidney Ruff-Diamond (Sid James) wrote a letter to Queen Victoria, using the salutation 'Dear Vicky'. The Princess was, apparently, far from amused. But she couldn't have failed to laugh, like Angela Douglas, at one of the closing scenes – arguably, the most famous from the entire film series when Sir Sidney's palatial residence comes under attack from Bunghit Din and his men. As they continue to munch through dinner, the building is being razed to the ground around them. This, perhaps the *Carry Ons*' best piece of action, technically, was witnessed first-hand by Angela Douglas in her fourth and last appearance. 'I can remember every day just laughing and laughing. At the dinner party scene where the plaster, ceiling and chandeliers are all over the place, there isn't one shot of my face. They weren't able to film me as I couldn't stop laughing; tears were rolling down my face. Just watching Peter Butterworth was wonderful. He was brilliant, so clever. He was my absolute favourite, a darling. They were golden days. I think I could have gone on being the juvenile in the team for maybe another three or four movies, but said goodbye because I wanted to have a baby.'[72]

Stalwart Joan Sims, who played Sid James's screen wife Lady Ruff-Diamond, was equally pleased with the film, although not so keen about the location shooting. She recalled: 'The Khyber Pass sequences were shot on location in Snowdonia, a place which, while undeniably spectacular, did nothing for me at all. I've always suffered from a fear of heights, and being perched on the side of a mountain was not exactly my idea of fun.'[73] She didn't take kindly to being bumped all the way to the set in a Land Rover, either.

VII

If *Up the Khyber* is regarded as Talbot Rothwell's best script, *Camping* must be close behind for entertainment. Technically, it's not the best, and the storyline isn't the most extravagant, based around the isolated adventures of the campers who spend their holidays at Paradise Camp Site, where the proprietor Josh Fiddler (beautifully played by Peter Butterworth) lives up to his name. But the film exudes the warmth associated with the best of the *Carry On* films and, personally, it's one of my favourites.

Although set in summer, *Camping* was shot during the autumn. As is widely known by now, the Orchard at Pinewood was used to represent the campsite, and to disguise the fact that recent heavy rain had turned the patch into a mudpit a clever plan was hatched to spray the mud green to resemble lush grass – and it worked. Recalling the uncomfortable conditions, Dilys Laye, who was seen as Anthea Meeks, says: 'As we shivered in our summer clothes, Gerry Thomas used to say: "Children, think sun!"'

It wasn't the easiest thing to do when it was freezing cold and extremely wet. As Kenneth Williams recalled: 'Our PT lessons in the open air were dreaded by the girls. Barbara [Windsor] complained, "My boobs are all goose pimples and my open-toed sandals are sinking into the mud while I'm trying to be buoyant in a bikini."'[74]

The other well-travelled story relating to *Camping* is the famous bikini scene starring Barbara Windsor. Playing Babs, one of the nubile young women from the finishing school Chayste Place, she loses her bikini top while undertaking morning exercises with the rest of the girls. Lesley Duff, playing one of Babs's friends, remembers watching the scene. 'With the special effects we have today, it wouldn't have been a problem, but I remember someone from the team using a fishing rod for the job. They placed the hook on the front of the bikini top and had to time it so that when Barbara bent her arms, it popped off. One time, the back didn't undo and Barbara was pulled over into the mud – we all killed ourselves with laughter.'

Eventually, the fishing-rod trick worked but, as Barbara Windsor explained, it was important for the censor's sake not to show any bosom. 'The second take was wonderful – it went flying, I got my hands on the boobs and thought, "This is good". I didn't flash a boob or anything. And then Kenny [Williams] had to say: "Take her away, Matron, take them away". Hattie got hold of my right arm, pulled it – and, of course, I flashed the right boob, so they had to go for another take. The third take was fine, not flashing anything. And evidently, when it was shown in front of the censor, he said: "I don't think Barbara Windsor's right bosom is going to corrupt the nation!" And they let it go.'[75]

Camping was released in February 1969 although originally it was due to go into production at the close of 1966. However, Peter Rogers wasn't happy with Rothwell's initial draft and wanted it reworked. It was worth putting in the extra effort because the film recouped the production costs within days, quickly becoming a box-office winner. Even so, critics still dished out their normal fare of mixed reviews. A common theme in a lion's share of the articles was the obvious observation that by now you know what you're getting with a *Carry On* film and you either love or hate them. If you loved them, chances were you probably enjoyed it best when they spotlighted the medical profession, affording audiences a rich dollop of laughs.

There had been a nine-year gap between the medical romps *Nurse* and *Doctor*, but Rogers and Thomas didn't leave it so long this time before revisiting the wards. After the success of *Doctor*, it was the following year, 1969, when we returned, this time to the Long Hampton Hospital. Accident-prone Dr Nookey, played by Jim Dale in his last *Carry On* until the ill-fated *Columbus* two decades later, is popular with the nurses and patients but despised by certain senior members within the hospital; so determined are they to see the back of him that they even resort to lacing his drinks so that he becomes drunk, makes a fool of himself and ends up facing disciplinary action. Dr Carver and Matron (Kenneth Williams and Hattie Jacques) are two of Nookey's biggest foes, as well as Dr Stoppidge, an unusually acerbic characterisation for Charles Hawtrey. All three receive their come-uppance, though, when Nookey, banished to the far-off, monsoon-swept Beatific Islands, comes across a serum which induces drastic weight loss, making him a rich man upon his return to the UK when he sets up a private clinic dispensing the serum to millions of overweight people.

Talbot Rothwell signed a contract to write the screenplay, for a £5,000 fee, on 1 November 1968, but his first draft required further work so he rewrote it, expecting to deliver by the end of January 1969. When the script was submitted, it was passed to Rank's legal adviser, Hugh J. Parton, for reading; he, however, raised a few concerns. Knowing Rothwell had penned a script for *Doctor in Clover* that had been rejected by Betty Box, he highlighted potential concerns regarding copyright infringement, namely that the dialogue attributed to Doctor Carver (Kenneth Williams) was reminiscent of Sir Lancelot Spratt from the *Doctor* films. Parton questioned whether this was a deliberate attempt to parody the character. Also, after acknowledging that Dr Nookey's exile to the remote Beatific Islands Medical Mission and the discovery of the slimming serum make up the bulk of the film, he felt that he'd read such storylines before, perhaps in Rothwell's rejected *Doctor* script or in one of author Richard Gordon's books.

Rogers and Rothwell assuaged Parton's concerns and both elements were used in the film. Cameras began turning on 17 March and continued until the beginning of May, with location work in Maidenhead and interior scenes shot on Pinewood's C, F and G stages. Filming finished one day ahead of schedule but wasn't without incident, as actress Alexandra Dane, given the unfortunate character name of 'Stout Woman', can testify. When Dr Nookey causes mayhem by damaging the hospital's electricity supply, the 'Stout Woman' is using an exercise machine which spins out of control. 'I had a nasty accident and suffered back problems for some time after. I was leaning back on the machine which was made to look like it was out of control and it came out of the floor resulting in me going to hospital.'

Carry On Again Doctor was released in August and was welcomed by the reviewers, with Ian Christie in the *Daily Express* extolling the film series's value. He wrote: 'What I like about the *Carry On* series is its enormous extravagant and basically innocent vulgarity. The effect is not all that easy to achieve, and one should not be misled by the simplicity of the humour into thinking that any fool could do it. The films may be bawdy and rude but they are never really dirty, and producer Peter Rogers and director Gerald Thomas are adept at treading the fine tightrope that divides the two.'[76]

The medical profession, by now, was a well-tilled environment – not that it prevented the team dropping in again with *Matron*, five films later. Hospitals, nurses, bedpans, patients – there was a seemingly inexhaustible supply of targets for comedy and the team had, once again, carried it off with aplomb.

The use of the flashback hadn't been employed in a *Carry On* film until *Up the Jungle*, which began as *Jungle Boy*, came along in 1970. It was filmed entirely as a flashback, reliving an expedition into the depths of the African jungle by the venerated ornithologist Professor Tinkle (Frankie Howerd) in search of the extremely rare Oozalum bird; also on the trip was Lady Bagley (Joan Sims), who returned to the spot where she had lost, feared drowned, not only her husband but her baby boy, many years earlier.

Enticing Frankie Howerd back into the *Carry On* clan – a replacement for Kenneth Williams – was satisfying for Peter Rogers, who'd previously cast him in *Doctor*. In return for picking up a £9,000 pay packet at the end of the six weeks, Howerd delivered another fine display despite, at times, appearing a little too individualistic in his style, something which had earlier prompted Peter Rogers to raise the matter with his agent, Beryl Vertue at Associated London Scripts; Vertue passed on the producer's comments to her client.

Feeling the need to put Rogers's mind at rest and allay any concerns, Howerd wrote from The Sheraton Hotel in Malta, where he was holidaying, stating that he would be on his best behaviour during filming.

Although no one expected the film to be shot in real jungle, the artificiality of the studio-based alternative is a disappointing element of the film – as is the dearth of genuine humour, with many situations and jokes simply being too obvious to elicit a real belly laugh. There was also a noticeable shift towards more blatant sexual innuendo, such as the appearance of the Lubidubies, an all-female tribe from Aphrodisia symbolised by the statuesque figure of Leda (Valerie Leon), who want to get their hands on any available men for mating purposes. Yes, there are amusing moments but the 1970s had opened disappointingly with one of the weaker offerings in the *Carry On* series.

One positive aspect of the film, though, was the arrival of a new face in the team: 22-year-old Jacki Piper, playing the meek and mild maid of Lady Bagley. It was the first of four appearances, during which she'd forge a successful screen partnership with Richard O'Callaghan. The introduction of new faces from time to time was occasionally due to circumstance, at other times deliberate. While making *Up the Jungle*, Gerald Thomas stated: 'We built up a group of artists that was almost a repertory team, but they are interchangeable, and none of them are really indispensable, although I'd hate to lose any of them. But we do change them occasionally and bring in a newcomer just to give it a bit of a spark.'[77]

Piper was still cutting her film-making teeth when she was invited to Pinewood to meet Peter Rogers and Gerald Thomas, having just played Roger Moore's secretary in *The Man Who Haunted Himself*. She recalls reading for a part in *Up the Jungle* which, at one point, Peter Rogers had hoped to call *Carry On Tarzan*. 'I said to them: "You can't possibly employ me, I haven't done much film work because I've come from the theatre." At which Peter roared with laughter.' That didn't matter because Rogers and Thomas were eagle-eyed when it came to identifying artistes who'd suit the *Carry Ons*, and Piper was offered the role of June, earning £600 in the process.

She has nothing but happy memories of making the film, but

one particular moment sticks in her mind. 'Before shooting one day, Gerald Thomas said to me: "I'm afraid I've got something unpleasant to tell you."' Piper feared she was about to be given her marching orders, so was relieved to discover the director only wanted to warn her about having to endure a bucket of water being thrown over her. Unfortunately things didn't go to plan. 'I had this hairpiece on and they threw the water so forcefully that everything was struck off: hair, eyelashes – everything. They had to dry me down and throw the water again, this time gently.'

Equally uncomfortable were the burns she suffered, along with Terry Scott (who played Cecil, the Jungle Boy, a role originally envisaged for Jim Dale) while swinging on ropes in various scenes, à la Tarzan and Jane. 'We had to wear these trusses for when we were swinging on the ropes. We got terribly cut between our legs and had to go and see the nurse; we could barely walk properly with them on.'

Jacki Piper enjoyed working with Terry Scott, although she thinks he was concerned initially about her lack of film experience. In the end, they got on 'famously', she says, which is just as well because of what happened on the edge of the man-made pond. 'We were filming the scene sincerely but noticed everybody laughing at us. We decided to take no notice and completed the scene. I discovered later that Terry had fallen out of his loincloth and was on view.'

Also on set that day was Nora Rodway, who was assisting her husband, make-up designer Geoffrey Rodway. In the scene, Scott crashed at the feet of Jacki Piper because he never mastered the art of swinging between the trees. 'Terry was wearing nothing but a leopard-skin nappy fastened with an enormous safety pin,' recalls Rodway. 'As well as Jacki, Terry was the only one who didn't know that in the fall his loincloth had slipped sideways and he was lying there on the artificial grass exposing his private parts for all to see. The first I knew about it was when I heard Gerald's voice, saying: "Nora, you're needed over here to powder something off!" So off I trotted with my powder puff and then the laughter exploded and Terry himself joined in which was very noble of him.'

Reception from the media upon the film's release in March 1970 was lukewarm, most critics agreeing with the *Daily Telegraph*'s Patrick

Gibbs who found the film 'woefully flat despite the presence of Frankie Howerd and a pleasing newcomer in Jacki Piper.'[78]

Piper was in good form again for her next role, Sally Martin in *Loving*, which started out as *Carry On Courting*. So impressed were Peter Rogers and Gerald Thomas that before she'd even finished *Up the Jungle* they were requesting her services for the next picture, which saw Sidney and Sophie Bliss (Sid James and Hattie Jacques) running a successful dating agency, Wedded Bliss, presenting the image of a happily married couple to their prospective clients despite not having tied the knot and fighting like cat and dog. If the previous scriptwriter, Norman Hudis, hadn't been happy with the *Regardless* script, believing it resembled nothing more than a series of sketches, the same assessment could be directed towards Rothwell's fourteenth script. The plot was fairly threadbare, loosely hanging on the Blisses' agency, from which a collection of sketches involving their clients emerged; the only time the various faces were united was during the closing scene when the Blisses ask all the couples they've matched over the years to their own wedding reception, only to see it turn into a farce when a food fight breaks out with plenty of custard pies being tossed around the room.

The closing scene involving the food fight took three days to shoot and meant that Peter Howitt, the set dresser, was rushed off his feet whipping up real cream for the myriad cakes. 'You can't just throw anything, such as phoney cream, because you need to know what ingredients are in it, otherwise if someone got it in their eyes, it could cause an infection. So we did it with real cream because it's pure. I bought lots of cream, whipped it up and put it in and on top of sponges, so we could throw them. I must have made hundreds. By the end of the three days, though, the studio stunk because all the cream had gone off.' Howitt and the rest of the crew didn't come away unscathed, either. 'We were all covered in it because the actors threw it at anyone. I was standing by the camera when they all started giggling, then started throwing the cream at us.'

The late Patsy Rowlands, one of the stars of the film with her sterling performance as Mr Snooper's dowdy housekeeper Miss Dempsey, in probably her last ever interview shared her memories of the wedding reception scene with me. 'Because we didn't finish the filming on the same day, we had to leave the studio as it was, covered in cream and cakes, for continuity purposes. It had to be identical to how it was the day before; but when we arrived the following morning the cream had gone off and the smell was dreadful. You couldn't wear your shoes or you'd slide across the floor, which is just as well because the previous day I'd worn a pair of sandals and by the end they were ruined.

'I also remember waiting all day for Kenneth [Williams] to push my head into the middle of a cream cake. There was retake after retake, every time stopping just before my bit. My head didn't know whether it was coming or going! Eventually they filmed it and it was a horrible experience. Cream was everywhere. As we're speaking, I'm actually wiping my face with my hands – the memory is so vivid.' Rowlands's character was often cast alongside Kenneth Williams's, either playing his housekeeper or his secretary. 'I found him [Kenneth] difficult to work with,' admitted Rowlands. 'Once he knew you were all right, you had a friend for life, but it took a while to reach that point. We didn't have any arguments or anything, it's just that I was very much in awe of him when I started, which doesn't always make for an easy ride.' Williams's unpredictability wasn't easy to cope with. Patsy Rowlands recalls the day some visitors were arriving to watch a *Carry On* being made. 'As soon as Gerry Thomas knew this, he was going to change the order of scenes around but didn't have time. It meant that they'd be arriving when Kenneth Williams was in a scene. I remember Gerry saying: "Now, Kenneth, you behave when they come around." Because he was more than likely to drop his trousers or do something else in front of these people.' Fortunately, the message sunk in and Williams was on best behaviour – that day, anyway.

Peter Howitt, reflecting on the budget he was allocated to dress the sets, says: 'For very little money, they were very organised.' He also had to count the pennies when dressing the set on the next film, *Henry*, another historical romp, this time an apocryphal story about two wives Henry VIII didn't actually have, and about which the censor, on reviewing the film, commented: 'This is a difficult film to reduce to the 'A' category as practically every joke has a sexual meaning.'[79] When it came to the set-dressing for this period costume comedy, Howitt, again, had little money. He recalls a banquet scene. 'I had a phoney stuffed pig which I used to put glazing on every day to make it look real, and we kept using the same old chickens. I washed off the glazing at the end of the day, put them in the fridge overnight, got them out next morning, reglazed them and put them back on the set. This went on for about a week. We could just about afford real fruit, though.'

Deciding to play a joke on Howitt, Gerald Thomas approached him during a tea break and asked if he'd like a sandwich. 'I replied, "Thank you, very much." Hattie then appeared, saying: "Yes, Peter, have a sandwich." Next, Sid came along and said: "I'll get you one." Then someone brought me a cup of coffee. I wondered what was the matter with everyone, then saw them head towards the table and start cutting one of the chickens. I quickly shouted: "Oh, no, thank you, not for me." Gerald turned to me, smiling, saying: "Well, you could have killed all the actors!"'

The narrative of *Loving* might have struggled finding its way through the film at times, but just as I liked Hudis's *Regardless*, I have a soft spot for *Loving*, too, and Dick Richards in the *Daily Mirror* was also a fan, stating Rothwell 'whipped up some funny situations'.[80] And while Ian Christie in the *Daily Express* noted that the only aspect of the *Carry On*s that didn't age were the jokes because they were old when first used, he asked who cared, adding: 'The fun lovers who have flocked to the cinema and made the other films so successful will no doubt flock to this.'[81] Meanwhile, over at the *Sunday Mirror* the critic complimented Rothwell for coming up with some 'fresh situations and gags and the plot, such as it matters, is better shaped then usual.'[82]

Peter Buckley in *Films and Filming* singled out Richard O'Callaghan for praise – his on-screen relationship with the delightful Jacki Piper is one of the film's best aspects. The London-born actor was cast as Bertrum Muffet, an undertaker's assistant who turns to the Wedded Bliss Agency for help in finding romance, although his credentials as an ineffectual, puny individual with hobbies including making models out of milk-bottle tops make Mr and Mrs Bliss's job almost impossible; it is only a case of mistaken identity that brings him to the attention of Sally Martin. Still, romance blossoms and they eventually marry.

Reflecting on being one half of the young love interest in *Loving*, O'Callaghan recalls being taken to London's Dorchester Hotel in a white Rolls-Royce. 'I was appearing in *Three Months Gone* at the time. It was making quite a smash and I was playing a northern Bertrum Muffet-like character. My agent called and said Peter Rogers and Gerald Thomas wanted to see me. I was doing a matinée that day so it was arranged that they'd pick me up from the theatre during the break.' Chauffeured to the Dorchester, he enjoyed tea and a chat before returning to the theatre. The Bertrum Muffet characterisation was similar to what he was being offered at that point in his career. 'I'd just reached thirty but probably looked a good deal younger than that and was very naive. I was used to playing characters like him so it wasn't difficult bringing Bertrum to life.'

O'Callaghan was soon issued with his props, including the tinfoil aeroplanes. 'There was a wonderful props man on the production who said to me: "There's your briefcase over there." When I opened it and saw it was full of planes made out of milk-bottle tops I fell about laughing and couldn't believe they'd gone to the trouble of making them – it must have taken someone hours!' O'Callaghan 'loved' appearing with Jacki Piper in *Loving* and, later, in *At Your Convenience*. He said: 'I guess Peter and Gerald thought we worked well together.'

As well as the Piper-O'Callaghan partnership, Imogen Hassall's sole *Carry On* performance, playing the shy, 24-year-old Jenny Grubb who was transformed into a hip, cleavage-showing, miniskirt-wearing sex bomb, was equally impressive. Tragically, the actress's short career came to an abrupt end in 1980 when, aged just thirty-eight, she was found dead after a large overdose of drugs.

Sandwiched between *Loving* and *At Your Convenience* – originally titled *Carry On Comrade* and *Carry On Working* – was *Henry*, which had only been given the slot when the latter was temporarily halted. *At Your Convenience* is set at W.C. Boggs and Son, a company which manufactures toilet ware. Unsurprisingly, the world of toilets and bidets was an apposite setting for Talbot Rothwell's barrage of lavatorial-style innuendoes and farce.

Filming began on 22 March 1971 and explored the day-to-day events at the factory. While management attempts to keep orders flowing in a tough economic climate, the workers are constantly striking, thanks, largely, to the pugnacious shop steward Vic Spanner who brings the workforce out over the slightest thing, including the scrapping of drinking tea outside normal breaks. The militant Spanner was astutely played by Kenneth Cope of *Randall and Hopkirk* fame. Reflecting on his role, he recalls a scene where Bernard Bresslaw – playing Spanner's sidekick Bernie Hulke – arrives at Spanner's house on a motorbike. It took some achieving, as Cope explains. 'Bernard couldn't ride and was terrified. I think he'd told the production team that he could. He had to ride round this corner to my front door, switch off the engine, park the bike, leave it on its stand and come up to the front door. We heard the bike revving up around the corner before stalling. Bernie didn't appear for about seven takes. Eventually he managed to get it into view but then drove too far past the mark. This went on for what seemed like all day. In the end, a couple of guys pushed the bike into shot. What made it funnier was that poor old Bernie's visor misted up and he couldn't see anything. Before the end of the scene, the bike had fallen over, too. My ribs were aching with laughter that evening – so were Gerald Thomas's!'

Teamed up again after their successful screen relationship in *Loving* were Jacki Piper and Richard O'Callaghan – Myrtle Plummer and Lewis Boggs – who would have made an ideal pairing for future productions if circumstances had permitted. In the film, employees at the Boggs factory forget their differences and embark on a trip to the seaside for the firm's outing; filmed in Brighton, this was one of the highlights of the picture, with the cast revelling in the seaside-postcard environment. Piper enjoyed her sojourn on the coast, although she saw two of her colleagues nearly come a cropper in the ghost train, as she explains. 'Bernard Bresslaw and Maggie Nolan's car, which was behind mine, didn't emerge from the tunnel; it had derailed and they were on the floor in the dark. Apparently they'd both lunged to the side as it went around a corner and tipped the car over. It was funny, really.'

Although he played his part superbly, Richard O'Callaghan didn't enjoy his time on *At Your Convenience* as much as *Loving*. 'The character wasn't as naive as Bertrum [in *Loving*] and I didn't enjoy playing him as much.' And as for other aspects of the film, he adds: 'It seemed so right-wing, and although it was only jokey, it was very much poking fun at trade unions.' He did, however, enjoy the time in Brighton, partly because it afforded him the chance to speed along in a sports car. 'I didn't get to drive it much but I've always loved driving and being behind the wheel of a sports car for the first time was very enjoyable.'

Time is a great healer and although *At Your Convenience* would eventually be regarded as another perfectly acceptable entry in the series, it took a while to achieve that status. It was released into an era when trade unions possessed bite and power in Britain, and the film's big mistake was that it poked fun at the unions primarily, and in doing so made the very audience the films appealed to, largely working-class, the butt of the joke – and the low box-office receipts showed that the public weren't pleased. As Nina Hibbin, who admitted to enjoying the films, remarked in the *Morning Star*: 'There has been a ripe and earthy working-class slant to the series which has given it special appeal – and phenomenal box-office returns. But now it has turned round and bitten the hand that has been feeding it all these years. It has betrayed its own roots.'[83]

VIII

Rogers and Thomas returned to the wards more than they did to any other setting; it was a reliable environment for laughter. The best comedy always emanates from a closed environment and it worked again in *Matron*. After three successful hospital-based films, and the initial poor reception from the cinema-going public of *At Your Convenience*, it was no surprise when Rogers and Thomas eked out a few more laughs and double entendres from bedpans, busty nurses and all things medical.

It was over five years since scriptwriter Norman Hudis had jetted off to the United States, but he was in the frame for writing the

Matron screenplay, largely because its premise was in the tradition of those realistic themes that he'd helped to pioneer. Unfortunately, we weren't to see a return for the original writer. Hudis says: 'There was no difficulty with the Writers' Guild of America in the sense that the body was obstructive; the Guild merely adhered to its rules covering writing done while a member-writer is geographically in the US. Crucially, these require the employer, in such a circumstance, to pay an additional 11% of the fee to the Guild's Pension and Health Insurance Schemes. Peter [Rogers] declined. The deal, therefore, didn't get Guild approval. I have to underscore that this is a completely defensible position by a producer who, philosophically, won't contribute to benefits which, in his view, the writer should take care of himself. No hard feelings. Peter doesn't need my approval to conduct his business and career as he sees fit. This is his unchallenged right. So none of this is personal. When Peter subsequently asked me to write *Again Nurse*, the Guild relaxed its rule because, as a "special case", I was the writer of the original *Nurse* and would be writing *Again* in London.'

With Hudis out of the equation, Talbot Rothwell was assigned the project: his contract was issued in May 1971 and the script delivered that August. Filming was completed between 11 October and 26 November with the finalised product whizzed off the Rogers-Thomas production line in May 1972, with small-time villain, Sid Carter (Sid James) and his crooks planning to steal contraceptive pills from Finisham Maternity Hospital and flog them abroad. The job of securing a plan of the building and details of where the pills are stored is given to Sid's recalcitrant son Cyril Carter (Kenneth Cope), who eventually gives in and, disguised as a student nurse, sets to work.

Cope was making his second and last appearance in the films and enjoyed himself. 'Cyril was a lovely part. I had some say in the costume and chose suspenders because I thought they'd be funnier than tights.' When the team stopped for lunch, rather than change out of his nurse's uniform and waste fifteen minutes, he nipped over to the restaurant wearing his outfit, make-up and wig. 'I loved walking down the corridors in Pinewood because the high heels made a hell of a noise on the floor. Once, dressed as a nurse, I passed three guys in the corridor and went straight into the gents – that didn't half make them look!'

Even lunchtimes were often a ball. Cope recalls: 'In the restaurant at Pinewood, we'd do things like pretend to be French. I couldn't actually speak French, like many of the others, so we adopted the accent while talking to each other. We were outrageous.'

Appearing in a cameo role, aptly named 'The Twitching Father', was Jack Douglas, making the first of eight film appearances. His unique style had been perfected over many years spent on stage. He recalls: 'Joe Baker and I, as young men, appeared at Butlin's in Clacton. I used to play the character of Alf but without the twitch. I played a conjuror and asked for someone in the audience to come up and help, which was Joe's cue, dressed as a little boy, to come up on stage. One evening, with about 1,500 people in the audience, the theatre doors were locked by the Red Coats because it was full. Unfortunately, Joe couldn't get in, so I was left with a twenty-minute slot to fill. My brain was working at seventy miles an hour and I picked up a tray and put on bits of junk. I happened to look to my right and noticed Eric Winston, the famous band leader, who had a little twitch. So, in desperation, I said: "I shall now make these articles disappear . . ." Then I did my twitch and threw them up in the air. They fell on the floor and I just picked them up, ignoring what had happened. Luckily, by this time Joe had got in and came down to the front of the house, only to hear all these people falling about laughing – and I was supposed to be the straight one.'

Douglas's introduction to the *Carry On* films began when his agent, Michael Sullivan, phoned and asked whether he wanted the good or bad news first. 'I asked for the good news first and he told me I was in the next *Carry On* picture, which pleased me. I then asked what the bad news was and he told me I wasn't getting paid. He told me he'd persuaded Peter Rogers to put me in a little scene in the maternity ward and if it worked I'd be in the next film.' The archives show that Douglas was, in fact, paid £25 but he believes this was to cover expenses. Being the newcomer, Douglas was apprehensive about joining the established team for *Matron*. He needn't have worried, however, because he was made to feel at home from day one. 'I thought they might resent me, but suddenly Sid James came over and introduced himself and asked if I fancied a coffee. Then Kenneth Williams got me some biscuits. It wasn't long before I felt I'd been part of the team from the beginning. They were, without doubt, the most unselfish comedy team I'd ever worked with.' While the film was Douglas's first, the series bade farewell to Jacki Piper, who played Sister. Pregnant by this time, she left the acting scene for a while to raise a family. Most of the usual faces were cast in the film, although Peter Butterworth was busy in a television series and so was unable to play Freddy, one of Sid Carter's gang, so Bill Maynard stepped into his shoes.

Whereas Pinewood and Maidenhead Town Hall had been used to represent hospitals in previous *Carry Ons*, the spanking new quarter of a million-pound maternity unit at Heatherwood Hospital, Ascot was utilised this time for the unit's two-day visit. As soon as the characters are established the film picks up momentum and cruises along to an amusing climax with a chase sequence through the wards and corridors at the maternity hospital.

After the disinfectant and starched uniforms of Finisham Maternity Hospital, the cast headed for the sun – well, almost – for their next offering. By the 1970s the package-holiday business was booming with increasing numbers jumping on a plane and heading for sunnier climes. So no one flinched, therefore, when the industry became the focus for the *Carry On* treatment. In this, my favourite from the Rothwell era, we see Stuart Farquhar, a holiday courier at Wundatours, played by Kenneth Williams, and his sexy assistant Moira Plunkett (Gail Grainger) escort a naive bunch of holiday-makers, including landlords Vic and Cora Flange (Sid James and Joan Sims); sexy Sadie Tomkins (Barbara Windsor); mother's boy Eustace Tuttle (Charles Hawtrey); the incessant complainer Evelyn Blunt (June Whitfield) and her henpecked, sex-starved husband Stanley (Kenneth Connor) on a short break to the Med resort of Elsbels which boasts an unbeatable sunshine record – that is, until the motley crew turns up and endures a sudden downpour which not only puts a dampener on their trip but brings the hotel crashing down around them. The final scenes in the so-called Med resort are akin to the dinner-table scene in *Up the Khyber*. This time, though, it's the poorly built hotel which collapses during the farewell dinner and dance.

The script was delivered in March 1972, by which time it had undergone several amendments. In Rothwell's initial story outline, Joan Sims's character was called Clara, not Cora, while other differences included Elsbels being on the Costa Bomm; Kenneth Williams's character being called Kenneth Stuart-Farquhar rather than just Stuart Farquhar and Hawtrey's character being called Charles Makepeace, an old-fashioned solicitor. There was also a character called Lady Joan Baugham, travelling with her 17-year-old son, who was down on her uppers and spent the entire time scrounging off other travellers, while Robin Tweet's friend was to be called Cyril not Nicholas, and they were to walk around hand-in-hand the entire time. Meanwhile, in charge of the flight to Spain was an aged captain who drained the confidence from his passengers by asking them to move to the back of the aeroplane to counterbalance the weight when a problem occured. And to top it all, on the return flight the decrepit plane came a cropper and ended up crashing in the sea, leaving the holidaymakers no alternative but to jump on to a raft. Fortunately, everyone was picked up by the *Waverley*, a cross-Channel ferry.

If any actor thought the title *Abroad* meant a jolly in the sun, they were mistaken. Playing Evelyn Blunt was June Whitfield's favourite *Carry On* role, despite her initial disappointment upon learning where the film would be shot. She says: 'When I was offered the role, I had visions of a trip abroad to make the film. I thought I'd have to stock up on sunblock and suntan lotion. But I needn't have worried because the so-called beach was, in fact, a corner of Pinewood's car park, with half a ton of builder's sand and some deckchairs to add authenticity. And it was cold and windy.'

Sally Geeson, who played Lily, a young girl travelling with her friend Marge and looking for a little holiday romance, concurs with Whitfield. 'It was freezing, and it didn't help when they turned on the fire engine hoses to represent rain – and all of this in the car park, where they built the front of the hotel.' Geeson was initially worried about joining the established team of actors. 'They all knew each other extremely well and had worked together so long. When you're a new person it's a bit nerve-racking. But I was young and went along and had a great time. Of course, it helped knowing Sid [James] from playing his screen daughter in *Bless This House*.'

Lily's friend Marge was played by Carol Hawkins; she enjoyed the first of her two *Carry On* appearances, although, like Geeson, didn't savour the thunderstorm scene. The actors were given strict instructions not to budge until they received their cue. 'You could see the firemen ready with the hoses, then the water being sprayed but we couldn't move. My cue seemed like an eternity,' laughs Hawkins, who suggests tongue-in-cheek that everyone should have been paid danger money for the scene where the hotel collapses. 'It was great fun filming that sequence.'

The idea of transporting the team to sunnier climes to film *Abroad* never crossed Peter Rogers's mind. The closely controlled finances never extended to such luxuries. If a spot within the grounds of Pinewood would suffice, Peter Rogers could save the pennies. And in doing so, he was unknowingly helping to develop the style associated with the *Carry Ons*; after all, there is a certain appeal about the team, for example, pretending to sun themselves in the Pinewood car park-cum-Elsbels Palace Hotel grounds. Something would have been lost if they had been lazing around on a real beach in the Med.

In Robin Tweet in *Abroad*, we saw the series's first gay character, travelling to Elsbels with Nicholas, played by David Kernan; but when Nicholas starts dating Lily, dear old Robin is left on his own. When the censor saw the film he asked Peter Rogers for a 'general lightening of homo theme'[84] and deletion of the line 'I shall take my ankle bracelet back.' But after the usual negotiating, the line remained in the film. John Clive, who brought Robin to life, can't understand why his character was needed in the film. He says: 'Kenneth Williams and Charles Hawtrey were both camping it up madly and David Kernan and I didn't know why they wanted us to come in and do the same sort of thing. Actors are always worried about their own positions and I didn't want Kenneth or Charles to think we were seeking to take over their roles in the film. I liked Kenneth Williams enormously and thought he was a fabulously funny guy, so I was a little bit careful with him and waited to see how we'd get on. After seeing the rushes, he came over to congratulate me, patting me on the shoulder and saying: "That was terrific, you two boys are going to be great in this." Another time I was in make-up and Sid James said virtually the same thing.'

Clive, too, recalls feeling like ice during the sunbathing scene. 'Trying to create the Mediterranean in the freezing cold of Pinewood was difficult but you just had to put up with it. But I have to say, we were blue with the cold in those bathing costumes because there was a chill wind round the place that day. We had to have body make-up plastered all over us because everybody was freezing. When we filmed the scene involving the rainstorm, everyone got soaked.'

Critics felt the team of regulars was strengthened, quite rightly, by the introduction of June Whitfield and Jimmy Logan, playing the loud-mouthed Scot Bert Conway who was expecting a dirty weekend before, much to his chagrin, he met his fellow tripsters. But all the occasional *Carry On* actors delivered a good display, including John Clive and Brian Osborne, whose cameo appearance saw him play a stallholder at the local market, the second of six appearances in the film series.

Osborne's decision to add additional lines to his snatch of dialogue initially confused Sid James, who readily admitted that ad libbing wasn't his forte. Osborne recalls: 'I thought my dialogue sounded boring so added the words "drinky, drinky" while trying to encourage Sid's character to taste the love potion I was selling. Sid James liked it and so did Gerald. He said: "Where did that come from? Keep it in!" We did another take and it worked fine.' The idea stemmed from a Spanish holiday that Osborne had enjoyed. 'Every morning we'd go down to the beach and this chap selling ice lollies and drinks could be heard miles away, shouting: "Lolly, lolly, licky, licky, drinky, drinky!" I whacked the line in and from then on was known as "drinky, drinky" by the crew.'

Just as with other scenes, shots of the local market were completed in inclement weather. 'Everybody sat in the coach with the engine running, heater on, wrapped in coats. We'd go out to rehearse and Gerald would tell us we could keep our coats on. He'd then say: "Right, camera running, coats off." You'd rush in, take your coat off and rush out to film the scene.'

The theme of a summer holiday, particularly one that didn't go to plan, struck a chord with viewers who could, again, relate to the subject matter and empathise with the poor souls forking out good money only to be let down by the bungling travel company. There was a good-time feel to the production but, unlike me, not everyone enthused about it. Judith Simons at the *Daily Express* acknowledged that a humorous film could be made about package holidays but claimed that *Abroad* wasn't it. She thought 'the development, with endless jokes about lavatory plumbing and shared bathrooms, could have been invented by an eleven-year-old.'[85] Kenneth Williams, meanwhile, classed the film as grim, remarking that even on day one 'there was an air of staleness over everything. A feeling of "I have been here before" and I thought the acting standard was rather bad throughout.'[86]

Yes, there might have been a feeling of déjà vu about many of the performances, puns, double entendres and so on, but there is cordiality coursing through the picture. The film, however, is tinged with sadness as it was to be Charles Hawtrey's last appearance. It was, perhaps, ironic that his final characterisation, Mr Tuttle, was fond of the bottle because Hawtrey's excessive drinking had finally taken its toll. Explaining why he had to go, Peter Rogers stated: 'He became rather difficult and impossible to deal with because he was drinking a lot. We used to feed him black coffee before he would go on. It really became that we were wasting time.'[87] Hawtrey's side of the story, however, was told rather differently. In 1980, he informed an interviewer, 'What did worry me was the dialogue. Instead of being double entendre there became only one meaning which was vulgar. I thought: you're going to lose a lot of people who are kind to you in the audience if you use dialogue like that. I thought that was the time to say "no". Of course, I was hated by lots of people.'[88]

The same inherent warmth that was present in *Abroad* was apparent in *Carry On Girls*, number 25 in the series. Spotlighting the wiggle and wobble of beauty contests, the gang subjects the contest at the core of the film to much ribtickling, with Kenneth Connor playing the Mayor of Fircombe, a prize pipsqueak whose weak leadership sees him allow a beauty pageant in the seaside town.

Angry about the decision, the Women's Lib element of the town council, led by the militant and strong-willed Augusta Prodworthy, played beautifully by June Whitfield, is determined to spoil the event. Prodworthy is ably supported by a bunch of women, including her right-hand woman in trousers, Rosemary. Donning a cardi and trousers and sporting greased-back hair, Rosemary was played by a wonderfully-disguised Patricia Franklin. 'I was shocked when they asked me to play the part,' she laughs. 'It seemed ridiculous for me to play it, but in the end I was a good sidekick for June. If the person playing it had been tall and butch, it would have looked unbalanced. It was great fun.'

Organiser of the beauty contest is Sid Fiddler, played by Sid James, who'd just been voted Best Actor for 1972 by Melbourne theatre critics for his performance in *The Mating Game*. The owner of the local amusement arcade feels the event will put Fircombe – called Bungcope in Rothwell's original treatment – on the map. The tensions created by staging the contest produce a rich vein of comedic opportunities which the team fully exploit. It's not everyone's favourite *Carry On* but I rate it highly as a worthy example of what the team do best, in this case taking the saucy seaside-postcard material which was in vogue during the 1960s and 1970s and mining it for all it is worth, resulting in a film full of all-round entertainment.

With occasional location shooting along Brighton's promenade and on its West Pier, which at the time was in a dangerous condition and closed to the public, the cavalcade of beauties includes Barbara Windsor as Hope Springs, Margaret Nolan as Dawn Brakes and Valerie Leon in her sixth and final film, as prude-turned-sexpot Paula Perkins. (Her surname was Prentiss and her profession was a teacher of archaeology in the original treatment.) The fiancée of Peter Potter (Bernard Bresslaw) becomes jealous when Peter is invited to organise the publicity campaign for the beauty contest. Annoyed at the thought of Peter ogling all those leggy lovelies, she decides to give him a taste of his own medicine by becoming a late entrant in the Miss Fircombe competition, donning horn-rimmed specs in the process. 'They were very old spectacles that I'd worn in real life while training to be a fashion buyer at Harrods before going into showbusiness,' recalls Leon. 'They were sold not long ago for charity, framed with a picture of me wearing them in *Girls*, and fetched a lot of money.'

A good supply of regulars – bar Kenneth Williams, who was appearing in *My Fat Friend* at the Globe Theatre, Hattie Jacques and Charles Hawtrey – were on show, coupled with wonderful support from the likes of Jack Douglas, who milked his 'Twitching Alf' character to the full as William, the porter-cum-doorman-cum-general dogsbody at Connie Philpotts's Palace Hotel. His twitching tendencies were perfectly delivered in a scene where William tries unsuccessfully to transfer a call from the hotel reception's switchboard, much to the disbelief of Sid Fiddler. The sequence works wonderfully, although Douglas admits James helped him survive a rare mistake. 'We were doing a scene and my mind suddenly went blank. Sid twisted my line and gave it back to me and we picked up from there – he was an amazing man,' says Douglas, who remembers indulging in a little ad libbing during the scene, only to discover, like Brian Osborne in *Abroad*, that James didn't ad lib. 'I fell about laughing and he replied: "No, don't laugh, it's true – I'm an actor. You'll get the same performance from me; you can set your watch by me every time I do something, but give me a line that I don't know and I'm dead." He was happy for me to do anything I liked, but asked how he'd know when I'd finished. I said: "I'll look you straight in the eyes and say: 'Pardon?'" We'd then pick up from where we'd left off.'

Before the film could be released, Rogers and Thomas faced the normal negotiations with the censor, in this case Stephen Murphy, who wanted selected lines removed, including 'Quick knee-trembler under the pier'; 'You have been in everything else' following the line, 'Not fit to be in husband's shoes'; 'You lecherous sod'; 'Anything else you want off?'; 'Which would you prefer, a short or long one' (Hope Springs), 'I should ask you that' (Peter) and a reduction in the screen time given to the cat fight between Barbara Windsor and Margaret Nolan, particularly the close-ups of Hope Springs trying to rip off Dawn Brakes's bikini bottoms. Rogers and Thomas largely complied with Murphy's request but felt, on reviewing the fight sequence, that there wasn't anything objectionable and

asked Murphy to reconsider. The censor still classed the fight unsuit-
able for 'A' certification and requested that the close-ups should be
cut, which Thomas reluctantly agreed to do to avoid holding up
the production schedule, despite reiterating his disappointment with
the assessment.

Filming proceeded as planned, with one of the best scenes saved
until last: while the bevy of beauties wobble down the catwalk, they
are soaked with water and goodness knows what else – it's pure
mayhem for the contestants, who play their parts to perfection.
Little did they know that Gerald Thomas was enjoying a jolly jape
at their expense. While a mild sprinkling of water was envisaged,
Thomas used five times the quantity of water and requested a
bombardment of soot and other items to add to the fun, just one
of many jokes played out during the making of the *Carry On* films.

Another semi-regular in *Girls*, which started out as *Carry On
Beauty Queen*, was the ever-reliable Patsy Rowlands, who played the
Mayor of Fircombe's indolent, slovenly wife, Mildred Bumble. Her
oft-understated performances received some credit from critics at
long last, with a journalist in *Films Illustrated* classing her as the
person who 'saves the film'.[89] He added: 'Miss Rowlands gives a
performance which is more than can be said for the rest of the cast
who appear so at ease in the series that they no longer worry about
characterisation. A pity, because they are all capable of so much
more.'[90]

Girls was one of the few *Carry On*s to make a serious social
comment, although whether this was Talbot Rothwell's intention is
questionable. Nonetheless, the women's puritanical stance against
the beauty contest was symbolic of the mood at the time, when a
wave of feminism saw such contests disrupted.

Overall, the media reaction was encouraging, with Arthur Thirkell
in the *Daily Mirror* classing it as one of the most inspired of the
long list of entries, while even the doubters among the journalists
had to take their hats off to the series's stamina and long-lasting
appeal to many millions of people. A journalist in *What's On* wrote:
'Even while I have, in all honesty, to admit that this isn't at all my
cup of celluloid tea, I am still lost in admiration for the way in
which Gerald Thomas and Peter Rogers cooked up the original

recipe and have kept it simmering ever since.'[91] His contemporary at the *Daily Express* lauded the 25th in the series, explaining that he'd laughed more than ever and regarded it as the best to date. The *Carry On*s had long become staple fare in British comedy and, despite their limitations, they remained as popular as ever among the cinema-going public.

IX

After a run of four contemporary subjects, the next film marked the last journey back in time – until the ill-fated *Columbus* sailed onto our screens eighteen years later. *Carry On Dick* was set in the 18th century when highwaymen were a constant bugbear along the roads of Britain, especially the legendary Richard Turpin, better known as Big Dick. All the regulars were cast, including Sid James as the dastardly villain and Kenneth Williams as Captain Fancey, who oversaw day-to-day running of the Bow Street Runners, tasked with tracking down the elusive criminal.

The script was based on a treatment by writers Lawrie Wyman and George Evans, a partnership which began in the days of *The Navy Lark*. They received £250 each for their efforts, although the archives reveal that they did, in fact, write a complete script for *Dick*, with their main character named Dick Twirpin. George Evans recalls suggesting the idea to Peter Rogers. 'He asked if we could come up with some subjects for a *Carry On*, and Lawrie came up with *Dick*. When we told Peter, he immediately said "wonderful" and that's how it all started.' It wasn't the first time Wyman and Evans had been in contact with Rogers. As writers of *The Navy Lark*, interest had been shown in making a film based around the successful premise, titled *The Navy Game*. But the idea never progressed beyond the initial stages. 'We wrote a screenplay but Peter didn't like it at all,' recalls Evans. 'He liked the second half of the script better so asked whether we'd write just a general naval comedy. We rewrote the first half and sent it in; Gerry Thomas loved it, but Peter didn't and decided against making it.'

So it was a return to period costume for the only *Carry On* production released in 1974. It was also the last time that Sid James would be seen on a *Carry On* film set, his absence from the next movie, *Behind*, occasioned by him touring Australia in a play. Then came his untimely death in 1976, just before *England* got off the ground. His presence would be sorely missed by everyone, including fans around the world. As Jack Douglas, who appeared in, among others, *Dick*, *Behind* and *England*, states: 'No one could believe it when Sid died. He was like a block of granite, such a solid person. We couldn't grasp the fact that he was no longer with us.'

Dick also marked the end of Talbot Rothwell's *Carry On* career. With Rothwell taken ill while writing the script – he died in 1981, aged 64 – Peter Rogers stepped in to complete the screenplay. The loss of Rothwell was 'tragic' says Douglas. 'He was a brilliant writer and a lovely chap. He had a certain magic and created the most wonderful situations. I often enjoyed long chats with him, especially when we finished filming and some of us went for a drink. He was very dedicated. When he was on the set he was the writer, and there was no messing about. But afterwards he was just a normal person.'

Filming ran from early March to mid-April, a particularly busy time for Sid James, Barbara Windsor, Kenneth Connor, Peter Butterworth, Bernard Bresslaw and Jack Douglas, who were performing simultaneously in the stage production *Carry On London* at the Victoria Palace. Each evening the actors would perform not once but twice, with filming scheduled so they could reach the theatre in time. With many scenes in the film involving horse-riding, everyone had to be careful. 'I'm terrified of horses,'[92] Windsor told a regional journalist who visited the set one sunny April afternoon. 'I don't mind so much if the horse just stands still, but as soon as it moves, I feel ill.'[93] Sid James, meanwhile, joked: 'These horses we're working with have appeared in so many films nobody dare say the word "Action" in their hearing, or they're off. We have to spell it out, "A-c-t-i-o-n" or say it in a whisper if we don't want the horses to start galloping.'[94]

Dick, which cost £228,000 to make, was released in July 1974, after Gerald Thomas confirmed to the British Board of Film Censors (BBFC) that the required cuts to dialogue had been made to obtain an 'A' classification. It was rare that the censors allowed a *Carry On* to pass through their fingers without requesting deletions, although John Trevelyan, Secretary of the BBFC for a time, once stated: 'I cannot pretend that these pictures are always free from censorship troubles! But so far they have never given us problems that have no satisfactory solution, and I think that Peter and Gerald can now anticipate our reactions with considerable accuracy, which is most helpful. Some years ago a well-known critic, when writing about one of the *Carry On* pictures, described it as "innocent vulgarity" and I think this was a very apt phrase.'[95]

What was deemed acceptable in society altered over the years and it is interesting to note that 15 years earlier, when *Nurse* was released, a critic questioned the granting of a 'U' certificate to the medical comedy. Although it is a harmless film and hardly full of suggestive material, Paul Dehn, writing in the *News Chronicle*, argued that: 'There is, of course, nothing commercially wrong about a film company having a bash at sexual innuendo for adults only, if they think it will pay off . . . But there is surely something very wrong with a Board of Censors who will permit such stuff to be passed as fit entertainment for an uninstructed child.'[96] How society has changed. By the time the censors were studying *Dick*, there were many more blatant sexual references to sort out. In his letter to Stephen Murphy at the BBFC, Thomas confirmed the deletion of requested lines, including Dick Turpin quoting a psalm with the phrase 'Goes a-whoring', the line 'There's nothing like an old mare for a comfortable ride' and 'I am far too busy to worry about how I am hung.' Despite such cuts, some of the remaining dialogue was still near the knuckle in what was, arguably, Rothwell's most blatant script.

The actors slotted back into their normal rhythm and fun was had by all, especially Jack Douglas, playing the ludicrously named Sergeant Jock Strapp, his biggest and favourite role in the series. Although what he hadn't been told was that he'd end up being thrown in a horse trough that was full of water. The scene unfolds at the old Cock Inn, a favoured watering hole among the criminal fraternity; while searching for clues to help trace Dick Turpin, an old lady, Maggie, announces that the highwayman has a distinctive birthmark on his 'diddler'. Sergeant Strapp is given the unenviable task of following every man into the toilet to see if they have the mark. His furtive glances, though, are noticed and after almost getting attacked for being a Peeping Tom he is thrown into the water – all in the line of duty. 'I thought the scene ended when the men noticed I was looking at them; Gerald didn't tell me there was a trough outside, into which the men dumped me. But Gerald, wonderful man that he was, made sure the water was heated because it was an extremely cold day. That was typical Gerald, but he wanted the expression of surprise and shock on my face – and got it! I could never have acted that sort of face.'

The film's release was met with largely wholesale approval: while many critics didn't go as far as admitting it was to their taste, they were prepared at least to acknowledge that it was now hard to knock the films' success and the sheer pleasure that they afforded fans. As Nigel Gearing, a critic writing in a trade magazine, suggested: 'Maybe their continuing appeal is beyond criticism – or, according to taste, beneath it.'[97] Russell Davies, in the *Observer*, wrote along similar lines, contemplating 'how much longer the Pinewood mob can sustain its famous immunity to criticism.'[98] Others, at long last, were beginning to realise and appreciate the reasons for the series's longevity, with Nigel Andrews in the *Financial Times* acknowledging that there had 'never been a film series in which the same themes and the same motifs were milked for the same effects over quite so long a period of time.'[99] He added that the appeal of this kind of comedy was its predictability, which is true, although in *Dick*'s make-up there was a discernible reduction in the laugh-out-loud moments while many performances were muted or surprisingly out of sorts. Among the weakest of the Rothwell scripts, the film lacked the bright demeanour associated with others in the series.

Some felt the same about *Behind*, which was shot between mid-March and mid-April 1975 and released by the end of the year. With Rothwell having written his last *Carry On* script, the job of penning this caravan-park adventure was passed to Dave Freeman, a Londoner who began his working life as an electrician and experienced his first taste of writing while serving in the navy. After the war, he joined the police force for five years before accepting a job booking cabaret acts at the American Officers' Club. It was there that he met Benny Hill, for whom he went on to write sketches.

In February 1973, Freeman, for a fee of £5,000, delivered a script titled *Love On Wheels*, which started off with a distinguished archaeologist, Roland Plumcott, giving a lecture. No action was taken on the script, but by the end of 1974 Freeman was busy rewriting it under a new title, *Carry On Behind*, for an additional £1,250, retaining the basic premise and characters from his original script. On the strength of the revised work and Rogers's casting plans, Rank provided a budget of £225,000, with Frank Poole looking forward to another successful partnership on the film. Knowing the screenplay was reminiscent of the earlier *Camping*, he closed his letter to Peter Rogers in February 1975 hoping that similarities with *Camping* wouldn't stop there – they would be reflected in the takings, too.

A pallid version of *Camping*, maybe, at a time when questions were being raised about whether the series was finally losing its way, yet it was still an amusing piece of work which offered memorable moments and performances. Although Sid James and Barbara Windsor were absent – James touring Australia in a play, Windsor trekking around New Zealand with her one-woman show – the likes of Connor, Williams, Butterworth, Sims, Bresslaw and Rowlands were on the cast sheet, together with London-born Windsor Davies, a former teacher and miner (and later the barking sergeant major in *It Ain't Half Hot, Mum*) and German model-turned-actress Elke Sommer.

With action centred around the Riverside Caravan Site, run by the diminutive Major Leep (Kenneth Connor), the film focuses primarily on two partnerships: firstly, Fred Ramsden (the role originally intended for Sid James but portrayed by Windsor Davies) and Ernie Bragg (Jack Douglas), friends who take a short caravan holiday after convincing their wives that they intend doing a little fishing, although 'birds' are what they're hoping to catch. The pairing resembles *Camping*'s Sid Boggle and Bernie Lugg, with Davies playing the sex maniac happy to deceive his wife in the hope of finding a younger model for a bit of fun, accompanied by an unsuspecting fool of a friend, in this case portrayed by Douglas.

The second partnership within the film arrives at the caravan site in the shape of Professor Crump (Kenneth Williams), an experienced archaeologist, and Professor Vooshka (Elke Sommer), a Russian archaeologist specialising in Roman remains. They travel to the caravan park when a Roman encampment is discovered next to the site, and much comedy is eked out of the amusing study of Crump and Vooshka, particularly the confusion caused by the Russian's haphazard command of the English language.

Sommer, who'd appeared in the 1967 Betty Box-produced crime thriller *Deadlier Than The Male*, agreed to appear in the film as a 'friendly gesture' towards Peter Rogers: 'Peter and Betty [Box] were very good friends of mine.' When Rogers asked her to play Vooshka, she admits she'd never heard of the *Carry On*s. 'I met my colleagues and what impressed me was that they were all incredible actors. We did this silly, groovy movie, but it brought a lot of joy and that's the main thing,' says the actress, now based in Los Angeles. She has happy memories of filming, apart from the weather conditions. 'It was freezing – we froze our behinds off!' she laughs. Patricia Franklin, who played Vera Bragg (Jack Douglas's screen wife) concurs with Sommer. 'When we filmed the scene outside the butcher's shop it snowed and Liz Fraser and I were in summer dresses. We had to wait for Marks and Spencer to open so they could buy us cardigans.'

Most of Sommer's scenes were alongside Kenneth Williams, who she describes as a 'very friendly, very intelligent' man. 'He was extremely knowledgeable. We talked about subjects to which I couldn't contribute much, things I had to learn about during the course of my life. He knew everything, though.' Sommer's solid performance was pinpointed by the press, with Felix Barker classing her 'especially good with her tongue-in-cheek seriousness'[100] and a critic in *Films Illustrated* rating *Behind* as the 'liveliest in many years, thanks largely to the injection of new blood provided by Elke Sommer.'[101] Settling into her role with ease, she explains: 'That is one of my fortes. I can fit into practically anything in life, I've never had a problem and am able to feel comfortable and make others feel comfortable, too.'

While Dave Freeman's effort, which took three weeks to plot and three to fill out, might have lacked some of the polish and vigour of his predecessor's work, it remained a funny script and Verina Glaessner in *Monthly Film Bulletin* went as far as to suggest that the advent of the new scriptwriter 'seems to have worked a small wonder, and the film emerges as the most consistently funny *Carry On* in many years.'[102] As usual, some people weren't so enamoured of the script but there were compensatory elements, such as the performances – and not just from Elke Sommer and the ever-reliable Kenneth Williams. Jack Douglas and Windsor Davies struck up a fruitful working partnership. 'There are times in showbusiness when you have a magic, and Windsor and I had that. We'd literally only just met, but from the moment we started working together it was like Laurel and Hardy bouncing off each other.'

Windsor Davies, who went on to play Sergeant Major Bloomer in *England*, felt accepted into the fold on his first appearance and enjoyed the experience. He said at the time: 'We have a lot of fun on the set, but filming's very disciplined. It's a hell of a lot of work, but everybody enjoys it. And Gerald Thomas, the director, is marvellous. He's very good in allowing us to insert small bits of invention and in allowing us to use our imagination.'[103]

Fans who didn't mind a little bit of nudity enjoyed watching actress Jenny Cox disrobing in the opening scene and, later, playing a stripper. The Welsh performer, however, didn't hold out much hope of securing the job when auditioned. She explained: 'Although I've appeared on stage in sexy comedies like *The Dirtiest Show in Town* and *Pyjama Tops*, most of my career has been spent in fairly serious roles. However, as acting jobs had been so scarce I decided to have a go as I've always wanted to be in a *Carry On*.'[104] Reaching the studios, however, was fraught with problems. 'I had a puncture on the way and was so flustered by the time I was ushered in to meet Peter Rogers and Gerald Thomas that I fell off my platform heels and landed at their feet. It was like a scene from a *Carry On*. Anyway, my trip across the office must have helped me get the job because they told me they'd rather have a funny lady playing a stripper than teach a professional stripper how to play a comedy role.' Cox explained that she studied for the role by secretly watching an erotic dancer who had been hired for a local rugby club social event; she must have been a fast learner because, after completing her act for the caravan site's cabaret evening, the regulars congratulated her with a resounding round of applause.

The initial strip scene, within a film inadvertently shown by Professor Crump, was lucky to survive the censor's examination; in fact, in May 1975 when viewed in respect of an application for 'A' categorisation, the censor, Stephen Murphy, requested three deletions: the removal of the line 'I feel a complete arse' as a man held a girl's bottom; the scene showing a glimpse of Linda Upmore's 'dangling breasts seen through caravan window'[105] and removal of scenes showing the bare-breasted dancer. While the first two were actioned, the dancing scenes were retained, all part of the bargaining that went on between film producer and film censor.

The *Carry On* machine, albeit a little slower now, continued to chug away and the 28th film, *Carry On England,* would be in production by spring 1976. Sadly, though, the film series had seen its best days.

Part 3
The Beginning of the End?

I

If a survey was conducted to identify the weakest and least-liked of the 31 *Carry On* films, it's probable that *England* and *Columbus*, followed closely by *Emmannuelle*, would be in pole positions. For many, 1976, the year when the vapid *England* was released, marked the beginning of the end for the *Carry On*s. Peter Rogers and Gerald Thomas had spent their careers paying little attention to what critics had to say about their offerings, which is just as well because most reviewers slated *England* on its release. Arthur Thirkell, in the *Daily Mirror*, wasn't impressed by the army-based picture at all, reporting that 'it's sad to say that another British institution, the *Carry On* series, is in a worse state than the economy.'[1] No holds barred, he branded the latest effort 'pathetic'[2], classing it 'British comedy fluttering the white flag, surrendering wit and imagination to the flabby forces of uninspired farce.'[3]

Reflecting on his relationship with the critics, and how they rated the films, Peter Rogers admits nonchalantly that he didn't worry about their opinions. 'They didn't like the films and were very rude about them, but it didn't make any difference – not a bit.' Rogers believed he could always predict what papers would report, and remembers an occasion when he jested with a journalist about penning his review for him. 'We always held a function for various members of the press, providing them with lunch and drinks. I knew what they were going to be like, and to one rather drunken character I said: "Don't worry, I'll write your notice for you, I know what you're going to say." So I didn't worry about them – in fact, some of the critics became friends, in a way.'

In his review of *England*, Thirkell acknowledged the stance that Rogers and Thomas took regarding his industry, but thought that perhaps this time they should take note. He wrote: 'Those genial chaps, producer Peter Rogers and director Gerald Thomas, remain unrepentant. Their attitude is that if the critics like their films they fear they might be on the wrong track. But I suspect that not only critics are going to give the thumbs-down, or some other hand sign, to this rubbish.'[4]

As Rogers would have expected, Arthur Thirkell wasn't alone in drubbing the latest *Carry On*, which saw the team return to khaki for the 28th film in the series, just as the original cast had done for the first picture, *Sergeant*, in 1958. But similarities with the inaugural production were in short supply and there was little to remind us of the catalogue of successes that had gone before.

Set in 1940, *England* spotlights the tomfoolery of the guys and gals posted to the experimental 1313 anti-aircraft battery. Rather than doing their bit for Britain with proficiency and dedication, they prefer to shirk their responsibilities and drive their captain to drink. When Captain Bull, played by David Lodge, makes way for the diminutive Captain S. Melly, portrayed by *Carry On* stalwart Kenneth Connor, it is anticipated that the new incumbent's tough-talking rhetoric will knock the belligerent bunch of slackers into shape – no such luck.

With the Rank Organisation financing only fifty per cent of the film, Peter Rogers and Gerald Thomas looked for potential partners. During early 1976, discussions took place with representatives of the rock band Pink Floyd, who'd expressed a desire to part-finance the production. Setting the end of April as the proposed start date for filming, Rogers and Thomas suffered a setback when on 1 April Pink Floyd's representative announced that the band had decided, reluctantly, not to proceed. By then, pre-production was well under way, and Gerald Thomas and Peter Rogers, so late in the day, were left with little alternative but to finance the remaining fifty per cent of costs themselves. Using their own funds was something they had avoided until now, with Thomas explaining that they 'didn't think it was a good policy because our finance is mainly used for our overheads between pictures and for the purchasing and promoting of other subjects, which is a very costly business.'[5]

Recording began on Monday, 3 May 1976, with scenes shot at Pinewood's Stage G involving Kenneth Connor and Windsor Davies. Most of the filming, which concluded on 4 June, took place in the

Orchard at the Pinewood lot, with a mobile anti-aircraft gun loaned by the Imperial War Museum adding a touch of realism.

Overall, critics didn't mince their words; few could muster a smile when they put pen to paper. But whereas previous opinions of those mocking the *Carry Ons* had borne little relation to the size of the audiences piling in to watch the latest instalment, the tide was changing: support from the public in terms of box-office receipts saw a marked decline, a worrying sign. But omens for the film's success weren't good from the beginning: by the time the cast assembled during May, Sid James, the linchpin of so many films, had died. In April 1976, while performing in a production of Sam Cree's *The Mating Game* in Sunderland, he'd collapsed – he was just 62. Such a loss inevitably cast a cloud over the entire *England* production, and as David Castell later concluded in the *Sunday Telegraph*, 'how sadly is missed the disarming vulgarity of Sidney James'.[6]

South African-born actress Olga Lowe, who'd played Madame Fifi in *Carry On Abroad*, was on stage with Sid at Sunderland's Empire Theatre when he suffered the fatal heart attack. A long-time friend, she had first worked with him at the tender age of 14 – an experience she'll never forget, for several reasons. 'We were doing a charity show in Johannesburg. I was the best tap dancer amongst a troupe of girls from my dancing class. Sid picked me to do the Snowman number with him, "Walking in a Winter Wonderland". We were dressed as snowmen, but with faces drawn on the back of our heads. So, in fact, we worked our tap dance with our backs to the audience, although the costumes gave the impression that we were facing the front.

'During the afternoon rehearsal, Sid hadn't done up his flies and his willy fell out. I could see it as I was dancing next to him, but the director and girls sitting out front couldn't, so everyone was astonished when I ran off the stage, crying. Everything came to a standstill! Doing up his flies, Sid shouted after me: "Come back here, you silly little bitch! You're going to see a lot worse than that in a few years' time." Everyone laughed and I returned, embarrassed. Sid dried my eyes, comforted me and we went on with the rehearsal.

'The second time I worked with him was when I joined the

South African Entertainment Unit. He was producing small concert party-type shows to entertain troops in South Africa and the Middle East; I was in one of the shows. Sid was then married to his second wife, Meg, who was also in the unit. We had a lot of fun. Sid was a wonderful character, living life to the full – there was never a dull moment with him.'

Olga's husband Keith Morris also appeared in *The Mating Season* on that fateful evening. 'I opened the show with the leading lady,' says Morris, 'and saw Sid in the wings with a whisky in his hand. He asked if I wanted a sip, which I politely refused, and I went back to my dressing room. I listened to Olga's entrance on the tannoy. She was playing the mistress and sat on the sofa with Sid, throwing off her shawl and exposing her bubbling boobs in typical *Carry On* style. During the scene, Sid's head went back on the sofa. At this stage, Sid had begun to play little practical jokes on all of us, like you do in a long run, so Olga continued, thinking he might have been mucking about.'

'I suddenly got this awful panic in my heart and knew something dreadful had happened,' adds Lowe. 'I went across to the wings, telling them something had happened to Sid and I'd do some ad libbing while they brought the curtain down. God knows what I said, but I kept talking to Sid until the curtain eventually came down. The manager went in front, by which time the audience was laughing because they thought a gag was being played on them. The company manager asked if there was a doctor in the house, which got another big laugh. Luckily, there *was* a doctor, who came backstage; by this time an ambulance had been called but Sid never recovered. Everyone was so shocked that we sat up half the night and had a few drinks. It was awful. The tour was cancelled immediately and we returned to London the next day.'

Joan Sims, who'd often been cast as Sid's henpecking wife or girlfriend in the *Carry On*s, regarded his death as the 'end of an era'. 'To me Sid was a complete gentleman, the ultimate pro and a great friend. I loved all the jokes and all the fun of working with him.'[8] She recalled an incident on the set of *Carry On Girls* which typified his altruistic tendencies, especially when protecting his contemporaries in the tightly knit *Carry On* clan. While visiting Pinewood

Studios, two MPs took the opportunity to watch a scene being shot. 'One of the MPs had clearly lunched a little too well and started making salacious suggestions to a couple of the actresses – in Sid's hearing,'[9] Sims recalled. 'Sid was always protective of all the *Carry On* team and would not put up with this sort of behaviour. He protested vehemently and demanded that they apologise. They did so – then made a hasty retreat.'[10]

Of course, James had been missing from *Behind*, due to touring commitments in Australia with *The Mating Season*, but his absence wasn't as palpable as it was in *England*. His memory hung like a shadow over Stage G as the cameras turned for the first time; gone was the dirty laugh, the captain of the team whose fighting spirit and sheer presence provided a stabilising influence over proceedings. To visiting journalists, invited along to see the new film in the making, his colleagues paid tribute. Jack Causey, the First Assistant, said: 'He was always a lovable man . . . as he became a star he never changed over the years.'[11] Peter Rogers, meanwhile, classed James as 'the head of the family. He was the father figure and everyone would go to him with their troubles.'[12]

Whether Sid James's presence in the cast would have made a difference to the film's fortunes is debatable because criticism was widespread: it wasn't just the experienced guys at the nationals queuing up to throw their four penn'orth into the mix. A reporter on the *West Hertfordshire and Watford Observer* felt that the film provided 'clear indications . . . that this once amusing comedy series has finally run out of steam.'[13] He added that *England* was likely to 'make you squirm in your cinema seat as the team try to resurrect or resuscitate a script suffering from a serious case of senility.'[14]

Pinpointing the script as one of the film's primary weaknesses was an important factor when considering why *England* and those it preceded lacked the inherent vitality permeating previous releases. This was the second script since the departure of Talbot 'Double Entendre' Rothwell, and the only one written by the successful writing partnership of David Pursall and Jack Seddon. Born in Kirkintilloch, Scotland, Pursall was demobbed from the Fleet Air Arm with the rank of commander and was introduced to film producers Frank Launder and Sidney Gilliat. Soon installed as their publicity director, he later joined the Rank Organisation's publicity team; but it wasn't until he returned to Pinewood as production publicity controller that he met his future writing partner, Jack Seddon, whose working life had begun as a regional journalist before progressing to the nationals. Eventually, Pursall and Seddon, both frustrated scriptwriters, ditched their jobs for the precarious world of freelance scriptwriting. Their talents were soon in demand and among their credits were the films *The Longest Day*, *The Alphabet Murders* and *Tomorrow Never Comes* and small-screen episodes for *The Liver Birds*, *Arthur and the Britons* and *Oil Strike North*.

England began life as a script for the second series of television's *Carry On Laughing*. The script, titled *The Busting of Balsy*, was dropped for TV but Rogers subsequently asked the writers to convert it for the big screen. Adapting television products for the cinema rarely works, and that was the case here.

Despite their skills in the art of scriptwriting, the writers' efforts to recapture the style and energy of former *Carry On* scripts failed. Jack Douglas, whose *Carry On* career began with a cameo appearance in *Matron* and continued with seven other roles, including Bombardier Ready in *England*, Lyons in *Emmannuelle* and Marco the Cereal Killer in *Columbus*, states that *Columbus* and *England* lacked the 'Tolly Rothwell magic, which was greatly missed'. He says: 'They weren't *Carry On* pictures, in my opinion. The beauty of *Abroad*, *Matron* and all the others was that they were all classics, but the new writers didn't have the magic that Tolly had.'

Members of the trade press also indicated this aspect as a weakness, with Derek Elley, a self-confessed admirer of the *Carry Ons*, commenting in *Films and Filming*: 'I have defended before, and will continue to defend, the many virtues of the *Carry On* series, but I must confess to being a trifle hard-pressed to find much of recommendation in this latest instalment.'[15] While he believed that Dave Freeman – who wrote the previous screenplay, *Behind* – had assumed the mantle from the much-missed Talbot Rothwell, the latest script, *England*, was let down by 'a feeble scenario by newcomers Seddon and Pursall, who just do not possess the necessary bawdy esprit to make the story of a mixed gun emplacement . . . really take off.'

Another factor that hampered the film's chances at the box office was it being shorn of so many regular faces. Much of the action centred around Patrick Mower and Judy Geeson, paid £2,500 and £2,000 respectively to portray Sergeants Len Able and Tilly Willing. Mower, then in his mid-thirties, was making his *Carry On* debut after forging a successful television career as James Cross in *Callan* and Tom Haggerty in *Special Branch*. Interviewed while filming at Pinewood, Mower expressed his delight at being asked to play one of the leading roles. 'When I was invited to join the comedy ranks, I jumped at the chance. I've always enjoyed doing comedy and recently have been trying to soften up my old image. I've found it great fun working with the *Carry On* gang. It's an education and a treat watching the way laughter-raisers like Kenneth Connor, Jack Douglas and Windsor Davies milk every situation. I have high hopes for it.'[16]

Judy Geeson was equally pleased to be joining the ranks of the *Carry On* team. She commented at the time, 'This is certainly one of the nicest things I've done. The atmosphere is so different from some of the films I've worked on, in that it's so relaxed and pleasant.'[17] Much of the credit for creating an atmosphere conducive to making good entertainment fell, of course, to director Gerald Thomas, but even his skills were unable to make up for the film's failings.

Continuity was not only exercised in terms of the production team and cast: the characters brought to life in every film were familiar, too. Fundamentally, familiarity is important in a product's longevity and one reason the *Carry On* films established a loyal band of followers, transcending generations, is that everyone looked forward to seeing the same clutch of actors, caught up in the same old scenarios. For *England*, though, notable absentees included Kenneth Williams, Charles Hawtrey, Barbara Windsor and Hattie Jacques. And among a scattering of regulars and semi-regulars, in the shape of Kenneth Connor, Joan Sims, Peter Butterworth, Windsor Davies and Jack Douglas much of the cast consisted of younger, less experienced faces in the world of big-screen comedy.

Initially, Peter Rogers hoped to assemble a cast including Windsor Davies, Kenneth Connor, Jack Douglas, Bernard Bresslaw, James Bolam, Adam Faith, Richard O'Sullivan, Kenneth Williams, Ian

Lavender; Joan Sims, Penelope Keith, Adrienne Posta, Michele Dotrice, Susan Penhaligon, Anne Aston and Carol Hawkins. Despite some of the originals being offered roles – like Kenneth Williams, who was unavailable to play the Brigadier – Rogers and Thomas deliberately sourced an injection of young blood. Thomas said: 'As is essential in all *Carry On*s, you have a certain amount of intimated sexual relations and we felt it was distasteful to have too great a discrepancy between our male characters and the young girls. We've had to lose some of our old actors, though a lot of them are still with us.'[18] He added that being based around the daily goings-on at an army unit, 'we had to have people believably between the ages of 20 and 40.'[19]

Peter Rogers added: 'Now with a few of them [the established faces] getting old, and one or two of them sadly fading away, we are bringing in a bit of new blood. We did so well with the last film, *Carry On Behind*, by adding Elke Sommer, Adrienne Posta and Windsor Davies to the regulars, and we have done so again now with Patrick Mower, Judy Geeson and Melvyn Hayes.'[20]

Although the introduction of newer faces had begun in the previous production, *Behind*, it was largely familiar names holding key posts: this wasn't the case in *England* and the influx of younger performers wasn't welcomed by many. Angela Haydon, writing in the *Monthly Film Bulletin*, felt that the *Carry On* films had reached a juncture. Although it had lost many of its originals, it had 'failed miserably to find acceptable substitutes'.[21] Even the casting of Connor and Davies couldn't make up for the loss of the other popular faces, remarked Nicholas Wapshott in *The Scotsman*, adding: 'It's hardly a *Carry On* at all.'[22]

Gerald Thomas noted that it was not only new personnel but a different stance in the scriptwriting that had been introduced. Stressing that it was time for change, he said: 'Over the last three or four [films], we realised that we had to do something fresh with the cast, the writing and the way we shot them. We do follow a straight line, in the sense that we try to keep faith with the audience, but the audience today wants a little more visual action. The *Carry On*s have latterly relied very heavily on spoken innuendo, but that's not sufficient today.'[23]

Not everyone felt the need to change. Russell Davies, for example, commented in the *Observer* that 'breasts are on parade this time, incidentally; gone is the mere coy bulbousness of seaside-postcard days.'[24] Other remarks from the press included the *News of the World* classing it 'one of the unfunniest',[25] and David Castell in the *Sunday Telegraph* feeling 'it isn't just the locations that have run out, it's the freshness and attack of the players.'[26]

Jack Douglas, like many of the critics reviewing the film, believes the golden rule in showbusiness was broken: if you have something that is successful, don't change it. 'They did on *England* and it didn't work. There were a lot of new faces and the approach to the film was different.' One piece of evidence to substantiate Douglas's views concerning the new approach was the inclusion of the first blatant nude scene. The inherent humour in the *Carry On*s was regarded as naughty, cheeky but inoffensive, with only fleeting moments of nudity, such as a momentary flash of Barbara Windsor's bottom, covered in soap suds, while standing under the shower in *Abroad*. Even as far back as *Constable*, the fourth film, in 1960, you saw the callow police constables' backsides as they ran from a shower. The scenes were integrated into the script and didn't shock or appear incongruous with the rest of the sequence. In *England,* though, a sequence depicting a group of busty females rushing topless from a billet and lining up, thrusting their chests forward, had everyone from the censor to the critics questioning the prudence of such a scene. Jack Douglas says: 'That wasn't what one expected of the *Carry On*s – Tolly [Rothwell] would never have written that. There were bare bums in *Carry On* but when you get a line-up of girls wearing skirts and nothing else, it's not a *Carry On*.'

The trouble was that Rogers and Thomas faced dichotomies: firstly, Sid James had died and the other regulars from the 'repertory company' were getting on. One now had to question, for example, how long the male characters could continue chasing young dolly birds without falling into the dirty-old-man-in-a-mac scenario. And times were changing and styles of comedy were evolving. Until now, Rogers and Thomas had produced films suitable for family viewing, with their primary objective being to attract a 'U' or 'A' certificate; but the 1970s marked the dawning of a new era with sex and nudity in films increasingly popular with cinema-goers, typified by the success of Robin Askwith's *Confessions of . . .* films. The shift in the *Carry Ons*' style was even reflected in contractual agreements with Rank: no longer was there an obligation to make the film suitable for family audiences, simply that Rogers and Thomas would try their best to attain a 'U' classification.

One of the actresses appearing topless in the film was Linda Regan, who was born into a theatrical family and has worked on stage and screen, including several series as April in Perry and Croft's holiday-camp sitcom *Hi-de-Hi!* Being cast as Private Taylor arrived early in her professional career. 'I was asked if I'd do a topless scene and agreed. It didn't bother me, it was just a rather twee scene,' says Regan, who acknowledges that many ardent fans of the films regarded the nudity as a step too far and not in keeping with the films' traditional style. As a newcomer to the *Carry On*s, she suggests that it was, perhaps, an attempt to move the films forward in life. 'I guess the only answer was how popular the film was, and I don't know the answer to that. I just wanted to work with all those good comedy people and thought it worth taking my clothes off in order to do so.'

England was released in October 1976 and failed to satisfy fans; shockingly, it was removed from the schedules of some cinemas just days after its initial screening, and it would be some time before the film clawed back just its production costs. But this didn't surprise reviewers who, from day one, had painted a gloomy picture of the film's chances of satisfying the sizeable audiences which had hitherto flocked to cinemas religiously to watch the next product off the *Carry On* production line. A scribe in *Screen International* confirmed that there was no way of gauging what impact the 'AA' certificate, which *England* was originally given, would have on the future of the film series, but thought that 'apparently the *Carry On*s are destined to go the way of the *Confessions* series, and is a taste of more sinful things to come. We are here treated to a largely streamlined and occasionally unclothed cast. Will this policy perpetuate the series ad infinitum?'[27] Meanwhile, Nigel Andrews in the *Financial Times* lamented the demise of the home-grown film industry and classed *England* as a 'bedraggled also-ran'[28]. Remarking that it came from the 'usually reliable stable of Peter Rogers and Gerald Thomas'[29] he felt it had 'the marks of defeat about it from the start'[30] and recommended a new scriptwriter, or a return to Rothwell, if the films were to remain the standard bearer of 'British low comedy'.[31] A critic in *Variety* classed the film unfunny and the 'dullest script of the series'.[32] Credit was forthcoming, though, for the cast, particularly for Kenneth Connor, Windsor Davies and Jack Douglas, for working tirelessly to generate some excitement from the 'flagging dialogue'[33] and for Gerald Thomas, who managed to deliver a film which the critic regarded as on a par with the previous pictures from a technical viewpoint.

Regardless of the film's failings, the popularity of the *Carry On*s meant that even performers cast in small parts tasted the series's influence. Canadian-born Peter Banks, who played Gunner Thomas, recalls being 'set upon in the nicest possible way' by autograph seekers in 1994 while performing in Chekhov's *The Cherry Orchard* at the Grand Theatre, Wolverhampton. 'Any fan mail I receive is always about *Carry On England*, even though I did very little in it. The play at Wolverhampton contained some big names, not least Susannah York. We were doing a midweek matinee, and just as I turned into the little street on which the stage door was situated, I noticed a crowd of people. Susannah happened to be in front of me, so I decided to hold back until everyone leapt on her, then I could nip in quietly. The trouble was, Susannah just walked by and no one batted an eyelid, which I thought was very strange. Then someone shouted: "There's Peter!" They were all *Carry On* fans. It was amazing.'

II

Gerald Thomas once proclaimed that the last *Carry On* would be the first to lose money, so the reaction at the box office and the consequences of *England*'s financial failings could have been crucial to the future of the films; it appeared as if the *Carry On* train had finally run out of steam and was ready to claim its place in the annals of British film history. But the stark experience of *England*, which Joan Sims described as containing 'none of the magic of earlier *Carry Ons*',[84] did little to deter Peter Rogers and Gerald Thomas from continuing, as long as the right ideas came along. Before embarking on another full-blown script, though, they decided to exploit the gems already gathered by releasing, in 1977, a compilation of the best bits from their back catalogue of 28 films. Titled *That's Carry On*, Kenneth Williams and Barbara Windsor were hired to introduce this cavalcade of memorable scenes which cost just £75,000, less than the original film, *Sergeant*, some nineteen years earlier.

Although some saw it as a valedictory chapter in the *Carry On* life story, it was the unexpected success of *That's Entertainment*, a 1974 trawl through the MGM archives, that made the *Carry On* films a natural target for such a project. Peter Rogers and Gerald Thomas struck a deal with Nat Cohen of EMI, but the proposed title, *The Best of Carry On*, jarred with Rogers and he proceeded to convince the other parties involved in the production that his original suggestion, *That's Carry On*, was a much better prospect; he also pointed out that what's deemed to be the 'best' is a subjective opinion and opting for 'best' in the title would make any sequel 'second best'. Accepting Rogers's suggestion, *That's Carry On* became the official title and Gerald Thomas and editor Jack Gardner, who had worked as assistant editor on sixteen previous *Carry On* films, devoted nearly six weeks to selecting what, in their view, were the best sequences. The trouble was that when they sat down to check their choices, they were horrified to find the film ran for six hours! After much cogitating, they streamlined the rough cut and the film was finally released. Although it didn't initially set the world alight, and was largely distributed as a second feature with *Golden Rendezvous*, a thriller starring Richard Harris, it was nonetheless a welcome addition to the *Carry On* library, reminding fans of the halcyon days when Norman Hudis and Talbot Rothwell's scripts had audiences rolling in the aisles. However, in doing so it also paradoxically highlighted the glaring weaknesses of *England* and subsequent films.

By the time *That's Carry On* entered the circuit in February 1978, pre-production was in full swing for the 30th film, *Emmannuelle*, written by Lance Peters. The 1974 soft-porn classic *Emmanuelle* – with just one 'n' – made 19-year-old actress Sylvia Kristel a household name. Reputedly watched by 500 million people, the original spawned several sequels and many imitations, including *Black Emmanuelle* (1976), *Yellow Emmanuelle* (1977) and *Emmanuelle and the Last Cannibals* (1978).

Taking a genre of film-making and making a spoof from it was something that Rogers and Thomas weren't averse to, having addressed, among others, the spy and horror genres in *Spying* and *Screaming!* respectively. But zeroing in on the world of soft porn and releasing a pastiche wasn't an obvious direction to take when contemplating their next film – that was, until a script from Lance Peters landed on their desks.

Although born in Auckland, New Zealand, in 1934, the author, producer and screenwriter grew up in Australia. After completing his education, he gained employment at Sydney's Tivoli Theatre before turning to singing and disc-jockeying on local radio. His talents extended to comedy and he started working as a stand-up comedian in clubs, penning his own material. He was soon offered a job at the local television station, writing scripts for programmes; finding that he enjoyed the role, he quit his stand-up routine to concentrate on writing. Between 1972–81, he based himself in the UK, when Bill Kenwright, who had played a reporter in *Matron* and now runs one of Britain's most successful film and theatre production companies, was interested in acquiring the rights of a stage play, *Mother's Little Murderer,* that Peters had written. Unfortunately, a deal failed to materialise but Peters didn't discard the script, knowing that when the chance arose he'd try his luck again, perhaps reworking it for the film medium. That opportunity took a leap forward when a fortuitous meeting with Jeremy Thomas, son of film director Ralph Thomas and nephew of Gerald, resulted in his script being passed to the *Carry On* office. 'They were interested in the writing, although not that particular film, which was a comedy-horror I'd written,' recalls Peters. Prior to meeting Thomas and Rogers, Lance Peters formulated another script idea. 'I used to wander around the West End, looking at what films were being screened, and I noticed that at that time there were lots of

Emmanuelle films in addition to the original version. All were serious soft-porn sex films, and I had the idea of writing one called *Green Emmanuelle*, about a sexpot from Mars who comes down to Earth and bonks everybody in England, in an unorthodox way. I wrote a film treatment, which I thought was extremely funny, so when I met Gerald and Peter to discuss the other script [*Mother's Little Murderer*], I told them about my new idea, and that it should be renamed *Carry On Emmanuelle* [the extra 'n' in the title was added later] and they bought the idea from me.'

A further meeting was arranged and Peters was told that the storyline as it stood, namely the Martian sexpot, wasn't right for a *Carry On* picture. However, Rogers and Thomas wanted him to write a script based on a French woman in London running amok, a satire of the *Emmanuelle* film. Peters accepted. 'I went to work and wrote an entirely new film treatment about the wife of a French ambassador to the Court of St James who was a rampant sexpot and virtually brought down the British Government. They liked it and commissioned me to write the screenplay in full.'

When it came to financing the film, Peter Rogers and Gerald Thomas found themselves working with a new partner. After Rank and, latterly, EMI's brief flirtation with the film series in the shape of *That's Carry On*, a new backer arrived in the form of Cleves Investments Limited, who advanced just under £400,000 for the making of the film. Although reports suggested that Rank had withdrawn from distributing the series, Gerald Thomas pointed out that there was nothing sinister in the parting of the ways with their long-term distributor and that they hadn't even approached Rank with the *Emmannuelle* project. In fact, he felt it was 'probably right not to offer it. From the inception, it was worked out between John Daly of Hemdale and ourselves. We have worked in the past with both EMI and Rank and it is surely a good thing to move around between distributors. In this British film industry, which I love and have never deserted, it's very difficult to get films set up and so one should be looking to make deals wherever one can.'[35] It was also felt that the film needed 'aggressive selling because I feel it will have worldwide appeal'[36] and 'a slightly more modern approach regarding distribution'[37].

Lance Peters, meanwhile, wrote the script and regarded it as 'far more sophisticated than any *Carry On* film they had done before.' But as soon as the first draft arrived at Rogers and Thomas's Pinewood offices, it was clear that the material was too blue for a *Carry On*. 'It was even ruder before they censored me, which was a dreadful thing to do. I wasn't happy about that: I didn't like being censored, I like being rude,' says Peters, smiling. 'I told Peter Rogers and Gerald Thomas that, in my view, they needed to upgrade the genre anyway.' Peters thought the tits and bums, coy laughter and side jokes were dated and what he'd written was a 'very sophisticated sex comedy'.

In all, Lance Peters wrote three drafts, each time having to replace explicit scenes with material deemed more suitable to a *Carry On*. When the third draft was delivered it still required surgery, despite having undergone various amendments. One of the scenes destined to be cut was set in a sausage factory where Emmannuelle was involved in a photo-shoot. Not only was the scene ditched but the two male characters as well.

Scene 74

Open on: close shot – Radish peering into still-camera viewfinder (set on tripod) From Radish's P.O.V.: (Through viewfinder) Emmannuelle, wearing nought but a string of sausages (bra and a G-string of sausages down below) is posing on a podium, in front of a moving sausage production line.

LORD SHARECROPPER:
How's the symbolism, Radish?

RADISH: (Peering through the camera)
There's a sausage in the way.

LORD SHARECROPPER: (To Emmannuelle)
Emmannuelle, dear. Could you move one of those sausages down there?

(Pointing) It's blocking your symbolism.

Emmannuelle puts her hand on one of the sausages covering her pubes.

LORD SHARECROPPER:
That's the one, cherrypot.

Emmannuelle moves the offending sausage a fraction.

LORD SHARECROPPER:
How's that, Radish, old colleague?

RADISH: (Still peering through camera)
Well, for sausage lovers it's fine. But for ordinary lovers . . . ?

LORD SHARECROPPER:
Emmannuelle, dear, I think he's worried that there's too much sausage and not enough meat. If you know what I mean.

Emmannuelle adjusts her sausage bra a fraction and allows a nipple to show through.

LORD SHARECROPPER:
How's that?

RADISH: (Looking through camera)
Better.

LORD SHARECROPPER:
'Tween you and I, ducky, I don't see where the attraction is in these silly booby things. But we have to cater to our butch readers.

EMMANNUELLE:
Don't you like girls at all?

LORD SHARECROPPER:
Well, some of them are all right to talk to.

RADISH: (Looking quite fed up)
Can you get her to clutch one of the sausages round her neck, as if she wants to eat it?

LORD SHARECROPPER:
Do as he says, petunia. He gets so angry.

Emmannuelle clutches a sausage as instructed.

Radish peers into the viewfinder again. Then looks up, still very dissatisfied.

RADISH:
Look! Why can't she put one in her mouth and sort of suck on it?

LORD SHARECROPPER:
Why not indeed? He's a perfectionist, see, sweetie. (**Confidentially**)

Emmannuelle is reluctant.

LORD SHARECROPPER:
They're not cooked, you know.

RADISH:
I didn't ask her to eat it.

EMMANNUELLE:
I don't like sausages.

LORD SHARECROPPER:
Don't let the British hear you say that, cherrypie. (**Shouts at Radish**)
She doesn't like sausages.

RADISH: (Getting very angry)
Stone the goldfish! Tell her to imagine it's a . . .

LORD SHARECROPPER:
Yes, of course. He said to tell you to imagine it's a . . .

Emmannuelle nods in understanding, puts the sausage in her mouth and sucks it like a . . .

LORD SHARECROPPER:
How's that?

RADISH: (Peering through camera)
Bloody disgusting!

LORD SHARECROPPER:
Good. He likes it. (Smiles with relief)

Radish starts clicking the camera.

Scene 75. Int. Montage of posed shots in sausage factory.
(a) Emmannuelle in her sausage bikini moving slowly along production belt. She smiles. FREEZE.
(b) Emmannuelle, naked except for three solitary, strategic sausages, standing up, leaning each arm on a gigantic 3-foot-long knife and fork. She smiles. FREEZE.
(c) Emmannuelle, in her sausage bikini, approaches a bed of sausages and sinks slowly down onto it. When she's fully reclining, she looks sideways and smiles. FREEZE.

RADISH: (Voice-over)
What are you going to call the spread?

LORD SHARECROPPER: (Voice over)
I'm not quite sure. How about – 'bangers and pash'?

RADISH: (Voice-over)
That's the worst idea I've ever heard!

(d)   Emmannuelle, still draped only with sausages and an open-mouthed expression of sensuality, is situated above the sausage-filling machine, which exudes a never-ending uncut sausage length that travels between her legs. She turns and smiles. FREEZE.

LORD SHARECROPPER: (Voice-over)
Our readers should love it.

(e)   Emmannuelle, wearing a dress made of sausages, which has two peepholes in the front allowing her breasts to poke through, is standing behind the weighing and dividing operator on the sausage production line. The operator is cutting appropriate lengths off the main sausage and twisting them into links.

Emmannuelle adopts a pained expression as she cuts. FREEZE.
(f)   Emmannuelle, naked, is bound and gagged by sausages to
a stake in front of a burning barbecue. She doesn't smile. FREEZE.

Scene 76. Sausage factory. Another Angle
Hiding behind a bowl-type chopping machine full of sausage
meat and spices, is Theodore, who is covertly taking photographs
of the photography session.

From Theodore's P.O.V. Lord Sharecropper winds up the session
as Emmannuelle flings her sausage-encased body down, exhausted.

LORD SHARECROPPER:
All right, precious, you can take your sausages off now.

Emmannuelle does just that.

Gerald Thomas turned to experienced television writer Vince Powell
to tone down Lance Peters's script, although contributions were also
made by Willie Rushton, for which he was paid £500. Powell, who
received £1,000, recalls: 'I got a call from Gerry, who I'd known for
some time. He asked whether I was busy and I told him I was. He
then said: "I've got a job for you: we have a *Carry On* script, *Emmannuelle*, but it's pornographic. Can you help?"' Powell agreed to look
at the script. 'It was like a blue movie, so I rang Gerry and said: "I
can only spare you about ten days because I'm going on holiday for
a month." Gerry was happy with that so I booked myself into the
Strand Palace Hotel in London and did a quick rewrite in ten days; I
was basically doing a doctoring job, taking out the very saucy bits that
wouldn't have got past the censor and thinking of more innuendo-
style jokes. I took it to Pinewood, they paid me and Peter Rogers
gave me a case of wine. I never saw the film but attended the end-
of-filming party at Pinewood, which was a nice occasion. To be
honest, I've tried to delete that period from my memory bank. I
just vaguely recall those long, seemingly endless days of rewriting in
my bedroom at the hotel, fortified by sandwiches and large whiskies
from room service. The only pleasant memory I retain is that of
Suzanne Danielle. I thought she was the best thing in the movie.'

Although the basis for many of Peters's original scenes was retained in the final script, Vince Powell often had to temper the content, such as the opening scenes involving Emmannuelle and the airline steward and, later, the gormless-looking mother's boy, Theodore Valentine, whom she escorts into a closet on Concorde to satisfy her insatiable sexual appetite. Lance Peters feels that among the scenes cut from his various drafts were some of the best, particularly one involving Emmannuelle playing tennis at Wimbledon. He recalls that it was deemed too expensive to shoot at the prestigious tennis club, as well as being too rude. 'Emmannuelle was playing tennis on Centre Court and had forgotten to put her panties on,' he says. 'Her opponent made sure she had to pick the ball up all the time. It was a teasing piece of nonsense, and I had lovely stock footage showing reactions from the Duke of Kent during a game, which I wanted to use. All these people were eating strawberries while Emmannuelle was playing tennis without her panties on. It was a very funny scene but it was cut – I was furious!'

The aforementioned scene was part of the fantasy sequence, for which a diluted version was rewritten for the final script; Peters's original version was much bluer and saw Mrs Dangle, played by Joan Sims, sharing her fantasy before Emmannuelle describes her intimate dreams on the tennis court. For Mrs Dangle, it was feeling the vibration from a washing machine that turned her on, as the following script extract reveals.

<u>Scene 57: Continued</u>
Mrs Dangle, sitting on the washing machine, sways gently from side to side with a pleasurable expression on her face.

<u>MRS DANGLE</u>: (Voice-over)
If you've never sat on a washing machine in motion before, I suggest you start now. During the actual washing cycle it's quite pleasant. A sort of low gentle vibration that worms its way up inside you, without achieving very much. But – wait for it.

Mrs Dangle is still sitting on the washing machine. Suddenly the machine makes a loud clicking sound and the cycle switches over to spin-dry.

MRS DANGLE: (Voice-over)
When the final rinse is over and the spin-dry starts, well, words can't describe it.

The machine begins to whirr and vibrate and Mrs Dangle starts to rock and tingle all over. Every vibration of the spin-dry seems to course through her. She throws her arms up in the air, holds her head back, opens her mouth, jerks her pelvis up and down and shrieks in ecstasy.

Scene 58: Street outside laundromat. Night.
LONG SHOT: lit-up laundromat in street of darkened shops. Mrs Dangle can be seen still sitting joyfully on top of her spin-drying washing machine. Her shrieks of delight are now a long way away, but continuing.

Scene 59: Kitchen of French Ambassador's Residence. Night
The group is still there. Coffee cups are empty, cakes have turned to crumbs and ashtrays are full.

LYONS:
Thank you, Mrs Dangle, for a truly unusual experience. Before you all rush out to the nearest laundromat, I think it's time we asked our guest of honour to recount her most unusual sexual experience for us.

All eyes turn towards Emmannuelle. She looks embarrassed. Hesitates.

LEYLAND:
Can't make up yer mind, eh, darlin'? Toss a coin.

EMMANNUELLE: (Modestly)
I fear, by comparison, mine may seem quite dull. I really don't have your imagination.

LEYLAND:
Don't you believe it, darlin'. One day they'll be queuin' up for the film rights of yours.

EMMANNUELLE:
Well, I have always been a tennis lover.

Scene 60: Outside of Centre Court building, Wimbledon
A great sudden burst of clapping is heard.

Scene 61: Centre Court gallery – Wimbledon
Close shot of Emmannuelle consuming last of ice-cream cone. Pull back to show she is sitting next to Emile. Behind them and around them are a packed stand of typical middle-class Wimbledon spectators. All the heads in the stand are turning from side to side in unison, following the ball. The heads rest. The crowd applauds.

UMPIRE'S VOICE:
Game to (Miss Evert and Mr Connors?) They lead 5 games to 3 and 1 set to love. New balls, please.

Scene 62: Centre Court.
Four famous professional players are in the midst of a mixed-doubles match. The server holds up the new balls for the others to see.

UMPIRE'S VOICE:
(Miss Evert?) to serve. Quiet, please.

She serves.

Scene 63: Centre Court Gallery – Wimbledon.
The heads in the grandstand begin to turn in unison again, as the rally continues. Except that Emmannuelle's head remains still. Then, from Emmannuelle's P.O.V.

Scene 64: The Centre Court.
Hold on the frilly lace panties worn by one of the women players, as she scampers across the court after the ball, then waits for the return.

Scene 65: Centre Court gallery – Wimbledon.
Emmannuelle's eyes start to glaze. Pull back to wider shot and

the whole gallery of people starts to blur. Slow ripple dissolve to:

Scene 66: The Centre Court.
Emmannuelle, in a brief tennis dress, prepares to serve in a mixed-doubles match. The other three players are famous professionals. The crowd sounds restive.

UMPIRE'S VOICE
Quiet, please. Mrs Prevert to serve.

SLOW MOTION: Emmannuelle tosses the ball up. From behind her baseline we see her bring her racket up and serve a fast low one down the centre. Her whole body bends forward with the exertion. The crowd gasps.

As her brief skirt whips up over her bottom, we see that Emmannuelle has forgotten to wear frilly lace panties. In fact, she has forgotten to wear *any*. The receiver returns the serve with a graceful backhand to Emmannuelle's forehand. Almost a passing shot. Emmannuelle bends low to retrieve it. The crowd gasps. Emmannuelle's dress is up again as she connects and plays a winner down the sideline.

UMPIRE'S VOICE:
Fifteen, love.

Emmannuelle serves again. Her skirt whips up. So does the chalk on the opposite centre line. An ace. The crowd applauds.

UMPIRE'S VOICE:
Thirty, love.

Emmannuelle serves again. It's in. The receiver returns it. It's too long. Emmannuelle lets it go. The linesman sitting behind Emmannuelle is looking straight ahead. From his P.O.V. Hold on Emmannuelle's skirt riding up. The return is over the baseline. The linesman's eyes are fixed on Emmannuelle's bottom.

UMPIRE'S VOICE:
Thirty, fifteen.

Now Emmannuelle's male partner is about to serve. Emmannuelle is at the net, bending over in readiness to intercept a volley. Her partner throws the ball in the air, but his eyes are on Emmannuelle's bare bottom at the net. He brings his racket down and catches the ball on the wood.

LINESMAN'S VOICE:
Fault.

Her partner serves again. Again he can't take his eyes off Emmannuelle's exposed bottom at the net.

LINESMAN'S VOICE:
Fault.

UMPIRE'S VOICE:
Double fault. Love, fifteen.

Cut to: Emmannuelle is waiting to serve again. But she has no balls. A ballboy collects them. Instead of bouncing them straight to her, he rolls them slowly along the court until they come to rest several yards in front of her. Emmannuelle is forced to bend down to pick up the balls. Another ballboy behind her almost goes cross-eyed as he stares at Emmannuelle's bottom. He gives the other ballboy a thumbs-up sign. Emmannuelle serves. The receiver returns it with a slow lob just over the net on Emmannuelle's side. She has to scramble low to retrieve it. The other 3 players all stop dead and watch Emmannuelle as she goes for it. She just gets there and lobs the ball slowly back over the net, then falls flat on her face with her skirt up. The other 3 players remain transfixed, their eyes on her bare bottom. Emmannuelle's return lob is in, and really quite easy to retrieve. But nobody bothers about the ball. The crowd applauds. Emmannuelle's partner, excited at their victory, grabs her hand and together they run to the net to congratulate the losers. Her partner jumps the net, then turns and encourages Emmannuelle to do the same. Emmannuelle jumps the net. Her skirt flaps up. FREEZE: for several seconds when she's above the net showing her bottom.

UMPIRE'S VOICE:
Game, set and match to Mrs Prevert and (**Mr?**), two sets to bum. (**Pause**) One.

The crowd applauds.

Ripple dissolve to:

Scene 67. Centre Court Gallery – Wimbledon.
Emile nudges Emmannuelle at the end of a brilliant rally. She snaps back to reality and joins in the applause. FADE OUT.

Although the launderette scene appears in the final version of the script, as Mrs Dangle recalls her most amorous experience, it bears no resemblance to what Lance Peters originally intended. Despite some of the editor's cuts hurting, Peters realises that releasing a film under the *Carry On* banner was good for marketing. 'It's still selling, even today; they've notched up some sales to different European cable outfits – here, there and everywhere.' In hindsight, he classes the film as a 'mixed bag', observing: 'It had some good moments and some very awkward moments, but it moved and had a lot of pace. I didn't agree with all the casting ideas, but that's another story. Apart from Suzanne [Danielle], it lacked a bit of glamour.'

With the script finally sorted, attention turned to casting. For the title role of Emmannuelle, Peter Rogers recalls 'hundreds of girls wanting to play the part'. Auditions were held in Floral Street, in the heart of London's Covent Garden. 'There were a hell of a lot of people lined up, so I said to Gerald, "For God's sake, we can't go through this lot."' Rogers and Thomas quickly whittled down the list to two. One of the names in the frame was actress Kelly Le Brock, whose film credits include 1984's *The Woman in Red*. 'I was only 16 years old and had just had my hair cut very short. I guess they thought I looked like Sylvia Kristel.'

Growing up this side of the Atlantic meant Le Brock not only knew all about the *Carry On* films, she classed herself as a true fan. 'I loved the team of people.'

When she learnt of the interest from Rogers and Thomas, she was flattered but in the end she knew it wasn't for her.

The role was finally offered to Suzanne Danielle, surprisingly one of her first acting jobs. London-born Danielle, just 23, realised she was competing with American Le Brock. 'She was very beautiful and I knew it was between us.' Danielle grew up in Romford, Essex, where she attended the Bush Davies Dance School developing an interest in acting as well as dancing. She gained early experience at Hornchurch Rep before a role in *Billy,* starring Michael Crawford, arrived. She'd made a couple of brief appearances, including a part in a small-screen production of *The Prince and the Pauper* and playing a disco dancer in the Joan Collins's movie *The Stud,* before being cast as the nymphomaniacal Emmannuelle Prevert, a role for which her modelling agent had suggested her.

During the audition, Danielle recalls telling Gerald Thomas a little white lie. 'He asked whether I could speak French. I told him my mother was French. I've often reflected on that but I've come up with the conclusion that it wasn't an actual lie because I didn't say I could actually speak French; I did lie, however, when saying my mother was French!' Having no knowledge of the language, she had to adopt a Gallic accent and did a sterling job. 'That's what fear does to you,' she jokes. 'I'd never in my entire life spoken with a French accent. And the first day of filming was with Kenneth [Williams]. It was a big, important scene and I just had to go for it.' So true was her performance that people thought she really was French. 'The next audition I had was with Eric and Ernie and they thought I was a French girl, too.'

The distributors, Hemdale, hoped that the new film would follow the more traditional *Carry On* style, after the unsuccessful digression from the tried and trusted format with *England,* and were keen for many of the mainstays to sign up, particularly Kenneth Williams who, after discussing the script with Gerald Thomas over lunch on 19 December 1977, rated the idea 'pretty dirty.'[38] When he eventually read the script, he was candid in his assessment, telling his diary that he found it 'monotonous and unfunny.'[39] He summed up by writing, 'It's so far away from the sort of story which a *Carry On* used to have. All this seems to do is attempt to shock.'[40] He saw no alternative but to decline any involvement in the film; his decision brought a swift response from Peter Rogers and Gerald Thomas, both of whom phoned Williams, trying to allay any concerns by confirming that he'd been sent an early script that needed revising and that any nymphomania was covered in an innocent way. A fortnight later, Williams visited his agent Peter Eade at his office to examine the revised script but branded it worse than before. To secure their man, Rogers offered to pay Williams £6,000, an increase of £1,000 from his normal fee. Eventually agreement was reached for £5,750 with a car to whisk him back and forth to the studio.

The first day's filming took place on Monday, 10 April 1978 with 'L' stage representing the ambassador's bedroom. But a few days later the production's progress was seemingly overshadowed by newspaper reports that Barbara Windsor had walked off the set, although she hadn't even set foot inside the studio. She had, however, been earmarked to play not only the fantasy figure in the sequences involving Leyland, Lyons and Richmond (Kenneth Connor, Jack Douglas and Peter Butterworth respectively) but also the nurse holding Emmannuelle's babies in the final scene. The *Daily Express* quoted Windsor as allegedly saying that she declined a part in the film because it was 'one long nude scene'[41], adding: 'I am not going to appear in the film because I think it's soft porn. They wanted me to strip off and I said "Definitely not" . . . I have always believed that the films should be good family entertainment. But this one has gone too far.'[42]

Meanwhile, Peter Rogers laughed away the alleged comments about the film's content, stating: 'You could hardly call this pornographic. These actors wouldn't want to be in anything like that. There was never any question of Barbara or anyone else stripping off – this will be family entertainment like all the other *Carry Ons*. Barbara would have been down to pants and bra. There was no question of her having to take everything off.'

As it happened, Windsor's agent had been in negotiations with Rogers over the roles but when the filming date for the hospital scene was moved, clashing with Windsor's holiday dates, which had already been passed to the production office, the actress felt that without the scene of her playing a nurse holding Emmanuelle's babies in the happy ending she wouldn't be able to appear in the film. Stalwarts of the *Carry On* films might have been surprised that other regulars were taking part in the film, although what they might not have realised was that Kenneth Williams, for example, had only been persuaded to join the cast by the promise of more money. His appearance generated a flood of letters from indignant fans concerned about his involvement in a picture that was supposedly pornographic. While thoughts in his diary suggested that, at times, he agreed with such views, publicly he defended the film. In an article, he wrote: 'Newspapers carried dreadful hints of erotic scenes being enacted in the studios. I was bemused. Where was all this courageous cavorting going on? I looked in vain: I could not find anything erotic.'[43]

Regarding the hullabaloo, a spokesman for Peter Rogers said: 'The film will have an "A" certificate. Any part of the film which might prevent it from getting one will be taken out. It is a send-up of the *Emmanuelle* films, but there is no full-frontal nudity. Everything is done by suggestion. It will be just like all the other *Carry On* films . . . all in the mind. Children will be able to see and enjoy it.'[44] Not so.

Correspondence between the British Board of Film Censors (BBFC) and Rogers and Thomas reveals that, at first, their desire was to obtain a 'U' certificate. To achieve that, the Censor requested certain cuts, including two shots of Emmannuelle in bed with her husband and her leg over him, Emmannuelle bending over and lifting her dress in front of a sentry and one with Kenneth Williams standing bare-bottomed.

Williams recalled his moments of nudity. 'There was one sequence which I thought might prove shocking; it was a scene in which my PT shorts fell down during my exercises, revealing my lower half. During the action, when I bent down to retrieve the shorts, the director cried out anxiously: "For heaven's sake keep your legs together!" and I began to feel apprehensive about propriety as well as my physical inadequacies.'[45] And while being interviewed for

Titbits, he recalled: 'I play a love scene naked on the bed. I told Gerald Thomas, "I don't want people seeing anything!" I was assured there would only be rear shots. I didn't want any of that frontal nonsense. Much too frightening, you know, to reveal as much as that.'[46] As for scenes exposing his bottom, he quipped: 'I was a bit worried about it because I'm no longer young and thought: "Who'd want to see a bum hanging in pleats?" But I'm very pleased with the result. A bit droopy but, on the other hand, like breasts, its pendulous nature can even add to the attraction. If my posterior stops the film getting a family certificate I think the censor either wants his head or his eyes seeing to.'[47]

The film was awarded an 'AA' certificate by the Board of Censors, preventing anyone under 15 seeing it. The Board stated that it differed from its predecessors because it 'relies almost entirely on sex jokes'.[48] The report's author thought it lacked the usual slapstick style of the genre and offered nothing to junior members of a family audience. 'It's not a question of cutting, since blue is the pervading shade.'[49]

Defending the film's content, Gerald Thomas said: 'There's more sex in it, there's no question about it . . . but it's titillating sex, as opposed to pornographic sex. It's by no means an attempt at making a *Confessions* type of film. They're much different, much cruder. We're vulgar, but never crude.'[50]

Filming began with scenes in and around the Ambassador's bedroom occupying the next five days on the schedule; it didn't take long for Suzanne Danielle, who was paid £2,750 for 21 days' filming, to settle into the role. 'I was absolutely bowled over, starring in a movie. I didn't appreciate just how big the stars I was working with were at that time – I was just a kid. But that probably helped because I wasn't worried. The entire cast was lovely, no one looked down their nose at me; no one had a feeling that I shouldn't be there.' Even Kenneth Williams, not one to suffer fools gladly and whose razor-sharp put-downs could have even mature performers quaking in their boots, complimented Danielle's performance in his diary. 'If he'd wanted to, he could have ruined everything for me, with just one word, one look, but didn't. He obviously thought I was pretty good, which is very satisfying for me because I didn't know what it would be like appearing in a comedy.'

Kenneth Williams wasn't the only actor to be impressed by Danielle's contribution. Jack Douglas, who played Lyons the butler, admits he got on 'like a house on fire' with the actress, and recalls his favourite moment in the film. 'It's when she was lying in bed and I entered the room wearing my dressing gown, saying: "Madam, there is a telephone call for you." When I passed the phone to her, I didn't realise that the wire had got caught around my neck, so when I handed the phone she pulled it – and me – towards her. For that scene she wasn't wearing a bra, and I went straight into her bust. When we'd finished, I asked Gerald whether he was happy with it, which he was. Then he asked me, so I replied: "No, I'd like to do it again another ten times!"'

Rather than adopt his usual 'Twitching Alf' character, Douglas played the butler straight. 'Yes, it was strange because Gerald asked me to play it as myself. I'd done all the others in character, which meant I was in disguise and could do whatever I liked.' Douglas admits *Emmannuelle* didn't possess the sparkle and magic of previous *Carry On*s. 'It was a good, entertaining film but not a true *Carry On*.' And as for remarks suggesting that earlier versions of the script verged on pornography, he says: 'One or two bits were a bit naughty for a *Carry On*.'

Even after Lance Peters's script had been revised by Vince Powell and Peter Rogers, scenes still necessitated that the lead actress should be in various stages of undress. To cater for this, Danielle's contract contained a clause stating that the 'artist agrees to appear nude in certain scenes, as discussed and agreed with the director.'[51] Danielle thanks not just the cast but, in particular, director Gerald Thomas for helping her to relax and rid her of nerves while filming. 'He just arranged everything and treated me like his daughter. If there was anything I was uncomfortable with, he'd just close the set; in fact, he anticipated everything, sometimes before I'd even thought of the problem.'

While making the film, when accusations were flying around that it had trodden beyond the line of decency, Danielle was interviewed by various members of the press. Regarding her role, she said: 'I don't strip. The furthest I go is for one scene with my bare back showing in a steamy bath.'[52] The *Sun*, meanwhile, reported Danielle hoping she had made a 'very sexy Emmannuelle'[53] but that 'everything is left to the imagination'.[54]

Reflecting on the film now, she doesn't regard it as her favourite *Carry On* and feels that the series was by then losing its way. 'It just got a bit too lewd. I haven't shown my children that film. I have a teenage son and I don't think he's seen it. I'm a little prude, always have been. But I'm proud I did the film, that I met Gerald and worked with the cast, including the great Kenneth Williams. I was one of the family at Pinewood.' Danielle admits, though, that she hasn't watched the film recently. 'It was on TV the other day but I didn't watch it. When it was on a little while before, Sam [Suzanne is married to golfer Sam Torrance] said: "There's a *Carry On* coming on, let's have a look." Of course, it starts and straight away it's a sex scene on Concorde. We watched ten minutes and then turned it off. I said: "You don't want to watch any of that stuff."'

Working with Danielle in the opening shot, set on Concorde, was Larry Dann, playing naive Theodore Valentine, who's seduced by Emmannuelle in the claustrophobic loo aboard the aircraft. It was Dann's fourth appearance in the series, having debuted as a schoolboy in *Teacher*. Appearances in *Behind* and *England* followed before he was offered the prominent role of the nerdish wimp besotted by the beautiful Emmannuelle. 'I was delighted to get the role because I thought: "This is good, we'll go on and do some more now, but of course that was it. I confess, I didn't particularly like the script, but you don't have any say in that. It wasn't the usual standard of *Carry On* humour: there weren't any double entendres, it was all single entendres.' Dann agrees that many scenes were too blatant. 'I can understand why it was like that because the picture-postcard-style humour had gone. But I enjoyed the role and was pleased when Vince Powell wrote extra scenes involving me and Beryl Reid; because they had such a talented actress as Beryl, they thought they'd include some extra material, which was nice for me as well.' Scriptwriter Lance Peters rates veteran actress Beryl Reid's performance as the best element of the film. 'I created this character, Theodore, a kind of stalker. He was a goofy character. I wanted Beryl to play his mother so she was offered the part.'

Larry Dann recalls his first day's shoot, beginning with the scene of Theodore arriving while Emmannuelle lies on a sunbed. At this point, he hadn't even met Suzanne Danielle. 'There's no preamble, you just turn up and do the scene. So, the first time I met Suzanne she was stark naked; she was terrific and handled the project brilliantly.'

It might have been the first scene he recorded, but Dann's initial scene on screen saw him being enticed into Emmannuelle's snare, whereby she seduces the callow Theodore in the WC, a scene Lance Peters parodied from the original *Emmanuelle* picture. He explains: 'The original French Emmanuelle sees a handsome stranger across the aisle on a Boeing and ends up seducing him in the WC of the plane. That was very serious in the original, but I sent it up like crazy: she lured the dark stranger into the bathroom and when they tried to make love there wasn't enough room and he ended up getting his foot stuck down the toilet and so on – it was a funny scene. The one original thing we had was a shot of Concorde and just at the right moment, when they had finally gotten together in the WC, Concorde's nose turned up; it was a good bit of symbolism.'

Newspaper critics weren't impressed when the film was released, typified by Geoff Brown in the *Financial Times*, who wrote: 'In their black-and-white days in the late 1950s, the *Carry On* films had a fruitful link with current fads and feelings: the jokes were barbed as well as broad. But time has taken its toll, and *Carry On Emmannuelle* is rootless entertainment, relying on the series's own traditions to see it through.'[55] Meanwhile, Kenneth Baily in the *Sunday People* classed it a 'very tired effort – and a bit sad.'[56]

Although the general consensus was unfavourable, there were one or two critics who offered a glimmer of hope, such as Richard Barkley in the *Sunday Express* who felt it had 'some good jokes and bits of buffoonery ... and Suzanne Danielle sails through the muddy waters with swan-like poise.'[57] Meanwhile, his colleague on the daily paper wrote of Danielle's performance, one of the high points from an otherwise tame offering, that 'considering the crass nature of the enterprise she carries off the role with something approaching style.'[58]

Picking a subject like the *Emmanuelle* films, or more broadly the sex industry as a whole, left Messrs Rogers and Thomas with an almost impossible task in terms of success. The reason its predecessor, *England*, had become arguably the least successful offering in the series was because it was first issued an 'AA' Certificate, thereby alienating much of the audience, those under 14, who had helped create its success initially. The effect was compounded by parents who'd previously viewed the *Carry Ons* as good family entertainment, an ideal excuse to fork out some money for a trip to the cinema, but now decided to stay away because they didn't want to go without their children. *England* was later re-edited and reissued with an 'A' certificate but by then the damage had been done.

Gerald Thomas, talking in February 1978, acknowledged that by attempting to produce a satire of the sex film they were tackling their biggest challenge to date. 'Make no mistake about it, this will be a sex film. We are out to titillate. This is no Disneyland job. But we are making the whole thing more difficult for ourselves by not going for an 'X' Certificate, or even an 'AA' . . . As for sex, we've always dealt with it on the suggestive rather than the implicit level.'[59] Of course, they didn't get their 'A' Certificate and felt the wrath not just of the critics but of their legions of fans, too. But it didn't deter Thomas and Rogers from a further foray, even if it was to be 14 years later.

III

If a film proposal pursued by Gerald Thomas and British producer John Goldstone (whose film credits include *Monty Python and the Holy Grail, Life of Brian* and *The Meaning of Life*) hadn't bitten the dust, the 31st *Carry On, Columbus*, might not have been conceived.

Goldstone had been approached by Paramount Pictures Corporation, which owned rights to the famous Bing Crosby-Bob Hope-Dorothy Lamour *Road to . . .* movies. Seven pictures were released

between 1940 and 1962, beginning with *Road to Singapore* and cul-
minating in *Road to Hong Kong*. An eighth title, provisionally called
Road to the Fountain of Youth, was to be filmed in 1978, but Crosby's
sudden death from a heart attack scuppered those plans. Paramount,
however, wanted to revisit the series, with two new faces stepping
into the lead roles. *Carry On* director Gerald Thomas was drafted in
to direct the picture, while Andrew Marshall (of *2point4 Children*
fame) and David Renwick (*One Foot in the Grave*) were the intended
scriptwriters. Various meetings took place to discuss the concept,
involving the central characters' adventures in Moscow where they
envisaged making their fortunes from the raft of business opportunities emerging from the former Soviet Union.

Gene Wilder and John Candy's names were in the frame for
casting but Renwick and Marshall eventually pulled out of discussions. Assailed by increasing doubts, and unable to see the project
materialising, Renwick didn't want to spend a lengthy period on a
script that would become a non-starter. And when Renwick's
concerns became reality, Goldstone and Thomas's attention turned
towards another *Carry On*.

John Goldstone recalls: 'In about 1990, I set up a new company
called The Comedy House, the purpose of which was to cross-
fertilise between America and England, using British comedy talent.
I'd worked with Peter Richardson from the start of the *The Comic
Strip* at the beginning of the 1980s, so I had connections with that
generation of comic talent: Rik Mayall, Nigel Planer – those people.
We developed some projects and during that time I met Gerald
Thomas while trying to develop the *Road to . . .* movie. While
working with him on that, the whole thing of 1992, the 500th
anniversary of Columbus's first sailing, seemed to become an interesting subject – particularly as two "serious" movies were being
made.' So when plans for the *Road to . . .* movie seemed to be
heading nowhere, Goldstone and Thomas, with Peter Rogers's
blessing, set their minds on making a new *Carry On*. 'Paramount
were funding the *Road to . . .* project, but like many things it took
so long to develop which is why Gerald and I went ahead and did
the *Carry On* film.'

Although *Carry On Columbus* was the third film released to

coincide with the anniversary, it was the only comedy; what Goldstone and Thomas wanted was to take a light-hearted look at the traditional story of Columbus, placing a different slant on the momentous occasion as an alternative treatment. The job of penning a screenplay was given to Dave Freeman, who'd written the script for *Behind* and for several instalments of the *Carry On Laughing* television series. He recalls receiving a call from Thomas. 'Gerry rang and said: "It's the quincentenary of Columbus. A couple of serious films are being made – do you think you could do a *Carry On*?" I agreed to have a go, even though I didn't have many of the originals to work with.'

Freeman compiled a storyline which sees Spanish map-maker Christopher Columbus determined to find a new route from Europe to the Far East without passing through the Sultan of Turkey's territory and paying exorbitant taxes. The Sultan, played by Rik Mayall, is irked on learning of Columbus's expedition, financed by the king and queen of Spain, so deploys his top spy, Fatima, to wreck Columbus's plans. Writing the script wasn't the easiest task for Freeman. 'When I was given the go-ahead there wasn't much time left to write it, about three weeks, because they wanted to release it during the summer. I could have done a better job but was being pushed and shoved in all directions by the producer and director. It wasn't a happy experience for me and I didn't like the end result; I thought a lot of it was miscast and the regulars were missed.'

With a dearth of familiar *Carry On* faces to choose from, Thomas and Goldstone were relieved to secure the services of Jim Dale as Christopher Columbus. Other occasional *Carry On* actors, including Jack Douglas, Bernard Cribbins, Leslie Phillips and Peter Gilmore, were joined by a clutch of contemporary comedians and comedy actors, such as Julian Clary, Rik Mayall, Alexei Sayle, Richard Wilson and Nigel Planer. 'There weren't many of the original cast still alive but Jim Dale had done some of the earlier ones and Gerald was still in touch with him,' recalls Goldstone. 'So we offered him the part of Christopher Columbus, and assembled the rest of the cast around him. I drew on my relationships with the new generation of comedians, but we brought in a few of the original *Carry On* cast, too. I think, though, that some were reticent about doing it.

Of course, if someone like Kenneth Williams was still alive I'd love to have used him. We wanted Frankie Howerd in it, too, but, sadly, he died that year.'

Jim Dale accepted the lead role as a favour to Gerald Thomas but also in the hope of reviving the spirit which emanated from the earlier films. Sadly, it never happened. He recalled: 'The story wasn't very strong and the jokes were feeble.'[60]

From the beginning, the idea of blending old faces and new, with their respective styles of performing, was a potential hazard and something that troubled Gerald Thomas initially, although his fears appeared to dissipate when the production began. He remarked: 'It was a problem I thought we might have. The new generation tend to be stand-up comics and individual performers but they have worked with us very well. The whole thing is a team from top to bottom.'

John Goldstone adds: 'They certainly seemed to play off each other; again, with comedy, it's that difference. I suppose in the real scheme of things, the best comedy is comedy of reality. Therefore, when you're involved in a movie that relies on verbal jokes as much as visual jokes, you're inevitably stretching reality. What you discover is that the generation that came from *Carry On* were much more out of music hall and a different type of comedy than the generation that we put them with; they came from a different direction.'

One of the original faces who felt uneasy about the film was Jack Douglas, who played Marco the Cereal Killer. 'I didn't like it from the word go,' he admits. 'For me, it just didn't work. Many of the new faces didn't want to be part of us [the remaining originals from the previous films] at all. They just went on, did their bit, got into their cars and went home. They never came with us for a drink or even sat with us. If we were having lunch, they'd go and sit at the other end of the room. They wanted to do their own thing, therefore it was like having two separate casts. People say to me, "There must be a film you did that you never liked," and I reply, "Yes, *Carry On Columbus!*"'

Many critics agreed with Douglas. With the cast lacking so many of the originals, there was little resemblance to previous films. Derek Malcolm reported in the *Guardian* that the film was 'but a shadow of what it might have been'.[61] Regarding the new faces, he added: 'Carry On Columbus conclusively shows that the modern generation of comics are totally unable to compete, at least on these particular terms, with those we know from the past and once sadly under-rated.'[62] Hugo Davenport in the Daily Telegraph felt the new personnel always faced an uphill struggle to blend with the stalwarts 'so deeply ingrained in British consciousness that they're now an institution'.[63] Like Malcolm, he felt that the bonding hadn't worked. 'It would be nice to say that they had carried off the new Carry On in the traditional style . . . but, well, they haven't. The new recruits look out of place or uncomfortable.'[64]

Many other critics echoed these views, rating the film by giving it a rapid thumbs-down, with Nigel Andrews in the Financial Times writing: 'A few early puns raise a faint smile. But the film is soon bare of wit in the script . . . and barer still of that wild, honking energy in the acting that once . . . covered the naked bits in the dialogue.'[65]

A scriptwriter must be iron-skinned not to take critics' often barbed comments to heart. But someone like the experienced Dave Freeman knew it was par for the course. In hindsight, he didn't rate the project as one of his happiest. And it was his script, written in haste, that took its fair share of criticism. Sheila Johnston in the Independent wrote: 'A large part of the blame goes to the third-rate script: the best Carry Ons revel in the inventiveness (or rather, the awful predictability) of their puns – their verbal agility and the infinite lewdness of language. Here, there are a couple of memorable exchanges . . . but most of the entendres are distressingly singular.'[66]

Of all the cast, though, at least the leading name, Jim Dale, was the recipient of occasional praise. Yet despite negativity from the press and some of the actors involved, or who chose not to be involved, Carry On Columbus earnt more at UK box offices than the other two Columbus-related films released during this period: the John Glen-directed Christopher Columbus: The Discovery and Ridley Scott's 1492: Conquest of Paradise.

Inevitably, anyone brave enough to attempt a film under the Carry On banner realises that their effort will be judged against the original pictures: they weren't technical masterpieces, and as Gerald

Thomas once said, there isn't anything to tax one's intelligence, they're just meant to make you laugh. Their inimitable style and repertory-company feel generated an unrivalled charm and when a familiar, well-loved situation is revisited, whether on the big or small screen, there is a risk that it won't, in the audiences' eyes, fare well. One of the key problems was that all too often the new generation of actors failed to generate the gusto, bravado and team spirit that had been honed over the years by their predecessors.

Admirably, Goldstone and Thomas wanted to maintain, as far as possible, the *Carry On* tradition. On reflection, however, Goldstone questions 'whether in 1992 *Carry On* had the same resonance as more contemporary comedies. What had happened latterly, certainly in the previous two or three *Carry On* movies, was that they started to lose their edge.' Whether this impacted on his own film, he's unsure. 'A few years had passed by the time *Columbus* was released. I think generally, the style of *Carry On* films had been superseded by the *Comic Strip* performers and their more contemporary, irreverent kind of comedy. What we felt at the time was: it was still important to try and keep the *Carry On* spirit and not to make it contemporary.'

Assessing the film more than 15 years later, Goldstone says: 'In terms of a *Carry On*, I was pretty pleased with it at the time. I suppose if we'd had more time to write it then it could have been better. But Gerald felt confident going ahead with the script, and I obviously trusted his judgement because his life had been *Carry On*. You can never regret, it's what it is, and we did the best we could; just in terms of the actual cast line-up, it's still a pretty impressive group of names.'

There were equally impressive names on the crew list, too, including Alan Hume as Director of Photography, who'd worked on nineteen other *Carry Ons*. When asked to join the team, Hume – although realising that many of the old faces had died – thought it would make a 'funny' addition to the series. 'But it wasn't,' he says. 'It was a nothing film. There was no Kenny Connor, Kenny Williams or Hattie Jacques – they were all gone or not keen. Other comics were cast who weren't funny, and not a team. Even the writing wasn't the same; the series was beginning to grind to a halt.'

Even with Gerald Thomas in the director's chair, the almighty chasm caused by so many notable absentees couldn't be bridged, despite the valiant attempts of Jim Dale, Jack Douglas and others. Furthermore, perhaps too many years had passed since the last excursion, and the *Carry On* days were over. But if nothing else, *Columbus* afforded Goldstone the opportunity to realise one of his career ambitions: to work with Thomas. 'It's was a wonderful experience,' he recalls. 'Working with him was one of the greatest pleasures of my life – he was extraordinary. We got on so well, I just loved him. He had a great sense of comedy and the *Carry On*s had a structure to them that he was enormously familiar with so we applied that to the *Columbus* story.' In true *Carry On* fashion, even the new faces were made aware that the script in a *Carry On* is the bible. The actors had to play it straight – there was no room for scene-stealing ad libs. 'He was so organised and knew exactly what he had to do every day. We got the film done in really good time. Also, the atmosphere on set was so good because he exuded confidence and happiness.'

Concerning views from some of the old stagers that the atmosphere on set was far from rosy, with the new and old not mixing, Goldstone states: 'I hadn't really thought about that. The older actors were all good friends anyway and had worked together. In a way, the younger ones were a bit in awe of them.'

Regardless of how successful one perceives *Columbus* to be, John Goldstone is proud to have been involved in a *Carry On* film. Of the series's remarkable popularity over the decades, he comments: 'Their success has been largely in the UK. Apart from the odd English-speaking country, I don't think they travelled much further than that because they're quintessentially English. With *Columbus* we tried selling it to the States but it wasn't successful. It sold in the usual territories, though. We made it on a very reasonable budget, on the basis that it was capable of recouping out of England alone, so it did really well.' As to why the series became such a phenomenal success, he comments: 'They come out of music hall, out of seaside postcards, and there is something very English about the nature of that comedy. In the heyday of the *Carry On*s, it was quite a high point for British cinema-goers who'd flock to see the latest film. It just hit a nerve at the right time and, I feel, was unique to Britain.'

Whether you liked or loathed *Columbus*, its success will forever be compared to the true classics, like *Up the Khyber* and *Camping*, and the same will apply to any future efforts.

Part 4

False Starts and Fresh Hopes

We have nearly completed our journey through the many chapters of *Carry On* history, but it's worth pausing momentarily to pay our respects to those ideas that failed to make the grade or where plans were scuppered for whatever reason. We're talking about the unmade *Carry Ons*.

Ever since *Sergeant* took its first breath, way back in the 1950s, myriad ideas were considered by Messrs Rogers and Thomas as potential entries in the series. Whilst, to date, 31 projects have made it to the big screen and, at the time of writing, a 32nd is in the pipeline, other ideas were pondered over before their fate was decided. Just occasionally an idea would strike a chord and be examined further with a scriptwriter commissioned to prepare a script; some prospective projects, meanwhile, nearly made it to the finishing line before falling at the final hurdle.

You can forget the final hurdle, though, when discussing the fire service-based *Carry On Smoking* because it failed to progress beyond the first; that idea was scotched before a scriptwriter was even assigned because it was reckoned that to extract comedy out of a subject like fire seemed inappropriate. Norman Hudis remembers discussing the matter with Gerald Thomas and Peter Rogers. 'I said, and obviously Gerry and Peter agreed, that it's risky, if not tasteless, to try and get comedy out of fire. There was a Robb Wilton sketch, once upon a time, about an inept fire brigade but, first, he was a much-loved comedian and, second, it was on radio and didn't, therefore, actually show an incompetent, slapsticking fire brigade while something blazed in the background to the peril of life and property.'

It wasn't the only potential idea Hudis recalls discussing. One, *Carry On Flying*, even reached script stage in 1962, with Hudis basing it on his own experiences while serving with the RAF during the Second World War; Jim Dale was in the frame for the anchor role but the project remained grounded. 'And I remember flying to Guernsey for the première of *Teacher* and distributor Stuart Levy suggesting *Carry On Vicar* to me. I said: "Nice idea, except: you're Stuart Levy, your partner is Nat Cohen; director Gerry Thomas and I share your religion. So *Carry On Vicar* would add up to four Jews poking fun at the Church of England." Nothing more was heard of this notion.'

A subject close to Hudis's heart that he wishes he'd been afforded the opportunity to explore in a *Carry On* script is journalism. '*Carry On Fleet Street* would have made a good title, although it would have been about newspapers rather than Fleet Street itself. I would have gone back to my old days as a 16-year-old, and written a script about a local paper. It would have been interesting and, in my view, successful but I didn't get the chance.'

Many discussions and proposals headed straight into a cul-de-sac and never saw the light of day; however frustrating it might have been, Hudis has been in the business long enough to know it was par for the course in the world of scriptwriting and film-making. 'With regard to the masses of scripts, synopses, presentations and outlines scribbled by the likes of me which never mature into production, it's a natural hazard of the business and, anyway, we're in good company. Mozart's 18th Piano Concerto is but one example of the work of an unmistakable master, written to impress Emperor Joseph II and generate employment for Amadeus, which utterly failed in that purpose. Coming up to date, twelve directors turned down *M*A*S*H* and number thirteen was not unlucky – Robert Altman took it on and shaped a classic.'

But of all the false dawns that Norman Hudis was involved in, none came closer to reaching the silver screen than *Carry On Again Nurse*, a script he wrote in 1988 after returning from Hollywood at Peter Rogers's behest to revisit the medical wards, nearly three decades after writing arguably the most successful of all: *Carry On Nurse*.

Arriving from the States, Hudis was whisked away in a chauffeured car to The Bull, a pub in the Buckinghamshire village of Gerrards Cross, for a reunion lunch with Rogers and Thomas. 'It was uncannily like old times in that, within 30 minutes, we'd agreed, as quickly as we did for all my *Carry On*s, the premise of the script-to-be: a beloved old London hospital, threatened with closure by NHS cuts, is saved, mostly by the unconquerable combined British forces of sentiment and slapstick.'[1]

Hudis was delighted that his services were in demand again. 'It was a question of being cast correctly. Like a correctly cast actor, you correctly cast a writer. They want to do *Nurse* again, so who do you call? The guy who did it before.'

Concerning the film not being produced, Hudis says: 'The powers-that-be, now the unlamented powers-that-were, decreed that the budget of £1,500,000 was excessive for such a parochial subject. This prudent decision did not prevent them from backing such parochial British films as *Four Weddings and a Funeral, Lock, Stock and Two Smoking Barrels* and *The Long Good Friday,* all of which fared very well outside Britain. Far less profitably, they lavished money on intense introspective movies about intellectuals practising joyless adultery in Hampstead, sometimes innovatively telling these stories backwards. To turn down our film, they were, in my view, plainly, simply and obtusely wrong. I still find that script probably the most inventive, affectionate and well-paced *Carry On* I ever wrote, which would have provided what may well have been the final and thoroughly characteristic appearances of the entire regular cast.'

How delightful it would have been to see Hudis's screenplay concerning a London hospital brought to life by most of the old favourites, including Kenneth Williams who was earmarked to play a surgeon; Joan Sims, the matron; Charles Hawtrey, a patient who believes that he's an esteemed author and Kenneth Connor as a hospital porter. The medical profession provides ample comedic potential, and the medical-based *Carry Ons* have proved among the most popular, which is why the profession was also nearly revisited in the late 1970s when writers George Layton – who played the doctor in *Behind* – and Jonathan Lynn submitted an unmade script of the same title.

Despite the two previous films in the series, *England* and *Emmannuelle,* bombing, Hudis is adamant that *Again Nurse* would have become a resounding success. And he wasn't alone in his conviction: Peter Rogers and Gerald Thomas were equally emphatic in believing that the project, if financed, would have been a winner. The decision not to proceed still rankles with Hudis, who, for the first time of writing a *Carry On* script, would have received a five per cent cut of the profits. 'I resent, to this day, those who judged it too expensive at £1,500,000.'

Carry On Spaceman, meanwhile, was banished into orbit when Peter Rogers decided it wasn't the right subject to pursue, Talbot Rothwell's *Carry On Escaping* proceeded to script stage before coming to a halt, *Carry On Yank* was put into cold storage, never to reappear, and *Carry On Robin Hood* was simply a title Rogers registered with the Film Producers' Association and never pursued. But staying on an American theme, in the late 1980s a script titled *Carry On Dallas*, a spoof on the successful 1980s soap, was penned by Vince Powell, a scriptwriter who alone and also with his writing partner Harry Driver wrote numerous sitcoms for British television. Their partnership began in Manchester where Powell worked as a club comic. Deciding he needed a partner to form a double act and 'share the boos and catcalls', he advertised in the local rag for a 'straight man' and two days later Driver, who worked the clubs with monologues, knocked on his door. Their act, however, was short-lived because Driver contracted polio, but when Powell later met producer John Ammonds, who most famously produced Morecambe and Wise's numerous series, Powell and Driver's small-screen writing careers began with the 1960 series *Here's Harry*, starring former ventriloquist Harry Worth. Various projects followed, including *Pardon the Expression, George and the Dragon, Bless This House, Nearest and Dearest* and *Never the Twain*.

For the *Dallas* script, Powell focused on the Screwing family, later changed to the Rammings after deciding that the former name was too coarse; the storyline follows the family's fortunes as they discover not oil, but fertiliser. Eventually crooks tried to elbow their way in on the act and a battle ensues. The script opens with the Ramming family, the rich owners of Northspoon Ranch who emigrated from Britain to Dallas to seek their fortune not from oil but sewage farming, mourning the loss of Bert, head of the family, who has drowned in one of his own sewage tanks.

The company is placed in the hands of the oldest son, ruthless R. U. Ramming, who doesn't see eye to eye with younger brother Nobby. But when Nobby starts believing there is oil under the sewage farm, the skulduggery starts in earnest with feuds erupting everywhere. Even a figure from the past, Windy Bumstead, who'd started the sewage farm with Bert Ramming and retained a five per cent share, arrives on the scene; after the partnership made its first million, Ramming not only cheated Windy out of his share of the spoils and kicked him out, but snatched his fiancée, Miss Leonie, too. Now, hearing of Bert's death, Windy seeks revenge.

Someone else wanting a piece of the action is Jimmy Riddle of Riddle Oil. After secret soil tests reveal oil does exist under the Rammings' sewage farm, he offers Windy $10,000 if he marries his former sweetheart, owner of 45% of Northspoon shares, and, secretly, transfers them to Riddle. In case Windy double-crosses him, the oil tycoon hires two heavies to kill the sons, R.U. and Nobby, allowing him to follow a different tack by pressurising their widows into selling their shares to him.

As it transpires, Windy does double-cross Riddle because by the time Miss Leonie announces to her family, much to their chagrin, that not only is she marrying him but he'll run the farm, Windy has rekindled his love for her and doesn't intend executing Riddle's devious plan. He later becomes the family's saviour: when R. U. and Nobby are kidnapped by Riddle's henchmen, and a $1,000,000 ransom is demanded, Windy comes to their rescue, endearing himself to everyone in the process.

The script took three weeks to write, with Powell tapping away at his typewriter from 8 a.m. until 10 p.m. He recalls: 'People like Sid James and Barbara Windsor were lovely to write for: they made it easy because often they played the same character in every film.' Casting offers were issued, and several of the intended cast were interviewed on *TV-am*, but the film never materialised. 'Peter said it was the funniest *Carry On* he'd ever read and everyone was set to do it,' says Powell. 'Then Gerry Thomas made a fatal mistake: he sent a copy to Lorimar Productions, who produced the American series; they thought we were taking the mickey out of their show and threatened legal action so the idea was dropped, which is a shame because it was a funny script and would have been a big success.'

A year later, Powell met director Gerald Thomas and was asked to write *Carry On Down Under*: a businessman in Australia wanted to finance a new *Carry On* and so the production wheels were set in motion. Thomas travelled down under to source suitable locations, followed by Powell who happened to be travelling to Australia on business with Thames Television. While there he met the film's financier on several occasions and began work on the script.

The part-completed screenplay, published later in this book, was set, initially, in Sydney, Australia, at the turn of the century with Charlie Gay, an old prospector, riding into town elated because he's struck it rich via an opal mine he's unearthed; his delight is short-lived, however, when he drops dead in the local bar. Fast-forwarding to the modern day, a firm of solicitors discovers Gay's will in a cupboard, in which he bequeaths the mine to his son, Bernard, or his descendants, last heard of in London. When a notice placed in a newspaper by the solicitors is spotted by Cynthia Smallpiece and Miles Gay, who've been engaged 15 years, Cynthia reminds Miles that he had a distant relative who was deported to Australia for robbing a bank. Seeing nothing but dollar signs before their eyes, they plan to claim the inheritance, praying that Miles's long-lost brother, Brian, the black sheep of the family, hasn't spotted the article. But Brian's eagle-eyed girlfriend Rita notices it and they too are eager to get their mitts on the money. Both brothers seek legal advice and after being told to get to Australia within two days to avoid forfeiting their claim, they jet off – only to find themselves sitting together on the plane.

After the plane is delayed arriving in Australia, a frantic rush ensues to reach the solicitor's office, both couples reaching the office as it is shutting. But when the will is read, it transpires that no one knows the mine's exact location; the only clues are contained in a poem and the first brother solving the puzzle secures the loot. Yet, as they soon discover, they aren't the only ones after the money.

Powell had nearly finished the script when he received bad news: the finance had fallen through and the project had been scrapped. Some time later, Peter Rogers, Gerald Thomas and Vince Powell tried rescuing the project by rewriting the script, setting it in the Yukon at the time of the Gold Rush; sadly, the project never progressed beyond the discussion stage.

That wasn't Powell's last involvement with the *Carry Ons*. Before waving goodbye to the 1980s, he was commissioned to write a further script, titled *Carry On Nursing*. 'Peter told me the most successful *Carry On* was *Carry On Nurse* and he wanted another one about a hospital,' recalls Powell, who suggested basing it at a training hospital for nurses. He wrote the script but, alas, it was never made. 'By the time they got around to making it, some of the regulars had died, so the idea was dropped.'

As the *Carry On* films have become embedded in the national psyche, and there have been continual television repeats and constant remarketing of the films on DVD, financiers and producers remain steadfast in their belief that there remains scope for revisiting the series. Perhaps their efforts will make the grade, but those venturing forth do so at their peril, because there are certainly choppy and dangerous waters in the *Carry On* world.

Many believe it's impossible to recreate the magic that the original films oozed, regardless of cast and crew. Vince Powell once suggested to Peter Rogers that he started a new series, titled *Tales Of . . .* 'I have long held a theory that the title itself is now counter-productive and is the reason that *Columbus* failed, as will any future *Carry On* films. The very title, *Carry On*, to the British film-going public, evokes so many happy memories of that incomparable and irreplaceable team of laughter-makers, such as Sid James, Hattie Jacques, Kenneth Williams, Peter Butterworth, Bernard Bresslaw and Kenneth Connor, that any substitutes are unacceptable.'

Yet ambitious people still attempt to make *Carry On* films, with *London* the latest to be considered. Only time will tell whether the project makes it to the screen, but it's certainly been a long time in the making: we have to travel back to July 2003 for the first official announcement. With a script written by Brian Leveson, Paul Minett, Peter Richardson and Peter Richens, the plot centres on Lenny's Limos, a limousine company hired to ferry celebrities to the Herberts, the British equivalent of the Oscars; reportedly, 'in true *Carry On* style, the scenario descends into mayhem and double entendres as gangsters, starlets and three hapless drivers career through London's famous West End in top-of-the-range limos.'[2]

A star-studded event was convened at the House of Commons, with fans, past performers and well-known faces posing for photos and raising their glasses to the new enterprise; it was hoped that filming would begin in and around the capital and at Pinewood Studios early in 2004. Among the cast members provisionally signed up who attended the event was soap actress Danniella Westbrook, tagged as the new Barbara Windsor.

But filming didn't begin as planned and by the end of 2004, with no start date in sight, Westbrook and Shaun Williamson, whose credits include playing Barry in *EastEnders*, had left the fold; delays starting the project meant that the actors, who couldn't keep declining other work indefinitely, had accepted alternative offers and were now unavailable. Other personnel changes saw producer James Black replaced by George Pavlou and then Chris Chrisafis.

A further refining of the project led to another press release in May 2006 when a progress report confirmed that Intandem Films and Chris Chrisafis were hoping to start shooting that summer, with character names in true double-entendre fashion including magazine publisher Sir Desmond Uppingham Knightly, LA film chief I. P. Freely and London criminal-cum-nightclub owner Tony Le Berc. Three actors confirmed were Shane Richie, ex-footballer-turned-actor Vinnie Jones and Swedish beauty Victoria Silvstedt.

All, as one would imagine, were flattered and excited about being offered roles. Richie, for the press release, said: 'Like many people I grew up with the *Carry On* movies and was thrilled to be asked to star in the new film. The original films . . . kept us all laughing for over thirty years, so it's a great honour not only to be asked to be part of the new film but also to be carrying on a wonderful tradition.'[3] Vinnie Jones, meanwhile, echoed Richie's thoughts, saying: 'It [the *Carry Ons*] really kept me laughing through my youth so it's great news that I'm part of that tradition and able to introduce it to my own kids.'[4]

An executive at Intandem Films acknowledged the power of the *Carry On* image and hoped to establish an entirely new audience for the films, as well as pleasing the faithful followers. The then director, Peter Richardson, said that *Carry On* fans around the world 'should be thrilled that this great British institution is returning in all its glorious vulgarity and will feature Britain's best comic actors who are standing by to camp it up for all they're worth. I am proud to be involved in such a politically incorrect and extremely funny film.'[5]

At the time of writing this chapter, the new *Carry On* film is still at preproduction stage and it's anyone's guess whether it eventually makes it. Only time will tell whether *London* earns the right to sit alongside the better examples in the long history of the *Carry Ons*.

Epilogue

What does the future hold for the *Carry On* phenomenon? If I ever doubted the enduring appeal of the films, I only have to recall a recent occasion when my seven-year-old daughter Hollie not only chose to watch the *Carry On Camping* DVD in preference to her own selection of children's discs, but also found the film highly amusing. It was heartening to see her take a real interest in the picture and for it to evoke genuine laughter; she found many scenes hilarious, particularly when Charles Hawtrey, Terry Scott and Betty Marsden become tangled while desperately trying to undress under canvas. In fact, Hollie is already a *Carry On* fan and delights in watching many of the films; but the allure of the canon, for all ages, is exemplified by the fact that although my daughter has by now seen the tent scene in *Camping* numerous times it always raises a chuckle.

The *Carry On* films aren't to everyone's liking and, as this book reveals, many critics lampooned the cheap, bawdy, double-entendre-laden approach over the years, scoffing at the predictable, unchallenging make-up. What they forget, of course, is that the astute film-makers' output must have ticked all the right boxes because millions of cinema-goers and, latterly, armchair viewers have convulsed with laughter over the antics of Kenneth Williams, Charles Hawtrey, Hattie Jacques, Sid James and the rest of the crowd. Sure, later films struggled but the fact that the films' appeal has transcended generations and has worked on many levels, from children enjoying the visual comedy to adults relishing the double entendres, means that five decades later they're still admired and valued by many, testament to their rightful inclusion in the British film industry's rich heritage.

Regular events are still hosted at Pinewood Studios, home of the film series, where fans flock for a glimpse of Peter Rogers, to hear Jack Douglas recollect his experiences of working on eight films, numerous television shows and two stage productions or gaze in awe as another face from *Carry On*'s history regales them with stories and anecdotes.

In May 2006, scriptwriter Norman Hudis was guest of honour at an event commemorating not only his work on the first six *Carry Ons* but the plethora of scripts he wrote for Peter Rogers during his Pinewood days. After the screening of clips and the trailers of his six *Carry Ons*, the Californian-based writer was mobbed by fans clamouring for his autograph. Despite being a veteran of the showbusiness world, Hudis was still pleasantly surprised by the reception he received that night.

Rogers, meanwhile, knows better than anyone just what his films mean to a great number of people, yet his shy, retiring demeanour masks his true feelings regarding the films' phenomenal success. When asked if his movies, even after 50 years, make him a proud man, he replies: 'It's nothing to be proud of – that's vain and conceited. I'm gratified, but I wouldn't say I'm puffed with pride – heavens, no. It's too important for that.' Whereas thousands of other film entries during this era have fallen by the wayside, it's noticeable that the *Carry Ons* remain accessible and relevant to newer audiences, something Rogers puts down to 'basics'. 'That's the common denominator. The scripts contain real people; you wouldn't think so, but they are. We also avoided topical issues because topicality doesn't last long. If we'd fallen into that trap, the films would have been five-minute wonders.'

Far from being five-minute wonders, they're here to stay. A thorough and consistent approach in producing, casting, directing and executing carved out a successful formula that, save for the occasional film, served everyone well in terms of good old-fashioned entertainment.

It seems unlikely that any attempt to rekindle the *Carry On* magic by even the most talented producers and directors will work. I hope I'm proved wrong, but the original films were of their time: that their style and sense of humour were viewed with deep affection and will, no doubt, continue to be so is evidence of the skills of all concerned; most of the 31 films remain fixed in time, never fading with age or in the glare of more sophisticated humour. The *Carry Ons* occupy a space in contemporary life, just as they have done for decades, and will, hopefully, continue to entertain their audiences for years to come.

Yes, they were cheap, full of predictable jokes and situations, obvious characterisations and a fair dollop of continuity errors – you only need to watch *Camping* and you'll see what I mean – but that's why we love them. Long live the *Carry Ons*!

Extra . . . Extra . . . Extra

i)   The *Carry On* Canon – At A Glance   203

ii)   The *Carry On* Canon – In Depth   205

iii) *Carry On Down Under* – The Uncompleted
      Script   265

iv)   *Carry On Sergeant* – First Treatment and
      Development Ideas   313

i)

The *Carry On* Canon – At A Glance

Films

Sergeant (1958)
Nurse (1959)
Teacher (1959)
Constable (1960)
Regardless (1961)
Cruising (1962)
Cabby (1963)
Jack (1963)
Spying (1964)
Cleo (1964)
Cowboy (1965)
Screaming! (1966)
Don't Lose Your Head (1966)
Follow That Camel (1967)
Doctor (1968)
Up the Khyber (1968)
Camping (1969)
Again Doctor (1969)
Up the Jungle (1970)
Loving (1970)
Henry (1971)
At Your Convenience (1971)
Matron (1972)
Abroad (1972)
Girls (1973)
Dick (1974)
Behind (1975)

England (1976)
That's Carry On (1977)
Emmannuelle (1978)
Columbus (1992)
London (still in pre-production at time of compiling this chapter)

STAGE

London! (1973–75)
Laughing – with The Slimming Factory (1976)
Wot A Carry On in Blackpool (1992)

TELEVISION

Christmas (1969)
Again Christmas (1970)
Christmas (1972)
What A Carry On! (1973)
Christmas (1973)

CARRY ON LAUGHING series

The Prisoner of Spenda (1975)
The Baron Outlook (1975)
The Sobbing Cavalier (1975)
Orgy and Bess (1975)
One in the Eye for Harold (1975)
The Nine Old Cobblers (1975)
The Case of the Screaming Winkles (1975)
The Case of the Coughing Parrot (1975)
Under the Round Table (1975)
Short Knight, Long Daze (1975)
And In My Lady's Chamber (1975)
Who Needs Kitchener? (1975)
Lamp-posts of the Empire (1975)
Carry On Laughing's Christmas Classics (1983)

ii)

The *Carry On* Canon – In Depth

FILMS

CARRY ON SERGEANT

DETAILS:
Nat Cohen and Stuart Levy present a Peter Rogers Production
Distributed by Anglo-Amalgamated Film Distributors Ltd
Based on a story, The Bull Boys *by R.F. Delderfield*
Released as a U certificate in 1958 in black and white
Running time: 83 mins

CAST

William Hartnell	Sergeant Grimshawe
Bob Monkhouse	Charlie Sage
Shirley Eaton	Mary Sage
Eric Barker	Captain Potts
Dora Bryan	Norah
Bill Owen	Corporal Bill Copping
Charles Hawtrey	Peter Golightly
Kenneth Connor	Horace Strong
Kenneth Williams	James Bailey
Terence Longdon	Miles Heywood
Norman Rossington	Herbert Brown
Gerald Campion	Andy Galloway
Hattie Jacques	Captain Clark
Cyril Chamberlain	Gun Sergeant
Ian Whittaker	Medical Corporal
Gordon Tanner	1st Specialist
Frank Forsyth	2nd Specialist

Basil Dignam	3rd Specialist
John Gatrell	4th Specialist
Arnold Diamond	5th Specialist
Martin Boddey	6th Specialist
Anthony Sagar	Stores Sergeant
Alec Bregonzi	1st Storeman
Graham Stewart	2nd Storeman
Alexander Harris	3rd Storeman
Pat Feeney	4th Storeman
Edward Judd	5th Storeman
Ronald Clarke	6th Storeman
David Williams	7th Storeman
Terry Scott	Sergeant Paddy O'Brien
John Mathews	Sergeant Mathews
Edward Devereaux	Sergeant Russell
Leigh Madison	Sheila
Bernard Kay	Injured Recruit

Following appeared as Recruits:
Jack Smethurst
Haydn Ward
Brian Jackson
Graydon Gould
Don McCorkindale
Jeremy Dempster
Leon Eagles
Terry Dickenson
Malcolm Webster
Henry Livings
Patrick Durkin
Derek Martinus
James Villiers
Michael Hunt

PRODUCTION TEAM
Screenplay by Norman Hudis
Additional material by John Antrobus

Music composed and directed by Bruce Montgomery
Played by the Band of the Coldstream Guards
Director of Photography: Peter Hennessy
Produced by Peter Rogers
Directed by Gerald Thomas

CARRY ON NURSE

DETAILS:
Nat Cohen and Stuart Levy present a Peter Rogers Production
Distributed by Anglo-Amalgamated Film Distributors Ltd
Based on an idea by Patrick Cargill and Jack Beale
Released as a U certificate in 1959 in black and white
Running time: 86 mins

CAST
Shirley Eaton ....Nurse Dorothy Denton
Kenneth Connor..............................Bernie Bishop
Charles Hawtrey ....Humphrey Hinton
Kenneth Williams.............................Oliver Reckitt
Hattie Jacques..................................Matron
Leslie Phillips....................................Jack Bell
Terence Longdon ....Ted York
Wilfrid Hyde-White ....The Colonel
Joan Sims...Nurse Stella Dawson
Harry Locke......................................Mick
Susan Shaw......................................Jane Bishop
Joan Hickson ....Sister
Bill Owen ....Percy Hickson
Irene Handl ....Madge Hickson
Susan Beaumont..............................Frances James
Brian Oulton ....Henry Bray
Susan Stephen..................................Nurse Georgie Axwell
Cyril Chamberlain ....Bert Able
Michael Medwin...............................Ginger
Norman Rossington...........................Norm
Jill Ireland..Jill Thompson

Ed Devereaux	Alec Lawrence
Ann Firbank	Helen Lloyd
Frank Forsyth	John Gray
John Mathews	Tom Mayhew
Graham Stewart	George Field
Patrick Durkin	Jackson
David Williams	Andrew Newman
June Whitfield	Meg
Marianne Stone	Alice Able
Hilda Fenemore	Rhoda Bray
Martin Boddey	Perkins
Marita Stanton	Rose Harper
Rosalind Knight	Nurse Nightingale
Leigh Madison	Miss Winn
Stephanie Schiller	New Nurse
Christine Ozanne	Fat Maid
Charles Stanley	Porter
Anthony Sagar	1st Ambulance Driver
Fred Griffiths	2nd Ambulance Driver
Shane Cordell	Attractive Nurse
John Van Eyssen	Stephens
John Horsley	Anaesthetist
Lucy Griffiths	Trolley Lady
Jeremy Connor	Jeremy Bishop

PRODUCTION TEAM

Screenplay by Norman Hudis
Music composed and directed by Bruce Montgomery
Director of Photography: Reginald Wyer
Produced by Peter Rogers
Directed by Gerald Thomas

CARRY ON TEACHER

DETAILS:

Anglo-Amalgamated present a Peter Rogers Production
Distributed by Anglo-Amalgamated Film Distributors Ltd

Released as a U certificate in 1959 in black and white
Running time: 86 mins

CAST

Ted Ray	William Wakefield
Kenneth Connor	Gregory Adams
Charles Hawtrey	Michael Bean
Leslie Phillips	Alistair Grigg
Kenneth Williams	Edwin Milton
Hattie Jacques	Grace Short
Joan Sims	Sarah Allcock
Rosalind Knight	Felicity Wheeler
Cyril Chamberlain	Alf
Richard O'Sullivan	Robin Stevens
George Howell	Billy Haig
Roy Hines	Harry Bird
Diana Beevers	Penny Lee
Jacqueline Lewis	Pat Gordon
Carol White	Sheila Dale
Paul Cole	Atkins
Jane White	Irene
Larry Dann	Boy

PRODUCTION TEAM
Screenplay by Norman Hudis
Music composed and directed by Bruce Montgomery
Director of Photography: Reginald Wyer
Produced by Peter Rogers
Directed by Gerald Thomas

CARRY ON CONSTABLE

DETAILS:
Anglo-Amalgamated present a Peter Rogers Production
Based on an idea by Brock Williams
Released as a U certificate in 1960 in black & white
Running time: 86 mins

CAST

Sidney James	Sergeant Frank Wilkins
Eric Barker	Inspector Mills
Kenneth Connor	Constable Charlie Constable
Charles Hawtrey	PC Timothy Gorse
Kenneth Williams	PC Stanley Benson
Leslie Phillips	PC Tom Potter
Joan Sims	WPC Gloria Passworthy
Hattie Jacques	Sgt Laura Moon
Cyril Chamberlain	Thurston
Shirley Eaton	Sally Barry
Joan Hickson	Mrs May
Irene Handl	Distraught Woman
Terence Longdon	Herbert Hall
Freddie Mills	Crook
Jill Adams	WPC Harrison
Brian Oulton	Store Manager
Victor Maddern	Criminal Type
Joan Young	Suspect
Esma Cannon	Deaf Old Lady
Hilda Fenemore	Agitated Woman
Noel Dyson	Vague Woman
Robin Ray	Assistant Manager
Michael Balfour	Matt
Diane Aubrey	Honoria
Ian Curry	Eric
Mary Law	1st Shop Assistant
Lucy Griffiths	Miss Horton
Peter Bennett	Thief
Jack Taylor	Cliff
Eric Boon	Shorty
Janetta Lake	Girl with dog
Dorinda Stevens	Young Woman
Ken Kennedy	Wall-Eyed Man
Jeremy Connor	Willy
Tom Gill	
Frank Forsyth	

John Antrobus
Eric Corrie
Anthony Sagar ....Citizens

PRODUCTION TEAM
Screenplay by Norman Hudis
Music composed and directed by Bruce Montgomery
Director of Photography: Ted Scaife
Producer: Peter Rogers
Director: Gerald Thomas

CARRY ON REGARDLESS

DETAILS:
Anglo-Amalgamated present a Peter Rogers Production
Released as a U certificate in 1961 in black & white
Running time: 90 mins

CAST
Sidney James.....................................Bert Handy
Kenneth Connor..............................Sam Twist
Charles Hawtrey ....Gabriel Dimple
Kenneth Williams.............................Francis Courtenay
Joan Sims...Lily Duveen
Liz Fraser ....Delia King
Terence Longdon ....Montgomery Infield-Hopping
Bill Owen ....Mike Weston
Esma Cannon ....Miss Cooling
Fenella Fielding.................................Penny Panting
Hattie Jacques...................................Sister
Stanley Unwin ....Landlord
Ed Devereaux ....Mr Panting
Cyril Chamberlain............................Policeman
Ambrosine Phillpotts ....Yoki's Owner
Joan Hickson ....Matron
Molly Weir ....Bird Owner
Sydney Tafler ....Strip-club Manager

Eric Pohlmann .... Sinister Man
June Jago .... Sister
Norman Rossington .... Referee
Terence Alexander .... Trevor Trelawney
Jerry Desmond .... Martin Paul
Eric Boon .... Young Man
Jimmy Thompson .... Mr Delling
Anthony Sagar .... Bus Conductor
Howard Marion-Crawford .... Wine Organiser
Fred Griffiths .... Taxi Driver
Bernard Hunter .... Wine Waiter
David Lodge .... Connoisseur
Nicholas Parsons .... Wolf
Michael Nightingale .... Wine bystander
Patrick Cargill .... Raffish customer
Kynaston Reeves .... Testy old man
Fraser Kerr .... Houseman
Douglas Ives .... Fanatic patient
Maureen Moore .... Pretty probationer
Victor Maddern .... 1st Sinister passenger
Denis Shaw .... 2nd Sinister passenger
Betty Marsden .... 'Mata Hari'
Freddie Mills .... Lefty
Tom Clegg .... Massive Micky McGee
Joe Robinson .... Dynamite Dan
Lucy Griffiths .... Auntie
Ian Whittaker .... Shop Assistant
Julia Arnall .... Trudy Trelawney
Jack Taylor .... MC/Policeman
George Street .... Club Receptionist
Cyril Raymond .... Army Officer
Nancy Roberts .... Old lady
Michael Ward .... Photographer
Ian Wilson .... Advertising Man
Madame Yang .... Chinese lady
Judith Furse .... Formidable lady
David Stoll .... Distraught manager

Carole Shelley.....................................Helen Delling
Charles Julian ....Old man in Ruby Room
Ian Curry...Leonard Beamish

PRODUCTION TEAM
Screenplay by Norman Hudis
Music composed and directed by Bruce Montgomery
Director of Photography: Alan Hume
Producer: Peter Rogers
Director: Gerald Thomas

CARRY ON CRUISING

DETAILS:
Anglo-Amalgamated present a Peter Rogers Production
Distributed through Warner-Pathe Distribution Ltd
From a story by Eric Barker
Released as a U certificate in 1962 in colour
Running time: 89 mins

CAST
Sidney James.......................................Captain Wellington Crowther
Kenneth Williams..............................Leonard Marjoribanks
Kenneth Connor...............................Dr Arthur Binn
Liz Fraser ....Glad Trimble
Dilys Laye...Flo Castle
Esma Cannon ....Bridget Madderley
Lance Percival ....Wilfred Haines
Jimmy Thompson..............................Sam Turner
Ronnie Stevens ....Drunk
Vincent Ball.......................................Jenkins
Cyril Chamberlain ....Tom Tree
Willoughby Goddard.........................Very Fat Man
Ed Devereaux ....Young Officer
Brian Rawlinson ....Steward
Anton Rodgers...................................Young Man
Anthony Sagar ....Cook

Terence Holland	Passer-by
Mario Fabrizi	Cook
Evan David	Bridegroom
Marian Collins	Bride
Jill Mai Meredith	Shapely Miss
Alan Casley	Kindly Seaman

PRODUCTION TEAM
Screenplay by Norman Hudis
Music composed and conducted by Bruce Montgomery and Douglas Gamley
Director of Photography: Alan Hume
Producer: Peter Rogers
Director: Gerald Thomas

CARRY ON CABBY

DETAILS:
Anglo-Amalgamated present a Peter Rogers Production
Distributed by the Rank Organisation
Based on an original idea by S.C. Green and R.M. Hills
Released as a U certificate in 1963 in black & white
Running time: 91 mins

CAST

Sidney James	Charlie Hawkins
Hattie Jacques	Peggy Hawkins
Charles Hawtrey	Terry 'Pintpot' Tankard
Kenneth Connor	Ted Watson
Esma Cannon	Flo Sims
Liz Fraser	Sally
Bill Owen	Smiley
Milo O'Shea	Len
Jim Dale	Expectant Father
Judith Furse	Battleaxe
Renée Houston	Molly
Ambrosine Phillpotts	Aristocratic Lady

Amanda Barrie..Anthea
Carole Shelley..Dumb Driver
Cyril Chamberlain..................................Sarge
Norman Chappell.....................................Allbright
Peter Gilmore ....Dancy
Michael Ward..Man in tweeds
Noel Dyson ....District Nurse
Normal Mitchell.......................................Bespectacled Businessman
Michael Nightingale ....Businessman
Ian Wilson..Clerk
Peter Byrne...Bridegroom
Darryl Kavann...Punchy
Don McCorkindale ....Tubby
Charles Stanley...Geoff
Marion Collins..Bride
Peter Jesson...Car Salesman
Frank Forsyth ....Chauffeur
Valerie Van Ost
Marian Horton...Glamcab Drivers
(Uncredited Glamcab drivers: Elizabeth Kent, Dominique Don, Carole
Cole, Anabella MacCartney, Audrey Wilson, Beverly Bennett, Heather
Downham, Jean Hamilton, Christine Rodgers, Sally Ann Shaw and
Maris Tant)

PRODUCTION TEAM
Screenplay by Talbot Rothwell
Music composed and conducted by Eric Rogers
Director of Photography: Alan Hume B.S.C.
Producer: Peter Rogers
Director: Gerald Thomas

CARRY ON JACK

DETAILS:
Anglo-Amalgamated present a Peter Rogers Production
Distributed through Warner-Pathe Distribution Ltd
Released as an A certificate in 1963 in colour
Running time: 91 mins

CAST

Kenneth Williams	Captain Fearless
Bernard Cribbins	Midshipman Albert Poop-Decker
Juliet Mills	Sally
Charles Hawtrey	Walter Sweetley
Percy Herbert	Mr Angel, the Bosun
Donald Houston	1st Officer Jonathan Howett
Jim Dale	Carrier
Cecil Parker	1st Sea Lord
Patrick Cargill	Spanish Governor
Ed Devereaux	Hook
Peter Gilmore	Patch
George Woodbridge	Ned
Ian Wilson	Ancient Carrier
Jimmy Thompson	Nelson
Anton Rodgers	Hardy
Michael Nightingale	Town Crier
Frank Forsyth	2nd Sea Lord
John Brooking	3rd Sea Lord
Barrie Gosney	Coach Driver
Jan Muzurus	Spanish Captain
Vivian Ventura	Spanish Secretary
Marianne Stone	
Sally Douglas	
Dorinda Stevens	
Jennifer Hill	
Rosemary Manley	
Dominique Don	
Marian Collins	
Jean Hamilton	Girls at 'Dirty Dick's'

PRODUCTION TEAM

Screenplay by Talbot Rothwell
Music composed and conducted by Eric Rogers
Director of Photography: Alan Hume
Producer: Peter Rogers
Director: Gerald Thomas

CARRY ON SPYING

DETAILS:

Anglo-Amalgamated present a Peter Rogers Production
Distributed through Warner-Pathe Distribution Ltd
Songs: 'Too Late' by Alex Alstone and Geoffrey Parsons;
'The Magic of Love' by Eric Rogers
Released as an A certificate in 1964 in black & white
Running time: 92 mins

CAST

Kenneth Williams	Desmond Simkins
Barbara Windsor	Daphne Honeybutt
Charles Hawtrey	Charlie Bind
Bernard Cribbins	Harold Crump
Jim Dale	Carstairs
Eric Barker	The Chief
Richard Wattis	Cobley
Dilys Laye	Lila
Eric Pohlmann	The Fatman
Victor Maddern	Milchmann
Judith Furse	Dr Crow
John Bluthal	The Head Waiter
Renée Houston	Madame
Tom Clegg	Doorman
Gertan Klauber	Code Clerk
Norman Mitchell	Native Policeman
Frank Forsyth	Professor Stark
Derek Sydney	Algerian Gent
Jill Mai Meredith	Cigarette Girl
Angela Ellison	Cloakroom Girl
Hugh Futcher	Bed of Nails Native
Norah Gordon	Elderly Woman
Jack Taylor	
Bill Cummings	Thugs
Anthony Baird	
Patrick Durkin	Guards

Virginia Tyler
Judi Johnson
Gloria Best..Funhouse Girls
Audrey Wilson
Vicky Smith
Jane Lumb
Marian Collins
Sally Douglas
Christine Rodgers
Maya Koumani................................Amazon Guards

PRODUCTION TEAM
Screenplay by Talbot Rothwell and Sid Colin
Music composed and conducted by Eric Rogers
Director of Photography: Alan Hume
Producer: Peter Rogers
Director: Gerald Thomas

CARRY ON CLEO

DETAILS:
Anglo-Amalgamated present a Peter Rogers Production
Distributed through Warner-Pathe Distribution Ltd
Released as an A certificate in 1964 in colour
Running time: 92 mins

CAST
Sidney James......................................Mark Antony
Kenneth Williams.............................Julius Caesar
Charles Hawtrey...............................Seneca
Kenneth Connor................................Hengist Pod
Joan Sims...Calpurnia
Jim Dale ....Horsa
Amanda Barrie..................................Cleopatra
Victor Maddern................................Sergeant Major
Julie Stevens.....................................Gloria
Sheila Hancock..................................Senna Pod
Jon Pertwee......................................Soothsayer

Brian Oulton ....Brutus
Michael Ward ....Archimedes
Francis de Wolff ....Agrippa
Tom Clegg...Sosages
Tanya Binning ....Virginia
David Davenport..............................Bilius
Peter Gilmore ....Galley Master
Ian Wilson..Messenger
Norman Mitchell..............................Heckler
Brian Rawlinson ....Hessian Driver
Gertan Klauber...................................Marcus
Warren Mitchell................................Spencius
Peter Jesson.......................................Companion
Michael Nightingale ....Caveman
Judi Johnson......................................Gloria's Bridesmaid
Thelma Taylor ....Seneca's Servant
Sally Douglas......................................Antony's Dusky Maiden
Wanda Ventham ....Pretty Bidder
Peggy Ann Clifford............................Willa Claudia
Mark Hardy..Guard at Caesar's Palace
E.V.H. Emmett..................................Narrator
Christine Rodgers, Gloria Best
and Virginia Tyler.............................Handmaidens
Gloria Johnson
Joanna Ford
Donna White
Jane Lumb
Vicki Smith ....Vestal Virgins

Uncredited 'Companions': Stuart Monro, Forbes Douglas, Billy Cornelius, Peter Fraser, Frederick Beauman and Keith Buckley

PRODUCTION TEAM
Screenplay by Talbot Rothwell
Music composed and conducted by Eric Rogers
Director of Photography: Alan Hume
Producer: Peter Rogers
Director: Gerald Thomas

CARRY ON COWBOY

DETAILS:
Anglo-Amalgamated present a Peter Rogers Production
Distributed through Warner-Pathe Distribution Ltd
Songs: 'Carry On Cowboy' and 'This is the Night for Love' – music by
Eric Rogers, lyrics by Alan Rogers
Sung by Anon
Released as an A certificate in 1965 in colour
Running time: 95 mins

CAST

Sidney James	Johnny Finger / The Rumpo Kid
Kenneth Williams	Judge Burke
Jim Dale	Marshall P. Knutt
Charles Hawtrey	Big Heap
Joan Sims	Belle
Peter Butterworth	Doc
Bernard Bresslaw	Little Heap
Angela Douglas	Annie Oakley
Jon Pertwee	Sheriff Albert Earp
Percy Herbert	Charlie
Sydney Bromley	Sam Houston
Edina Ronay	Dolores
Lionel Murton	Clerk
Peter Gilmore	Curly
Davy Kaye	Josh the Undertaker
Alan Gifford	Commissioner
Brian Rawlinson	Stagecoach Guard
Michael Nightingale	Bank Manager
Simon Cain	Short
Sally Douglas	Kitkata
Cal McCord	Mex
Garry Colleano	Slim
Arthur Lovegrove	Old Cowhand
Margaret Nolan	Miss Jones
Tom Clegg	Blacksmith

Larry Cross ....Perkins
Brian Coburn................................Trapper
The Ballet Montparnasse ....Dancing Girls
Hal Galili.....................................Cowhand
Norman Stanley............................Drunk
Carmen Dene ....Mexican Girl
Andrea Allen................................Minnie
Vicki Smith..................................Polly
Audrey Wilson ....Jane
Donna White................................Jenny
Lisa Thomas.................................Sally
Gloria Best...................................Bridget
George Mossman ....Stagecoach Driver
Richard O'Brien ....Rider
Eric Rogers ....Pianist

PRODUCTION TEAM
Screenplay by Talbot Rothwell
Music composed and conducted by Eric Rogers
Director of Photography: Alan Hume
Producer: Peter Rogers
Director: Gerald Thomas

CARRY ON SCREAMING!

DETAILS:
Anglo-Amalgamated present a Peter Rogers Production
Distributed through Warner-Pathe Distribution Ltd
Song: 'Carry On Screaming' by Myles Rudge and Ted Dick
Sung by Anon
Released as an A certificate in 1966 in colour
Running time: 97 mins

CAST
Harry H. Corbett ....Detective Sergeant Sidney Bung
Kenneth Williams.........................Doctor Olando Watt
Jim Dale ....Albert Potter

Charles Hawtrey ....Dan Dann
Joan Sims......................................Emily Bung
Fenella Fielding............................Virula Watt
Peter Butterworth ....Detective Constable Slobotham
Bernard Bresslaw...........................Sockett
Angela Douglas.............................Doris Mann
Jon Pertwee..................................Dr Fettle
Tom Clegg....................................Odbodd
Billy Cornelius.............................Odbodd Junior
Norman Mitchell..........................Cabby
Michael Ward ....Vivian (Window Dresser)
Frank Thornton............................Mr Jones (Shop Manager)
Frank Forsyth...............................Desk Sergeant
Anthony Sagar ....Policeman
Sally Douglas ....Girl
Marianne Stone.............................Mrs Parker
Denis Blake...................................Rubbatiti

PRODUCTION TEAM
Screenplay by Talbot Rothwell
Music composed and conducted by Eric Rogers
Director of Photography: Alan Hume
Producer: Peter Rogers
Director: Gerald Thomas

CARRY ON ... DON'T LOSE YOUR HEAD

DETAILS:
A Peter Rogers Production distributed through Rank Organisation
Song: 'Don't Lose Your Head' by Bill Martin and Phil Coulter
Sung by The Michael Sammes Singers
Released as an A certificate in 1966 in colour
Running time: 90 mins
(Note: the film was originally released without the Carry On moniker
but it was later reinstated.)

CAST

Sidney James	Sir Rodney Ffing / The Black Fingernail
Kenneth Williams	Citizen Camembert
Jim Dale	Lord Darcy de Pue
Charles Hawtrey	Duc de Pommfrit
Joan Sims	Desiree Dubarry
Peter Butterworth	Citizen Bidet
Dany Robin	Jacqueline
Peter Gilmore	Robespierre
Marianne Stone	Landlady
Michael Ward	Henri
Leon Greene	Malabonce
Hugh Futcher	Guard
Richard Shaw	Captain of Soldiers
David Davenport	Sergeant
Jennifer Clulow	1st Lady
Valerie Van Ost	2nd Lady
Jacqueline Pearce	3rd Lady
Nikki Van Der Zyl	Messenger
Julian Orchard	Rake
Elspeth March	Lady Binder
Joan Ingram	Bald-headed Dowager
Michael Nightingale	'What Locket?' Man
Diana MacNamara	Princess Stephanie
Ronnie Brody	Little Man
Billy Cornelius	Soldier
Patrick Allen	Narrator
Monica Dietrich	
Anna Willoughby	
Penny Keen	
June Cooper	
Christine Pryor	
Karen Young	Girls

PRODUCTION TEAM
Screenplay by Talbot Rothwell
Music composed and conducted by Eric Rogers

Director of Photography: Alan Hume
Producer: Peter Rogers
Director: Gerald Thomas

CARRY ON ... FOLLOW THAT CAMEL

DETAILS:
A Peter Rogers Production distributed through Rank Organisation
Released as an A certificate in 1967 in colour
Running time: 95 mins
(Note: the film was originally released without the Carry On moniker
but this was later reinstated.)

CAST
Phil Silvers .... Sergeant Ernie Nocker
Jim Dale .... Bertram Oliphant 'BO' West
Peter Butterworth .... Simpson
Kenneth Williams .... Commandant Burger
Charles Hawtrey .... Captain Le Pice
Joan Sims .... Zig-Zig
Angela Douglas .... Lady Jane Ponsonby
Bernard Bresslaw .... Sheikh Abdul Abulbul
Anita Harris .... Corktip
John Bluthal .... Corporal Clotski
Peter Gilmore .... Captain Bagshaw
William Mervyn .... Sir Cyril Ponsonby
Julian Holloway .... Ticket Collector
David Glover .... Hotel Manager
Larry Taylor .... Riff
William Hurndell .... Riff
Julian Orchard .... Doctor
Vincent Ball .... Ship's Officer
Peter Jesson .... Lawrence
Gertan Klauber .... Spiv
Michael Nightingale .... Nightingale the Butler
Richard Montez
Frank Singuineau

Simon Cain ....Riffs at Abdul's Tent
Harold Kasket...................................Hotel Gentleman
Edmund Pegge................................Bowler
Carol Sloan
Gina Gianelli
Dominique Don
Anne Scott
Patsy Snell
Zorenah Osborne
Margot Maxine
Sally Douglas
Angie Grant
Gina Warwick
Karen Young
Helga Jones.....................................Harem Girls

PRODUCTION TEAM
Screenplay by Talbot Rothwell
Music composed and conducted by Eric Rogers
Director of Photography: Alan Hume
Producer: Peter Rogers
Director: Gerald Thomas

CARRY ON DOCTOR

DETAILS:
A Peter Rogers Production distributed through Rank Organisation
Released as an A certificate in 1967 in colour
Running time: 94 mins

CAST
Frankie Howerd................................Francis Bigger
Kenneth Williams.............................Dr Kenneth Tinkle
Sidney James....................................Charlie Roper
Charles Hawtrey...............................Mr Barron
Jim Dale ....Dr Jim Kilmore
Hattie Jacques..................................Matron

Peter Butterworth ....Mr Smith
Bernard Bresslaw..............................Ken Biddle
Barbara Windsor..............................Nurse Sandra May
Joan Sims...Chloe Gibson
Anita Harris......................................Nurse Clarke
June Jago ....Sister Hoggett
Derek Francis....................................Sir Edmund Francis
Dandy Nichols.................................Mrs Roper
Peter Jones ....Chaplain
Deryck Guyler ....Surgeon Hardcastle
Gwendolyn Watts ....Mrs Barron
Dilys Laye...Mavis
Peter Gilmore ....Henry
Harry Locke......................................Sam
Marianne Stone ....Mum
Jean St Clair ....Mrs Smith
Valerie Van Ost................................Nurse Parkin
Julian Orchard.................................Fred
Brian Wilde ....Man from Cox and Carter
Lucy Griffiths ....Patient
Pat Coombs ....Patient
Gertan Klauber ....Wash orderly
Julian Holloway ....Simmons
Jenny White......................................Nurse in Bath and Nurse in
Nursing Home
Helen Ford ....Nurse
Gordon Rollings ....Night Porter
Simon Cain ....Tea Orderly
Cheryl Molineaux.............................Women's Ward Nurse
Alexandra Dane ....Female Instructor
Bart Allison......................................Grandad
Jane Murdoch ....Nurse
Stephen Garlick ....Small Boy
Uncredited actor ....Mr Wrigley, Bandaged Man
Patrick Allen ....Narrator

(Note: Jasmin Broughton was hired as a stunt double for Barbara Windsor)

PRODUCTION TEAM
Screenplay by Talbot Rothwell
Music composed and conducted by Eric Rogers
Director of Photography: Alan Hume
Producer: Peter Rogers
Director: Gerald Thomas

CARRY ON . . . UP THE KHYBER

DETAILS:
A Peter Rogers production distributed through Rank Organisation
Released as an A certificate in 1968 in colour
Running time: 88 mins

CAST
Sidney James.....................................Sir Sidney Ruff-Diamond
Kenneth Williams..............................The Khasi of Kalabar
Charles Hawtrey................................Private James Widdle
Roy Castle ....Captain Keene
Joan Sims...Lady Ruff-Diamond
Bernard Bresslaw...............................Bungdit Din
Peter Butterworth ....Brother Belcher
Terry Scott.......................................Sergeant Major Macnutt
Angela Douglas.................................Princess Jelhi
Cardew Robinson ....The Fakir
Peter Gilmore ....Private Ginger Hale
Julian Holloway................................Major Shorthouse
Leon Thau..Stinghi
Michael Mellinger.............................Chindi
Alexandra Dane ....Busti
Dominique Don.................................Macnutt's Lure
Derek Sydney ....Major-domo
David Spenser....................................Bungdit's Servant
Johnny Briggs ....Sporran Soldier
Simon Cain ....Bagpipe Soldier
Steven Scott......................................Burpa Guard

Larry Taylor ....Burpa at Door-grid
Patrick Westwood ....Burpa in Crowd
John Hallam ....Burpa on Rooftop
Wanda Ventham
Liz Gold
Vicki Woolf
Anne Scott
Barbara Evans
Lisa Noble
Eve Eden
Tamsin MacDonald
Katherina Holden ....The Khasi's Wives
Valerie Leon
Carmen Dene
June Cooper
Josephine Blain
Vicki Murden
Karen Young
Angie Grant
Sue Vaughan ....Hospitality Girls
Patrick Allen ....Narrator

PRODUCTION TEAM
Screenplay by Talbot Rothwell
Music composed and conducted by Eric Rogers
Director of Photography: Ernest Steward
Producer: Peter Rogers
Director: Gerald Thomas

CARRY ON CAMPING

DETAILS:
A Peter Rogers production distributed through Rank Organisation
Released as an A certificate in 1969 in colour
Running time: 88 mins

CAST

Sidney James	Sid Boggle
Kenneth Williams	Dr Kenneth Soaper
Joan Sims	Joan Fussey
Charles Hawtrey	Charlie Muggins
Terry Scott	Peter Potter
Barbara Windsor	Babs
Bernard Bresslaw	Bernie Lugg
Hattie Jacques	Miss Haggerd
Peter Butterworth	Josh Fiddler
Julian Holloway	Jim Tanner
Dilys Laye	Anthea Meeks
Betty Marsden	Harriet Potter
Trisha Noble	Sally
Amelia Bayntun	Mrs Fussey
Brian Oulton	Store Manager
Patricia Franklin	Farmer's Daughter
Derek Francis	Farmer
Michael Nightingale	Man in Cinema
Sandra Caron	Fanny
George Moon	Scrawny Man
Valerie Shute	Pat
Elizabeth Knight	Jane
Georgina Moon	Joy
Vivien Lloyd	Verna
Jennifer Pyle	Hilda
Lesley Duff	Norma
Jackie Poole	Betty
Anna Karen	Hefty Girl
Sally Kemp	Girl with Cow
Valerie Leon	Store Assistant
Peter Cockburn	Commentator
Gilly Grant	Sally G-String
Michael Low & Mike Lucas	Lusty Youths

PRODUCTION TEAM

Screenplay by Talbot Rothwell

Music composed and conducted by Eric Rogers
Director of Photography: Ernest Steward B.S.C.
Producer: Peter Rogers
Director: Gerald Thomas

CARRY ON AGAIN DOCTOR

DETAILS:
A Peter Rogers production distributed through Rank Organisation
Released as an A certificate in 1969 in colour
Running time: 89 mins

CAST
Sidney James.....................................Gladstone Screwer
Jim Dale ....Dr James Nookey
Kenneth Williams.............................Dr Frederick Carver
Charles Hawtrey ....Dr Ernest Stoppidge
Joan Sims...Mrs Ellen Moore
Barbara Windsor..............................Goldie Locks
Hattie Jacques...................................Matron
Patsy Rowlands ....Miss Fosdick
Peter Butterworth ....Shuffling Patient
Wilfrid Brambell...............................Mr Pullen
Elizabeth Knight...............................Nurse Willing
Peter Gilmore ....Henry
Alexandra Dane ....Stout Woman
Pat Coombs.......................................New Matron
William Mervyn ....Lord Paragon
Patricia Hayes ....Mrs Beasley
Lucy Griffiths ....Old Lady in Headphones
Harry Locke.......................................Porter
Gwendolyn Watts ....Night Sister
Valerie Leon.......................................Deirdre
Frank Singuineau...............................Porter
Valerie Van Ost..................................Out-Patients Sister
Simon Cain ....X-ray Man
Elspeth March ....Hospital Board Member

Valerie Shute	Nurse
Shakira Baksh	Scrubba
Ann Lancaster	Miss Armitage
Georgina Simpson	Men's Ward Nurse
Eric Rogers	Bandleader
Donald Bisset	Patient
Bob Todd	Plump Patient
Heather Emmanuel	Plump Native Girl
Yutte Stensgaard	Trolley Nurse
George Roderick	Waiter
Jenny Counsell	Night Nurse
Rupert Evans	Stunt Orderly
Billy Cornelius	Patient in Plaster
Hugh Futcher	Cab Driver
Faith Kent	Berkeley Nursing Home Matron

PRODUCTION TEAM
Screenplay by Talbot Rothwell
Music composed and conducted by Eric Rogers
Director of Photography: Ernest Steward B.S.C.
Producer: Peter Rogers
Director: Gerald Thomas

CARRY ON UP THE JUNGLE

DETAILS:
A Peter Rogers Production distributed through Rank Organisation
Released as an A certificate in 1970 in colour
Running time: 89 mins

CAST

Frankie Howerd	Professor Inigo Tinkle
Sidney James	Bill Boosey
Charles Hawtrey	Walter Bagley – King Tonka
Joan Sims	Lady Evelyn Bagley
Kenneth Connor	Claude Chumley

Bernard Bresslaw..............................Upsidasi
Terry Scott.......................................Cecil the Jungle Boy
Jacki Piper.......................................June
Valerie Leon.....................................Leda
Reuben Martin ....Gorilla
Edwina Carroll ....Nerda
Danny Daniels..................................Nosha Chief
Yemi Ajibade....................................Witch Doctor
Lincoln Webb ....Nosha with Girl
Heather Emmanuel...........................Pregnant Lubi
Verna Lucille MacKenzie ....Gong Lubi
Valerie Moore
Cathi March ....Lubi Lieutenants
Nina Baden-Semper..........................Girl Nosha
Roy Stewart
John Hamilton
Willie Jonah
Chris Konyils....................................Noshas

PRODUCTION TEAM
Screenplay by Talbot Rothwell
Music composed and conducted by Eric Rogers
Director of Photography: Ernest Steward
Producer: Peter Rogers
Director: Gerald Thomas

CARRY ON LOVING

DETAILS:
A Peter Rogers Production distributed through Rank Organisation
Released as an A certificate in 1970 in colour
Running time: 88 mins

CAST
Sidney James.....................................Sidney Bliss
Kenneth Williams.............................Percival Snooper
Charles Hawtrey ....James Bedsop

Hattie Jacques ....Sophie Bliss
Joan Sims ....Esme Crowfoot
Bernard Bresslaw ....Gripper Burke
Terry Scott ....Terence Philpot
Jacki Piper ....Sally Martin
Richard O'Callaghan ....Bertrum Muffet
Imogen Hassall ....Jenny Grub
Patsy Rowlands ....Miss Dempsey
Peter Butterworth ....Sinister Client
Joan Hickson ....Mrs Grubb
Julian Holloway ....Adrian
Janet Mahoney ....Gay
Ann Way ....Aunt Victoria Grubb
Bill Maynard ....Mr Dreery
Amelia Bayntun ....Corset Lady
Gordon Richardson ....Uncle Ernest Grubb
Tom Clegg ....Trainer
Lucy Griffiths ....Woman
Valerie Shute.....................................Girl Lover
Mike Grady ....Boy Lover
Anthony Sagar ....Man in Hospital
Harry Shacklock ....Lavatory Attendant
Derek Francis.....................................Bishop
Alexandra Dane ....Emily
Philip Stone ....Robinson
Sonny Farrar ....Violinist
Patricia Franklin................................Mrs Dreery
Hilda Barry.......................................Grandma Grubb
Josie Bradley ....Pianist
Bart Allison.......................................Grandpa Grubb
Anna Karen ....Wife
Dorothea Phillips...............................Aunt Beatrice Grubb
Lauri Lupino Lane.............................Husband
Bill Pertwee......................................Barman
Colin Vancao ....Wilberforce Grubb
Gavin Reed.......................................Window Dresser
Joe Cornelius ....Second

Len Lowe...Maitre d'Hotel
Fred Griffiths...................................Taxi driver
Ronnie Brody ....Henry
Kenny Lynch ....Bus Conductor
Robert Russell..................................Policeman

PRODUCTION TEAM
Screenplay by Talbot Rothwell
Music composed and conducted by Eric Rogers
Director of Photography: Ernest Steward
Producer: Peter Rogers
Director: Gerald Thomas

CARRY ON HENRY

DETAILS:
A Peter Rogers production distributed through Rank Organisation
Released as an A certificate in 1971 in colour
Running time: 89 mins

CAST
Sidney James.....................................King Henry VIII
Kenneth Williams.............................Thomas Cromwell
Charles Hawtrey ....Sir Roger de Lodgerley
Joan Sims...Queen Marie of Normandy
Terry Scott..Cardinal Wolsey
Barbara Windsor...............................Bettina
Kenneth Connor...............................Lord Hampton of Wick
Julian Holloway ....Sir Thomas
Peter Gilmore ....Francis, King of France
Peter Butterworth ....Charles, Earl of Bristol
Julian Orchard..................................Duc de Poncenay
Gertan Klauber.................................Bidet
David Davenport...............................Major-domo
Margaret Nolan ....Buxom Lass
William Mervyn ....Physician
Norman Chappell..............................1st Plotter

Derek Francis.............................Farmer
Bill Maynard...............................Guy Fawkes
Douglas Ridley ....2nd Plotter
Leon Greene
Dave Prowse ....Torturers
Monica Dietrich ....Katherine Howard
Billy Cornelius............................Guard
Marjie Lawrence ....Serving Maid
Patsy Rowlands ....Queen
Alan Curtis ....Conte di Pisa
John Bluthal ....Royal Tailor
William McGuirck ....Flunkey
Jane Cardew...............................Henry's 2nd Wife
Valerie Shute..............................Maid
Peter Rigby
Trevor Roberts
Peter Munt ....Henry's Courtiers

PRODUCTION TEAM
Screenplay by Talbot Rothwell
Music composed and conducted by Eric Rogers
Director of Photography: Alan Hume
Producer: Peter Rogers
Director: Gerald Thomas

CARRY ON AT YOUR CONVENIENCE

DETAILS:
A Peter Rogers production distributed through Rank Organisation
Released as an A certificate in 1971 in colour
Running time: 90 mins

CAST
Sidney James..............................Sid Plummer
Kenneth Williams........................W.C. Boggs
Charles Hawtrey ....Charles Coote
Hattie Jacques............................Beattie Plummer

Joan Sims...Chloe Moore
Bernard Bresslaw...............................Bernie Hulke
Kenneth Cope ....Vic Spanner
Jacki Piper...Myrtle Plummer
Richard O'Callaghan ....Lewis Boggs
Patsy Rowlands ....Hortence Withering
Davy Kaye ....Benny
Bill Maynard.....................................Fred Moore
Renée Houston ....Agatha Spanner
Marianne Stone ....Maud
Margaret Nolan ....Popsy
Geoffrey Hughes..............................Willie
Hugh Futcher ....Ernie
Simon Cain ....Barman
Amelia Bayntun ....Mrs Spragg
Leon Greene ....Chef
Harry Towb ....Doctor in Film
Shirley Stelfox.................................Bunny Waitress
Peter Burton ....Hotel Manager
Julian Holloway ....Roger
Anouska Hempel ....New Canteen Girl
Jan Rossini.......................................Hoopla Girl
Philip Stone......................................Mr Bulstrode

PRODUCTION TEAM
Screenplay by Talbot Rothwell
Music composed and conducted by Eric Rogers
Director of Photography: Ernest Steward B.S.C.
Producer: Peter Rogers
Director: Gerald Thomas

CARRY ON MATRON

DETAILS:
A Peter Rogers production distributed through Rank Organisation
Released as an A certificate in 1972 in colour
Running time: 87 mins

CAST

Sidney James......................................Sid Carter
Kenneth Williams...........................Sir Bernard Cutting
Charles Hawtrey.............................Dr Francis A. Goode
Hattie Jacques.................................Matron
Joan Sims..Mrs Tidey
Bernard Bresslaw...........................Ernie Bragg
Barbara Windsor............................Nurse Susan Ball
Kenneth Connor.............................Mr Tidey
Terry Scott.....................................Dr Prodd
Kenneth Cope ....Cyril Carter
Jacki Piper......................................Sister
Bill Maynard..................................Freddy
Patsy Rowlands ....Evelyn Banks
Derek Francis.................................Arthur
Amelia Bayntun.............................Mrs Jenkins
Valerie Leon...................................Jane Darling
Brian Osborne ....Ambulance Driver
Gwendolyn Watts...........................Frances Kemp
Valerie Shute..................................Miss Smethurst
Margaret Nolan ....Mrs Tucker
Michael Nightingale ....Pearson
Wendy Richard...............................Miss Willing
Zena Clifton...................................Au pair Girl
Bill Kenwright ....Reporter
Robin Hunter.................................Mr Darling
Jack Douglas...................................Twitching Father
Madeline Smith ....Mrs Pullitt
Juliet Harmer.................................Mrs Bentley
Gilly Grant ....Nurse in Bath
Lindsay March................................Shapely Nurse
Laura Collins ....Nurse

PRODUCTION TEAM

Screenplay by Talbot Rothwell
Music composed and conducted by Eric Rogers
Director of Photography: Ernest Steward

Producer: Peter Rogers
Director: Gerald Thomas

CARRY ON ABROAD

DETAILS:
A Peter Rogers Production distributed through Rank Organisation
Released as an A certificate in 1972 in colour
Running time: 88 mins

CAST

Sidney James	Vic Flange
Kenneth Williams	Stuart Farquhar
Charles Hawtrey	Eustace Tuttle
Joan Sims	Cora Flange
Peter Butterworth	Pepe
Kenneth Connor	Stanley Blunt
Hattie Jacques	Floella
Bernard Bresslaw	Brother Bernard
Barbara Windsor	Miss Sadie Tomkins
Jimmy Logan	Bert Conway
June Whitfield	Evelyn Blunt
Sally Geeson	Lily
Carol Hawkins	Marge
Gail Grainger	Moira Plunkett
Ray Brooks	Georgio
John Clive	Robin Tweet
David Kernan	Nicholas Phipps
Patsy Rowlands	Miss Dobbs
Derek Francis	Brother Martin
Jack Douglas	Harry
Amelia Bayntun	Mrs Tuttle
Alan Curtis	Police Chief
Hugh Futcher	Jailer
Gertan Klauber	Postcard Seller
Brian Osborne	Stallholder
Olga Lowe	Madame Fifi

PRODUCTION TEAM
Screenplay by Talbot Rothwell
Music composed and conducted by Eric Rogers
Director of Photography: Alan Hume B.S.C.
Producer: Peter Rogers
Director: Gerald Thomas

CARRY ON GIRLS

DETAILS:
A Peter Rogers Production distributed through Fox/Rank Distribution Ltd
Released as an A certificate in 1973 in colour
Running time: 88 mins

CAST
Sidney James......................................Sidney Fiddler
Barbara Windsor...............................Hope Springs
Joan Sims...Connie Philpotts
Kenneth Connor...............................Mayor Frederick Bumble
Bernard Bresslaw..............................Peter Potter
Peter Butterworth ....Admiral
June Whitfield ....Augusta Prodworthy
Jack Douglas......................................William
Patsy Rowlands..................................Mildred Bumble
Joan Hickson ....Mrs Dukes
David Lodge.......................................Police Inspector
Valerie Leon......................................Paula Perkins
Margaret Nolan ....Dawn Brakes
Angela Grant ....Miss Bangor
Sally Geeson ....Debra
Wendy Richard..................................Ida Downe
Jimmy Logan ....Cecil Gaybody
Arnold Ridley ....Alderman Pratt
Robin Askwith....................................Larry
Patricia Franklin................................Rosemary
Brian Osborne ....'Half a quid' Citizen

Bill Pertwee	Fire Chief
Marianne Stone	Miss Drew
Brenda Cowling	Matron
Zena Clifton	Susan Brooks
Laraine Humphrys	Eileen Denby
Pauline Peart	Gloria Winch
Caroline Whitaker	Mary Parker
Barbara Wise	Julia Oates
Carol Wyler	Maureen Darcy
Mavise Fyson	Francis Cake
Billy Cornelius	Constable
Edward Palmer	Elderly Resident
Michael Nightingale	City Gent on Tube
Hugh Futcher	'There's Fiddler' Citizen
Elsie Winsor	Cloakroom Attendant
Nick Hobbs	Stunt Double
Ron Tarr	Bearded Man in Audience

PRODUCTION TEAM
Screenplay by Talbot Rothwell
Music composed and conducted by Eric Rogers
Director of Photography: Alan Hume
Producer: Peter Rogers
Director: Gerald Thomas

CARRY ON DICK

DETAILS:
A Peter Rogers Production distributed through Fox/Rank Distribution Ltd
Released as an A certificate in 1974 in colour
Running time: 91 mins

CAST

Sidney James	Dick Turpin / The Rev. Flasher
Kenneth Williams	Captain Desmond Fancey
Barbara Windsor	Harriett

Hattie Jacques.....................................Martha Hoggett
Bernard Bresslaw...................................Sir Roger Daley
Joan Sims..Madame Desiree
Peter Butterworth ....Tom
Kenneth Connor ....Constable
Jack Douglas...Sergeant Jock Strapp
Patsy Rowlands.....................................Mrs Giles
Bill Maynard...Bodkin
Margaret Nolan ....Lady Daley
John Clive ....Isaak the Tailor
David Lodge..Bullock
Marianne Stone ....Maggie
Patrick Durkin......................................William
Sam Kelly ....Sir Roger's Coachman
George Moon ....Mr Giles
Michael Nightingale ....Squire Trelawney
Brian Osborne.......................................Browning
Anthony Bailey.....................................Rider
Brian Coburn and Max Faulkner.........Highwaymen
Jeremy Connor and Nosher Powell......Footpads
Joy Harrington ....Lady
Larry Taylor and Billy Cornelius..........Tough Men
Laraine Humphrys
Linda Hooks
Penny Irving
Eva Reuber-Staier ....'The Birds of Paradise'

PRODUCTION TEAM
Screenplay by Talbot Rothwell
Based on a treatment by Lawrie Wyman and George Evans
Music composed and conducted by Eric Rogers
Director of Photography: Ernest Steward
Producer: Peter Rogers
Director: Gerald Thomas

CARRY ON BEHIND

DETAILS:
A Peter Rogers Production distributed through Fox/Rank Distribution Ltd
Released as an A certificate in 1975 in colour
Running time: 90 mins

CAST
Kenneth Williams.............................Professor Roland Crump
Elke Sommer ....Professor Anna Vooshka
Bernard Bresslaw.............................Arthur Upmore
Kenneth Connor...............................Major Leep
Joan Sims.......................................Daphne Barnes
Windsor Davies ....Fred Ramsden
Jack Douglas...................................Ernie Bragg
Peter Butterworth ....Henry Barnes
Carol Hawkins..................................Sandra
Sherrie Hewson...............................Carol
Liz Fraser ....Sylvia Ramsden
Patsy Rowlands ....Linda Upmore
Ian Lavender...................................Joe Baxter
Adrienne Posta.................................Norma Baxter
Patricia Franklin...............................Vera Bragg
David Lodge....................................Landlord
Marianne Stone ....Mrs Rowan
George Layton ....Doctor
Brian Osborne ....Bob
Larry Dann......................................Clive
Georgina Moon ....Sally
Diana Darvey ....Maureen
Jenny Cox.......................................Veronica
Larry Martyn ....Electrician
Linda Hooks....................................Nurse
Kenneth Waller................................Barman
Billy Cornelius..................................Man with Salad
Melita Manger ....Woman with Salad
Hugh Futcher ....Painter

Helli Louise Jacobsen........................Nudist
Jeremy Connor ....Student with Ice Cream
Alexandra Dane ....Lady in Low-cut Dress
Sam Kelly ....Projectionist
Johnny Briggs ....Plasterer
Lucy Griffiths ....Lady with Hat
Stanley McGeagh..............................Short-sighted Man
Brenda Cowling...............................Wife
Sidney Johnson.................................Man in Glasses
Drina Pavlovic ....Courting Girl
Caroline Whitaker ....Student
Ray Edwards.....................................Man with Water
Donald Hewlett................................Dean

PRODUCTION TEAM
Screenplay by Dave Freeman
Music composed and conducted by Eric Rogers
Director of Photography: Ernest Steward B.S.C.
Producer: Peter Rogers
Director: Gerald Thomas

CARRY ON ENGLAND

DETAILS:
A Peter Rogers Production distributed by Fox/Rank Distributors Ltd
Released as an A certificate in 1976 in colour
Running time: 89 mins

CAST
Kenneth Connor...............................Captain S. Melly
Windsor Davies ....Sergeant Major 'Tiger'
                                            Bloomer
Patrick Mower ....Sergeant Len Able
Judy Geeson.....................................Sergeant Tilly Willing
Jack Douglas.....................................Bombardier Ready
Peter Jones ....Brigadier

Diana Langton.....................................Private Alice Easy
Melvyn Hayes.....................................Gunner Shorthouse
Peter Butterworth ....Major Carstairs
Joan Sims..Private Jennifer Ffoukes-
                                        Sharpe
Julian Holloway ....Major Butcher
David Lodge ....Captain Bull
Larry Dann..Gunner Shaw
Brian Osborne ....Gunner Owen
Johnny Briggs ....Melly's Driver
Patricia Franklin...............................Corporal Cook
Linda Hooks......................................Nurse
John Carlin..Officer
Vivienne Johnson.............................Freda
Michael Nightingale ....Officer
Jeremy Connor ....Gunner Hiscocks
Richard Olley ....Gunner Parker
Peter Banks.......................................Gunner Thomas
Richard Bartlett ....Gunner Drury
Billy J. Mitchell ....Gunner Childs
Peter Quince.....................................Gunner Sharpe
Paul Toothill ....Gunner Gale
Tricia Newby ....Private Murray
Louise Burton...................................Private Evans
Jeannie Collings...............................Private Edwards
Barbara Hampshire..........................Private Carter
Linda Regan ....Private Taylor
Barbara Rosenblat............................ATS Girl

PRODUCTION TEAM
Screenplay by David Pursall and Jack Seddon
Music composed and conducted by Max Harris
Director of Photography: Ernest Steward
Producer: Peter Rogers
Director: Gerald Thomas

THAT'S CARRY ON

DETAILS:
A Peter Rogers Production
Compiled by Gerald Thomas
A 1977 Rank/EMI film released through the Rank Organisation
Released as an A certificate in 1978 in colour and black and white
Running time: 95 mins

PRODUCTION TEAM
Original Screenplay by Tony Church
Archive Material by Talbot Rothwell, Norman Hudis, Sid Colin
and Dave Freeman
Music arranged by Eric Rogers
Director of Photography: Tony Imi
Producer: Peter Rogers
Director: Gerald Thomas

CARRY ON EMMANNUELLE

DETAILS:
Cleves Investments Ltd presents a Peter Rogers Production
A Gerald Thomas film distributed by Hemdale
Song: 'Love Crazy' by Kenny Lynch
Sung by Masterplan
Released as an AA certificate in 1978 in colour
Running time: 88 mins

CAST
Kenneth Williams............................Emile Prevert
Suzanne Danielle ....Emmannuelle Prevert
Kenneth Connor..............................Leyland
Jack Douglas...................................Lyons
Joan Sims..Mrs Dangle
Peter Butterworth ....Richmond
Larry Dann......................................Theodore Valentine
Beryl Reid...Mrs Valentine

Tricia Newby ....Nurse in Surgery
Albert Moses.......................................Doctor
Henry McGee......................................Harold Hump
Howard Nelson....................................Harry Hernia
Claire Davenport ....Blonde in Pub
Tim Brinton ....BBC Newscaster
Corbett Woodall ....ITN Newscaster
Robert Dorning ....Prime Minister
Bruce Boa ....US Ambassador
Eric Barker..Ancient General
Victor Maddern ....Man in Launderette
Norman Mitchell.................................Drunken Husband
Jack Lynn..Admiral of the Fleet
Michael Nightingale ....Police Commissioner
Llewellyn Rees ....Lord Chief Justice
Steve Plytas..Arabian Official
Joan Benham ....Cynical Lady
Marianne Maskell ....Nurse in Hospital
Louise Burton.....................................Girl at Zoo
Dino Shafeek......................................Immigration Officer
David Hart..Customs Officer
Gertan Klauber....................................German Soldier
Malcolm Johns....................................Sentry
John Carlin...French Parson
Guy Ward ....Dandy
James Fagan ....Concorde Steward
John Hallett..Substitute Football Player
Deborah Brayshaw.............................French Buxom Blonde
Suzanna East......................................Colette
Bruce Wyllie ....Football Referee
Philip Clifton.....................................Injured Footballer
Stanley McGeagh.................................Fleet Street Journalist
Bill Hutchinson ....1st Reporter
Neville Ware ....2nd Reporter
Jane Norman ....3rd Reporter
Nick White..Sent-off Footballer

PRODUCTION TEAM
Original Screenplay by Lance Peters
Music composed and conducted by Eric Rogers
Director of Photography: Alan Hume
Producer: Peter Rogers
Director: Gerald Thomas

CARRY ON COLUMBUS

DETAILS:
*Island World presents a Comedy House Production in association with
Peter Rogers Productions*
A Gerald Thomas film distributed by Island World
Released as a PG certificate in 1992 in colour
Running time: 91 mins

CAST
Jim Dale ....Christopher Columbus
Bernard Cribbins ....Mordecai Mendoza
Maureen Lipman ....Countess Esmerelda
Alexei Sayle.............................Achmed
Rik Mayall.............................The Sultan
Sara Crowe ....Fatima
Julian Clary.............................Don Juan Diego
Keith Allen ....Pepi the Poisoner
Leslie Phillips.............................King Ferdinand
Richard Wilson.............................Don Juan Felipe
Rebecca Lacey.............................Chiquita
Jon Pertwee.............................Duke of Costa Brava
June Whitfield ....Queen Isabella
Nigel Planer.............................The Wazir
Larry Miller ....The Chief
Jack Douglas.............................Marco the Cereal Killer
Andrew Bailey.............................Genghis
Burt Kwouk.............................Wang
Philip Herbert.............................Ginger

Tony Slattery	Baba the Messenger
Martin Clunes	Martin
David Boyce	Customer with Ear
Sara Stockbridge	Nina the Model
Holly Aird	Maria
James Faulkner	Torquemada
Don Maclean	Inquisitor with Ham Sandwiches
Dave Freeman, Duncan Duff, Jonathan Tafler, James Pertwee, Toby Dale, Michael Hobbs	Inquisitors
Peter Grant	Cardinal
Su Douglas	Countess Joanna
John Antrobus	Manservant
Lynda Baron	Meg
Allan Corduner	Sam
Nejdet Salih	Fayid
Mark Arden	Mark
Silvestre Tobias	Abdullah
Danny Peacock	Tonto the Torch
Don Henderson	The Bosun
Harold Berens	Cecil the Torturer
Peter Gilmore	Governor of the Canaries
Marc Sinden	Captain Perez
Charles Fleischer	Pontiac
Chris Langham	Hubba
Reed Martin	Poco Hontas
Prudence Solomon	Ha Ha
Peter Gordeno	The Shaman

PRODUCTION TEAM

Screenplay by Dave Freeman
Additional material by John Antrobus
Music composed and directed by John Du Prez
Song 'Carry On Columbus' written and produced by Malcolm McLaren and Lee Gorman
Director of Photography: Alan Hume B.S.C.

248

Executive Producer: Peter Rogers
Producer: John Goldstone
Director: Gerald Thomas

STAGE

CARRY ON LONDON!

DETAILS:
Louis Benjamin presented a Peter Rogers Production.
Previewed at the Birmingham Hippodrome 14 September 1973–29
September 1973. Performed at the Victoria Palace, London, 4 October
1973–March 1975.

CAST
Sidney James
Barbara Windsor
Kenneth Connor
Peter Butterworth
Bernard Bresslaw
Jack Douglas

PRODUCTION TEAM
Written by Talbot Rothwell, Dave Freeman and Eric Merriman
Additional Material by Ian Grant
Orchestra Directed by Richard Holmes
Based on the *Carry On* films as directed by Gerald Thomas
Manager and Stage Director: Alan West
Comedy Director: Bill Roberton

CARRY ON LAUGHING
With 'The Slimming Factory'

DETAILS:
A Don Robinson Production in association with Peter Rogers and Gerald
Thomas. Performed at the Royal Opera House, Scarborough 16 June–
September 1976

CAST
Liz Fraser	Milly
Kenneth Connor	Major Chambers
Beau Daniells	Mrs Babbington
Peter Butterworth	Willie Strokes
Jack Douglas	Alf Hardy
Linda Hooks	Hilde
Barbara Sumner	Alice Pringle
Anne Aston	Candy Maple
Danny O'Dea	Albert Waterman

PRODUCTION TEAM
Written by Sam Cree
Designer: Saxon Lucas
Theatre & General Manager: John Palmer
Company & Stage Manager: Tommy Layton
Director: Bill Roberton

WOT A CARRY ON IN BLACKPOOL

DETAILS:
A Mike Hughes production for Liver Promotions Ltd. Performed on the North Pier, Blackpool, 22 May 1992–25 October 1992.
From an original idea by Associate Producer/Production Manager, Martin Witts.

CAST
Bernard Bresslaw	Leading Man
Barbara Windsor	Leading Lady
Andrew Grainger	Juvenile Lead
Richard Gauntlett	Light Comedy Relief
Jacqueline Dunnley & Natalie Holtom	The Merry Maids
Jonathan Blazer & Julian Essex Spurrier	The Jolly Juveniles

PRODUCTION TEAM
Written by Barry Cryer and Dick Vosburgh
The Orchestra under the direction of Tim Parkin

Directed and Devised by Tudor Davies
Company Stage Manager: James Skeggs
Stage Manager: Sharon Curtis
General Manager: Peter Walters

TELEVISION

CARRY ON CHRISTMAS

DETAILS:
Made at Thames Television
Broadcast: 24 December 1969, 9:15 p.m.
Colour
Duration: 50 mins

CAST
Sidney James..............Ebenezer Scrooge
Terry Scott.................Dr Frank N. Stein / Convent Girl / Mr Barrett
and Baggie the Ugly Sister
Charles Hawtrey........Spirit of Christmas Past / Angel / Convent
Girl and Buttons
Hattie Jacques............Elizabeth Barrett / Nun and Bemused
Passer-by
Barbara Windsor........Cinderella / Fanny and Spirit of Christmas
Present
Bernard Bresslaw........Bob Cratchit / Frankenstein's Monster / Spirit
of Christmas Future / Convent Girl / Town
Crier and Policeman
Peter Butterworth......Dracula / Street Beggar / Convent Girl and
Haggie the other Ugly Sister
Frankie Howerd.........Robert Browning and Fairy Godmother

PRODUCTION TEAM
Written by Talbot Rothwell
Comedy Consultant: Gerald Thomas
Director: Ronnie Baxter
Producer: Peter Eton

By arrangement with Peter Rogers – creator and producer of the *Carry On* series.

CARRY ON AGAIN CHRISTMAS

DETAILS:
Made at Thames Television
Broadcast: 24 December 1970, 9:10 p.m.
Black and White
Duration: 50 mins

CAST
Sidney James...............Long John Silver
Terry Scott.................Squire Treyhornay
Charles Hawtrey........Old Blind Pew / Nightwatchman and Nipper
         the Flipper
Kenneth Connor ....Dr Livershake
Bernard Bresslaw........Rollicky Bill
Bob Todd...................Ben Gunn and Shipmate
Wendy Richard..........Kate
Barbara Windsor........Jim Hawkins

PRODUCTION TEAM
Written by: Sid Colin and Dave Freeman
Comedy Consultant: Gerald Thomas
Producer/Director: Alan Tarrant
By arrangement with Peter Rogers – creator and producer of the *Carry On* series.

CARRY ON CHRISTMAS

DETAILS:
Thames Television Production
Broadcast: 20 December 1972, 8:00 p.m.
Colour
Duration: 50 mins

CAST

Hattie Jacques............Fiona Clodhopper / Miss Harriet / Miss Molly Coddles and the Fairy Godmother

Joan Sims...................Lady Rhoda Cockhorse / Miss Esmerelda / Princess Yo-Yo and Clodhopper's Mother-in-law

Barbara Windsor........Milk Maiden / Eve / Maid / Miss Clodhopper and Aladdin

Kenneth Connor ....Club Chairman / Lieutenant Bangham – Inspector Knicker / General Clodhopper and Hanky Poo

Peter Butterworth ......Captain Alistair Dripping / Sir Francis Fiddler / Admiral Rene and Widow Holinone

Norman Rossington...Valet / Tardy dinner guest and Genie of the Lamp

Jack Douglas..............Mr Firkin / Adam / Ringworm the Butler / Charles Burke and The Demon King

Brian Oulton ....Oriental Orator

Billy Cornelius...........Waiter

Valerie Leon...............Serving Wench

Valerie Stanton ....Demon King's Vision

PRODUCTION TEAM

Written by Talbot Rothwell and Dave Freeman
Director: Ronald Fouracre
Producer: Gerald Thomas
Executive Producer: Peter Rogers
By arrangement with Peter Rogers – creator and producer of the *Carry On* series.

CARRY ON CHRISTMAS

DETAILS:
Thames Television Production
Broadcast: 24 December 1973, 9 p.m.
Colour
Duration: 50 mins

CAST

Sidney James...............Mr Belcher the Store Santa Claus / Seed Pod / Sir Henry / Sgt Ball and Robin Hood

Joan Sims...................Bishop's Wife/Adele/Virginia's Mum / Salvation Army Lady / Traffic Warden / Maid Marian / Ballet Dancer and Senna Pod

Barbara Windsor........Virginia / Crompet the Pit Cavegirl / Fifi / Lady Fanny / Ballet Dancer and Lady Frances of Bristol

Kenneth Connor ....Mr Sibley, the Store Manager / Bishop / Anthro Pod / Private Parkin / Will Scarlet and Ballet Dancer

Peter Butterworth ......Caveman Carol Singer / Ancient Gent / Dart Player / German Soldier / Friar Tuck and Ballet Dancer

Bernard Bresslaw........Bean Podkin the Cave Teenager / Captain Ffing-Burgh / Dart Player / Merry Man / Police Officer and Ballet Dancer

Julian Holloway.........Angle Leader and Captain Rhodes

Laraine Humphrys.....Bed Customer

PRODUCTION TEAM

Written by: Talbot Rothwell
Director: Ronald Fouracre
Producer: Gerald Thomas
Executive Producer: Peter Rogers

WHAT A CARRY ON!

DETAILS:
ATV Network Production
Broadcast: 4 October 1973, 9 p.m.
Colour
Duration: 50 mins
Introduced by Shaw Taylor

CAST
Sidney James
Barbara Windsor
Kenneth Connor
Peter Butterworth
Bernard Bresslaw
Jack Douglas

PRODUCTION TEAM
Director / Producer: Alan Tarrant

CARRY ON LAUGHING

The Prisoner of Spenda

DETAILS:
ATV Network Production
Broadcast: 4 January 1975, 8:45 p.m.
Colour
Duration: 21 mins

CAST
Sid James ....Prince Rupert / Arnold Basket
Barbara Windsor............................Vera Basket
Peter Butterworth ....Count Yerackers
Joan Sims.....................................Madame Olga
Kenneth Connor............................Nickoff
Jack Douglas ....Colonel Yackoff
David Lodge ....Duke Boris
Diane Langton...............................Tzana
Rupert Evans.................................Major
Ronnie Brody................................Waiter

THE BARON OUTLOOK

DETAILS:
ATV Network Production

Broadcast: 11 January 1975, 8:45 p.m.
Colour
Duration: 24 mins

CAST

Sid James ....Baron Hubert
Joan Sims..Lady Isobel
Barbara Windsor...............................Marie
Kenneth Connor...............................Sir William
Peter Butterworth ....Friar Roger
Linda Hooks.....................................Rosie
Diane Langton...................................Griselda
David Lodge.....................................Sir Simon de Montfort
John Carlin.......................................Ethelbert
John Levene......................................Soldier
Brian Osborne ....Gaston
Anthony Trent ....Herald

THE SOBBING CAVALIER

DETAILS:
ATV Network Production
Broadcast: 18 January 1975, 8:45 p.m.
Colour
Duration: 23 mins

CAST

Sid James ....Lovelace
Jack Douglas......................................Sir Jethro Houndsbotham
Barbara Windsor...............................Sarah
Joan Sims..Lady Kate Houndsbotham
Peter Butterworth ....Oliver Cromwell
David Lodge......................................Colonel
Brian Osborne ....Cavalier
Bernard Holley ....Captain

ORGY AND BESS

DETAILS:
ATV Network Production
Broadcast: 25 January 1975, 8:45 p.m.
Colour
Duration: 24 mins

CAST

Sid James...Sir Francis Drake
Hattie Jacques....................................Queen Elizabeth I
Kenneth Connor...............................King Philip
Barbara Windsor...............................Lady Miranda
Jack Douglas......................................Master of the Rolls & Lord
                                                     Essex
Victor Maddern................................Todd
McDonald Hobley............................Quaker Reporter
Simon Callow.....................................1st Crew Member
Brian Osborne...................................2nd Crew Member
John Carlin...Sir Walter Raleigh
Norman Chappell.............................Lord Burleigh

ONE IN THE EYE FOR HAROLD

DETAILS:
ATV Network Production
Broadcast: 1 February 1975, 8:45 p.m.
Colour
Duration: 24 mins

CAST

Jack Douglas......................................Ethelred
Kenneth Connor...............................Athelstan
Joan Sims..Else
Diane Langton....................................Isolde
David Lodge.......................................William the Conqueror
Linda Hooks.......................................Nellie
Norman Chappell.............................King Harold

Patsy Smart	Old Hag
John Carlin	Egbert
Brian Osborne	Herald
Paul Jesson	Messenger
Jerold Wells	Black Cowl
Billy Cornelius	
Nosher Powell	Pikemen

THE NINE OLD COBBLERS

DETAILS:
ATV Network Production
Broadcast: 8 February 1975, 8:45 p.m.
Colour
Duration: 24 mins

CAST

Jack Douglas	Lord Peter Flimsy
Kenneth Connor	Punter
Barbara Windsor	Maisie
Joan Sims	Amelia Forbush
David Lodge	Inspector Bungler
Victor Maddern	Charlie
Patsy Rowlands	Miss Dawkins
John Carlin	Vicar

THE CASE OF THE SCREAMING WINKLES

DETAILS:
ATV Network Production
Broadcast: 2 November 1975, 7:25 p.m.
Colour
Duration: 24 mins

CAST

Jack Douglas	Lord Peter Flimsy
Kenneth Connor	Punter

Joan Sims..Mrs MacFlute
Peter Butterworth ....Admiral Clanger
David Lodge......................................Inspector Bungler
Sherrie Hewson.................................Nurse Millie Teazel
Norman Chappell..............................Potter
Marianne Stone ....Madame Petra
John Carlin.......................................Major Merridick
Melvyn Hayes...................................Charwallah Charlie
Michael Nightingale ....Colonel Postwick

THE CASE OF THE COUGHING PARROT

DETAILS:
ATV Network Production
Broadcast: 23 November 1975, 7:25 p.m.
Colour
Duration: 24 mins

CAST
Jack Douglas ....Lord Peter Flimsy
Kenneth Connor................................Punter
Joan Sims..Dr Janis Crunbitt
David Lodge ....Inspector Bungler
Sherrie Hewson.................................Irma Klein
Peter Butterworth ....Lost Property Attendant
Norman Chappell..............................Ambulance Driver
Brian Osborne ....Harry
Johnny Briggs ....Norman
Vivienne Johnson..............................Freda Filey

UNDER THE ROUND TABLE

DETAILS:
ATV Network Production
Broadcast: 26 October 1975, 7:25 p.m.
Colour
Duration: 25 mins

CAST

Kenneth Connor	King Arthur
Joan Sims	Lady Guinevere
Peter Butterworth	Merlin
Bernard Bresslaw	Sir Pureheart
Jack Douglas	Sir Gay
Oscar James	Black Knight
Victor Maddern	Sir Osis
Norman Chappell	Sir William
Valerie Walsh	Lady Ermintrude
Billy Cornelius	Man-at-Arms
Desmond McNamara	Minstrel
Ronnie Brody	Shortest Knight
Brian Capron	Trumpeter
Brian Osborne	Knight

SHORT KNIGHT, LONG DAZE

DETAILS:
ATV Network Production
Broadcast: 16 November 1975, 7:25 p.m.
Colour
Duration: 25 mins

CAST

Kenneth Connor	King Arthur
Joan Sims	Lady Guinevere
Peter Butterworth	Merlin
Bernard Bresslaw	Sir Lancelot
Jack Douglas	Sir Gay
Susan Skipper	Mabel
Norman Chappell	Sir William
Brian Osborne	Herald – Knight
Desmond McNamara	Minstrel
Billy Cornelius	Man-at-Arms
Brian Capron	Trumpeter

AND IN MY LADY'S CHAMBER

DETAILS:
ATV Network Production
Broadcast: 9 November 1975, 7:25 p.m.
Colour
Duration: 25 mins

CAST
Kenneth Connor.........................Sir Harry Bulger-Plunger
Barbara Windsor.........................Baroness Lottie Von Titsenhausen
Jack Douglas..............................Clodson
Joan Sims....................................Mrs Breeches
Peter Butterworth.......................Silas
Bernard Bresslaw........................Starkers
Sherrie Hewson...........................Virginia
Andrew Ray.................................Willie
Carol Hawkins.............................Lilly
Vivienne Johnson........................Teeny

WHO NEEDS KITCHENER?

DETAILS:
ATV Network Production
Broadcast: 30 November 1975, 7:25 p.m.
Colour
Duration: 25 mins

CAST
Kenneth Connor.........................Sir Harry Bulger-Plunger
Barbara Windsor.........................Baroness Lottie Von Titsenhausen
Jack Douglas..............................Clodson
Joan Sims....................................Mrs Breeches
Bernard Bresslaw........................Klanger
Andrew Ray.................................Willie
Sherrie Hewson...........................Virginia
Carol Hawkins.............................Lilly
Vivienne Johnson........................Teeny
Brian Osborne.............................Newsboy

LAMP-POSTS OF THE EMPIRE

DETAILS:
ATV Network Production
Broadcast: 7 December 1975, 7:25 p.m.
Colour
Duration: 24 mins

CAST
Barbara Windsor...............................Lady Mary Airey-Fairey
Kenneth Connor...............................Stanley
Jack Douglas.....................................Dick Darcy
Bernard Bresslaw..............................Dr Pavingstone
Peter Butterworth ....Lord Gropefinger
Oscar James ....Witchdoctor
Reuben Martin ....Mabel the Gorilla
Wayne Browne..................................Native
Norman Chappell.............................Businessman
John Carlin.......................................Old Man
Michael Nightingale ....Neighbour

PRODUCTION TEAM FOR LAUGHING

Writers:
Dave Freeman (episodes 1–3, 6–8); Barry Cryer and Dick Vosburgh (4); Lew Schwarz (5, 9–13)

Music:
John Marshall and Richie Tattersall, except 9–11 by John Marshall, Richie Tattersall and Max Harris

Executive Producer:
Peter Rogers

Producer:
Gerald Thomas

Director:
Alan Tarrant

During the filming of *Henry* in 1970, scriptwriter Talbot Rothwell became the subject of *This Is Your Life*.

Sidney and Sophie Bliss's wedding day turned into a farce in *Loving*.

Sid James getting a little soaking, all in the line of duty.

Sid James became the linchpin for many of the *Carry On* films.

Sid James (Henry VIII) and Barbara Windsor (Bettina) stroll through the gardens at Pinewood while filming *Henry*.

Madame Desiree (Joan Sims) and her girls, 'The Birds of Paradise', alongside Dick Turpin (Sid James) in *Dick*.

Despite the chilly conditions, Bernard Bresslaw donned shorts, ready for filming a scene in *Carry On Behind*.

ofessor Vooshka's
ving left a lot to
desired in *Behind*.
ft to right:
e Sommer,
nald Hewlett and
nneth Williams).

nmer, Hewlett
l Williams are
ed by director

Preparing for the next scene
at the fictitious Riverside
Caravan Site, Bernard Bressla
checks his lines (*Behind*).

Jack Douglas, David Lodge a
Windsor Davies receive so
last minute direction fr
Gerald Thomas (*Behir*

ying Emmannuelle Prevert was one
Suzanne Danielle's first acting jobs
nmannuelle).

CARRY ON LAUGHING'S CHRISTMAS CLASSICS

DETAILS:
Introduced by: Kenneth Williams and Barbara Windsor
Thames Television Production
Broadcast: 22 December 1983, 7:30 p.m.
Colour
Duration: 24 mins

PRODUCTION TEAM
Created by Peter Rogers and Gerald Thomas
Original Material by Talbot Rothwell and Dave Freeman
Music by Eric Rogers
Director: David Clark
Producer: Gerald Thomas

iii)

Introduction to *Carry On Down Under* Script

In the late 1980s writer Vince Powell was commissioned to pen the following script. When an Australian businessman expressed interest in making a new *Carry On* film, director Gerald Thomas travelled to Australia to begin the process of sourcing viable locations. Powell, who also happened to be there on business, grabbed the opportunity to meet the financier behind the proposed film. On the strength of the meetings he began working on the script in earnest, but before he'd typed the final snatches of dialogue news filtered through that the finance hadn't materialised and the project was ditched. The following pages reveal how the film would have shaped up.

Carry on Down Under

A screenplay written by Vince Powell

1. OPENING TITLES
2. EXTERIOR. MAIN STREET. OLD SYDNEY TOWN. DAY
SUPER CAPTION
PROLOGUE.

SYDNEY – THE TURN OF THE CENTURY.
WHEN MEN WERE BOLD AND WOMEN WERE
GRATEFUL.
Underneath the captions we can see a horse and rider in the distance, galloping towards camera. It is CHARLEY GAY, a grizzled old prospector. He pulls his horse to a halt outside the SYDNEY TAVERN, leaps off, pulls out a pistol and fires several shots in the air.

CHARLEY (*Excitedly*): Yippee.

3. INTERIOR. SYDNEY TAVERN
A BARMAN is polishing glasses behind the bar.
At a table, a couple of SHEEP-HERDERS are playing cards.
ANNABELLE, a voluptuous and blowsy lady of easy virtue, is leaning against the bar. CHARLEY enters.

CHARLEY: I've done it. I've done it. After all these years, I've done it.
BARMAN: At your age you should be ashamed of yourself.

CHARLEY notices ANNABELLE and leers at her.

CHARLEY: Grrr.
ANNABELLE: Are you all right?
CHARLEY: I've been out in the bush for years. I've forgotten what a woman looks like. How about a kiss and a cuddle?

ANNABELLE: You must be joking. I wouldn't let you touch me with a boomerang.

CHARLEY: Don't be like that. (*To the barman*) A drink for the lady.

BARMAN: Lady?

CHARLEY: Yes.

BARMAN: You *have* been out in the bush for a long time.

ANNABELLE: Cheeky.

CHARLEY (*To the barman*): Come on, cobber – a drink, I said.

BARMAN: Let's see the colour of your money first.

CHARLEY (*Taking a handful of opals and putting them on the bar*): Will these do?

ANNABELLE (*Picking one up*): Opals.

CHARLEY: That's right. And there's plenty more where those came from. Old Charley Gay's struck it rich.

ANNABELLE (*Suddenly affectionate*): Oh you lovely man. (*Taking his arm*) Let's go into my private room. It's much more cosy in there.

CHARLEY: A minute ago you said you wouldn't touch me with a boomerang.

ANNABELLE (*Wickedly*): Who's talking about boomerangs. Come on, gorgeous.

ANNABELLE drags the not unwilling CHARLEY off through the curtained alcove. Almost immediately a pair of boots come hurtling out, followed in rapid succession by trousers, shirt, a dress and a pair of bloomers, all this to the accompaniment of cries of delight and ecstasy from CHARLEY and ANNABELLE. We hear the noise of bed springs, a loud wailful groan from CHARLEY, then silence. The BARMAN and the SHEEP-HERDERS look at each other. ANNABELLE emerges, wearing only a scarlet bodice and a suspender belt.

ANNABELLE: He's snuffed it.

BARMAN (*Crossing himself*): What a lovely way to go!

DISSOLVE TO.

4. ESTABLISHING SHOT OF MODERN SYDNEY SHOWING THE HARBOUR BRIDGE AND THE OPERA HOUSE

SUPER CAPTION
SYDNEY THE PRESENT

CUT TO.
5. CAPTION ON DOOR READING
BURKE, BURKE, BURKE AND BURKE, SOLICITORS.

MIX THROUGH TO.
6. INTERIOR. SOLICITOR'S OFFICE (SYDNEY). DAY
BURKE, an elderly solicitor, is sitting at his desk. His SECRETARY,
SANDRA, a young busty girl, enters, her arms full of files and
papers.

SANDRA: Excuse me, Mr Burke, shall I drop them here?
BURKE (*Lecherously*): Yes, please – but lock the door first!
SANDRA: I mean the files.
BURKE: Oh, I see. Yes, yes. Put them on the desk.
SANDRA (*Putting the files etc. on the desk. In doing so she leans forward,
displaying her cleavage*): Did you want me to take anything down
before I go?
BURKE (*Eagerly*): Yes, please, but lock the door first!
SANDRA (*Sighing*): Dictation! Mr Burke.
BURKE (*Disappointed*): Oh you're a lovely girl, Mavis.
SANDRA: It's Sandra.
BURKE: What is?
SANDRA: My name.
BURKE: They don't last long here, you know.
SANDRA: I'm not surprised. (*She bends over again and rummages
among the letters*) Oh, by the way, there's a couple of things I'd
like you to see.
BURKE (*Staring down at her ample bosom*): Yes, I can see them!
SANDRA (*Still searching*): I had them in my hand a minute ago.
BURKE: How delightful.
SANDRA (*Picking up the envelope*): There they are.
BURKE (*Looking at them and reading*): Charley Gay. Personal
effects. Last Will and Testament. Good grief. Where did you
find these?

271

SANDRA: In the stock cupboard. They'd fallen behind the shelves.

BURKE (*Opening one envelope*): They must have been lying there for years. (*Taking out a paper and reading*) Last Will and Testament of Charley Gay.

SANDRA: Do you think he's dead?

BURKE: Well, if he isn't he's nearly two hundred years old.

(*Reading*) All my worldly goods . . . including my opal mine to my only son Bernard or his descendants last heard of living in London, England.

MIX THROUGH TO.

7. ESTABLISHING SHOT OF LONDON, SHOWING THE HOUSES OF PARLIAMENT AND BIG BEN

CUT TO.

8. EXTERIOR STREET (AUSTRALIA FOR ENGLAND) DAY

A flower stall stands by the kerb. The wall behind is covered in hoardings. A telephone box can be seen, in which MILES GAY is speaking on the phone. CYNTHIA SMALLPIECE is standing by the flower stall.

CYNTHIA (Calling): Fresh daffs – 40p a bunch. Lovely lupins.

CYNTHIA bends down to adjust some flowers in a pot on the pavement. A middle-aged man enters frame.

MAN: Excuse me.

CYNTHIA (*Straightening up*): Yes, sir.

MAN: I've just been admiring your bloomers.

CYNTHIA: I beg your pardon!

MAN: The flowers.

CYNTHIA: Oh, I see. How silly of me. What can I get you?

MAN: A dozen red roses. For the wife.

CYNTHIA: Long or short?

MAN: Well about five foot two.

CYNTHIA (*Puzzled*): Five feet two?

MAN: In her stockinged feet.

CYNTHIA: Not the wife – the roses, sir – long or short stem?

MAN: Oh – long, please.

CYNTHIA (*Picking up two bunches of roses*): How's that?

MAN: Very nice.

CYNTHIA (*Wrapping them in a newspaper*): That will be just five pounds.

MAN (*Paying*): Can I put a card in?

CYNTHIA: Certainly. (*The man hands her a card. CYNTHIA reads it*) 'To Betty – Thank you for the happiest day of my life.' Oh. How romantic. Is it her birthday?

MAN: No.

CYNTHIA: A wedding anniversary?

MAN: No.

CYNTHIA: Well, what *is* the special occasion?

MAN (*Picking up the flowers*): It's her funeral!

The MAN leaves frame.

CYNTHIA (*Calling after him*): Male chauvinist pig!

GLADYS, an elderly LADY, enters frame. She is carrying a bundle of newspapers.

GLADYS: 'Ere you are, Cynthia dear. A few old papers.

CYNTHIA: Thank you, Gladys.

GLADYS: Where's lover boy?

CYNTHIA (*Indicating the phone box*): Miles is in the office.

ANOTHER ANGLE
MCU OF PHONE BOX.
MILES hangs up the receiver and steps out. He sticks a notice on the door of the phone box reading 'OUT OF ORDER' and moves across to the flower stall. GLADYS has now gone.

MILES (*Petulantly*): I'm fed up.

CYNTHIA: What's the matter, my pet?

MILES: You want to try being stuck in that phone box for half an hour. Especially after that cat's been in it. Why can't we sell this stall and buy a proper flower shop?

CYNTHIA: Darling, of course we can buy a little shop.

MILES: When?

CYNTHIA: Just as soon as you agree to marry me.

MILES (*Fussing with the flowers*): Don't start all that again. I've told you before. I don't like rushing into things.

CYNTHIA: We've been engaged for fifteen years. What are you trying to do – get in the Guinness Book of Records?

MILES: I'm not ready for marriage, Cynthia. It's the physical side I don't like.

CYNTHIA: Are you worried about it?

MILES: Worried about it? I'm terrified of it! All that thrashing about between the sheets. It's most unhygienic.

CYNTHIA: Oh, Miles – let's not wait any longer. I want to snuggle up to you in bed and mother you.

MILES: I don't know about 'mother me'. You'd very likely smother me.

CYNTHIA: I want you, Miles. I need you. Put your arms around me.

MILES: I don't think they'd reach.

CYNTHIA: Stop playing hard to get. (*Advancing*) Give me a kiss.

MILES (*Retreating*): Please, Cynthia – control yourself.

CYNTHIA (*Pressing MILES up against the stall*): I can't help it. You bring out the beast in me.

MILES: Stop it – you're crushing my hollyhocks.

CYNTHIA (*Crossly*): Oh, I don't know why I bother with you.

MILES: I'm sorry, Cynthia, I can't help it. It's something to do with my birth sign. I'm on the cusp.

CYNTHIA: There are times I think you might be on the turn.

MILES (*Picking up a watering can*): Cheeky.

MILES starts to water the flowers. CYNTHIA picks up a newspaper and glances through it. Suddenly she reacts.

CYNTHIA: Miles.

MILES turns sharply, still holding the watering can at an angle, and waters CYNTHIA'S bosom.

MILES (*Taking out a handkerchief*): I'm sorry – let me dry you off.

CYNTHIA (*As MILES dabs her bosom*): Yes, please.

MILES (*Handing her the hanky*): On second thoughts, do it yourself.

CYNTHIA: Oh, never mind. Didn't you tell me you had a great-great-grandfather who emigrated to Australia?

MILES: Well, he didn't exactly emigrate. He was deported.

CYNTHIA: Deported?

MILES: Yes. Old Charley was deported for something he didn't do.

CYNTHIA: What didn't he do?

MILES: He didn't run fast enough!

CYNTHIA: You mean he was a criminal?

MILES: He was the first man in England to open up a bank.

CYNTHIA: What was wrong with that?

MILES: He didn't own it!

CYNTHIA: Well, he's in the paper – look.

(*Reading*) 'Will any descendants of Charley Gay, late of Australia, please communicate with Messrs. Neil and Vickers Solicitors of Chancery Lane, where they may hear something to their advantage.'

MILES (*Excitedly*): Something to their advantage? Oh, I wonder what that means?

CYNTHIA: He could have left you a fortune.

MILES: We'd better get round to those solicitors now.

CYNTHIA: What about your brother Brian, the black sheep of the family?

MILES: He won't read it. The only paper he reads is the *Racing Times*. Anyway, I haven't heard from him in years. He's probably in prison by now.

CUT TO.

9. EXTERIOR. STREET. (AUSTRALIA FOR LONDON) DAY
BRIAN REDFORD is standing on the kerb. He is holding a white stick in one hand and a tin mug in the other. He is wearing dark glasses and around his neck hangs a sign proclaiming. 'Blinded with wife and six children'.

BRIAN (*Rattling his mug*): Spare a copper.

(*A man passes and drops a coin in*)
God bless you – whoever you are.

RITA COLLINS enters frame, waving a newspaper.

RITA: Quick – look at this paper.
BRIAN (*Dolefully*): I only wish I could, lady.
RITA: It's me, Brian – Rita.

BRIAN raises his glasses and peers at her.

BRIAN: What are you trying to do – get me arrested for false repre-
    sentation?
RITA (*Thrusting the paper at him*): Just read this.

BRIAN (*Reading*): Soho rapist strikes again. (*To Rita*) It wasn't me,
    Rita. I swear it.
RITA: Not that – there – in the Personal Column.
BRIAN (*Reading*): 'Will any descendants . . . Charley Gay . . .
    communicate . . . Neil & Vickers . . . something to their advan-
    tage.' (*To RITA*) Well, what are we waiting for?

BRIAN moves to where another MAN is standing – also with a
tin mug and a sign proclaiming, 'Deaf and dumb since birth'.

BRIAN (*Handing him the tin mug, white stick and notice*): Look after
    these, Harry, till I get back.
MAN: OK, Brian.

CUT TO.
10. CAPTION ON DOOR READING
NEIL & VICKERS, SOLICITORS.

MIX THROUGH TO.
11. INTERIOR OUTER OFFICE. (AUSTRALIA FOR
LONDON) DAY
A small office with a secretary's desk and a couple of chairs. There

is a door (L) and a door (R) leading to two other offices. MILES
and CYNTHIA enter from the corridor.

MILES (*Calling*): Hello – anybody in?

CUT TO.
12. INTERIOR. SOLICITOR'S OFFICE (AUSTRALIA FOR
ENGLAND) DAY
VICKERS – a neat, precise fussy little man – is sitting at his desk,
speaking on the telephone.

VICKERS (*Into phone*): I'm sorry, Mrs Fortescue, but the fact that
your husband has the unfortunate habit of breaking wind is not
grounds for divorce . . . Yes, I realise it must be distressing for you,
but there's nothing I can do. Try a doctor. (*He puts the phone down
and sighs. There is a knock at the door.*)
Come in.

MILES and CYNTHIA enter.

MILES: Excuse me. Are you Veal or Knickers?
VICKERS: I beg your pardon?
MILES: Sorry – Neil or Vickers. Do forgive me. I'm all of a
 dither.
VICKERS: I'm Mr Vickers. What can I do for you, Mr Dither?
MILES (*Confused*): Mr Dither? Who's Mr Dither?
VICKERS: You just said you were Oliver Dither.
MILES: All of a dither. (*To CYNTHIA*) The man's a fool.
VICKERS: Shall we start again from where you came in?
MILES: Very well. I'm Gay.
VICKERS: Don't worry, sir, none of us are perfect.
CYNTHA: His name is Gay. Miles Gay.
VICKERS: Ah. And you are . . . ?
CYNTHIA: Cynthia Smallpiece.
VICKERS: Quite so. Do sit down.

MILES and CYNTHIA sit down.

MILES: We've come to . . .

VICKERS: Don't tell me. Let me guess. (*To MILES*) *You* wish to get divorced. (*To CYNTHIA*) And *you're* here to provide grounds for adultery.

CYNTHIA: No – but it's a wonderful idea.

VICKERS (*Hopefully*): You haven't murdered anyone, have you?

MILES (*Meaningfully*): Not yet.

VICKERS (*Sadly*): Pity – I've never handled a murder case before.

CYNTHIA (*Waving the paper at Vickers*): We've come about the notice in the paper.

VICKERS (*Reading*): 'Soho rapist strikes again'. (*Happily*) Now, don't worry sir – I'm sure I can get you off. We'll plead provocation. But you must tell me all about it.

(*Lecherously*) I want *all* the details.

MILES (*Exasperated*): Now listen here, you silly old solicitor. I'm not a rapist and if I was I certainly wouldn't have you to defend me. I'd probably get life.

(*Showing him the paper again*)

I've come about this – there – look.

VICKERS (*Peering at the paper*): Ah yes – that little matter out in the Antipodes. I take it you're a descendant?

MILES: Yes, he was my great-great-grandfather.

CYNTHIA (*Anxiously*): How much has he left?

VICKERS: Not so fast, Miss Largepiece.

CYNTHIA: Smallpiece.

VICKERS: Quite so. (*To MILES*) I must have some proof of your identity, sir. Birth certificate, driver's licence . . . something like that.

MILES: Will a final demand from the Gas Board do?

VICKERS: I'm afraid not.

CYNTHIA (*Rummaging in her handbag and producing a passport*): What about a passport?

VICKERS (*Taking it*): Admirable.

CYNTHIA: Now, how much has he left?

VICKERS: It would appear that the late Charley Gay has left a fortune in opals.

MILES (*Excitedly*): Did you hear that, Cynthia – a fortune in opals? I'm rich, I'm rich. Now I can buy my own flower shop.

CYNTHIA (*Happily*): Very well – be like that then.

MILES (*To VICKERS*): When do I get this fortune?

VICKERS: The full details will be disclosed to you as soon as you arrive.

MILES: Arrive where?

VICKERS: Sydney – Australia.

MILES: Australia? How can I get to Australia?

VICKERS: I understand there are flying machines that undertake such hazardous journeys.

MILES: But I haven't got any money.

(*To CYNTHIA*) Cynthia. (*Suddenly turning on the charm*) Cynthia, my beloved.

CYNTHIA: Oh, it's 'my beloved' now is it?

MILES: I'll pay you back.

CYNTHIA: Tell me you love me.

MILES: I can't. (*Indicating VICKERS*) Not in front of him.

CYNTHIA (*Shrugging*): Please yourself.

MILES: All right – I do.

CYNTHIA: Say it.

MILES (*Muttering*): I love you.

CYNTHIA: I can't hear you.

MILES (*Shouting*): I love you.

CYNTHIA (*Sighing*): Oh, Miles, this is so sudden.

CUT TO.

13. INTERIOR OUTER OFFICE. (AUSTRALIA FOR ENGLAND) DAY

A pretty young SECRETARY is now sitting at the desk. BRIAN and RITA enter.

SECRETARY: Can I do anything for you?

BRIAN (*Winking*): You could do a lot for me, darling.

RITA (*Sharply*): Brian!

BRIAN: Only joking, Rita. (*Showing the paper to the SECRETARY*) We've called about this notice in the paper.

SECRETARY: Ah yes. Just one moment. (*She picks up an internal phone*) Excuse me, Mr Neil, there are two people here about the late Charley Gay . . . Very well.

(*To BRIAN*) Mr Neil will see you now. (*Indicating the other office door*) In there.

BRIAN: Thank you. (*Moves, then stops*) By the way, has anyone else been in about this matter?

SECRETARY: No, sir. You're the only claimant up to now.

BRIAN (*Gleefully*): Good – let's hope it stays that way.

BRIAN and RITA exit into the other office. MILES and CYNTHIA emerge from VICKERS's office accompanied by VICKERS.

VICKERS: Have a good trip.

MILES: Thank you.

VICKERS: Oh, there's just one more thing.

CYNTHIA: Yes?

VICKERS: The inheritance must be claimed in Australia within thirty days of the notice appearing in the paper.

CYNTHIA: When did it first appear?

VICKERS: Twenty-eight days ago!

CUT TO.

14. EXTERIOR PUB. (AUSTRALIA FOR ENGLAND) DAY

MILES is sitting at a table sipping a beer. CYNTHIA enters and flops down next to him.

CYNTHIA (*Calling waiter*): Gin and tonic and another beer, please. Well, that's everything done – visas, air tickets the lot. (*Showing him the air tickets*) We leave on the first flight in the morning. That will get us there in time to claim your inheritance before the deadline. (*Suddenly reacting*) Oh, oh.

MILES: What is it?

CYNTHIA: We've been spotted.

MILES: It's those starlings again. Dirty little things.

CYNTHIA: No, no – your brother Brian's just come in. He's seen us. He's coming over here.

MILES: For goodness sake, don't say a word about Australia.

BRIAN enters frame.

BRIAN (*Slapping MILES on the back*): Well, well – if it isn't my favourite brother. What a small world.

CYNTHIA: Too small.

BRIAN (*To CYNTHIA*): And how's the Incredible Hulk? Has Miles made an honest woman of you yet?

CYNTHIA: No, but he's going to very soon. When we get back.

BRIAN: Back from where?

MILES (*Hastily*): From where we're going.

CYNTHIA: We're having a little holiday.

BRIAN: Where?

MILES: Brighton.

CYNTHIA: Bournemouth.

MILES (*Hastily*): We're going to Brighton first, then we're going to Bournemouth.

ANOTHER ANGLE

RITA enters, looks round and spots BRIAN.

RITA (*Moving across*): Brian – I've managed to scrape up enough money for our tickets.

BRIAN (*Signalling frantically*): Rita – this is my brother, Miles.

RITA (*Flustered*): Oh – I don't believe I've had the pleasure before.

MILES: Well you should know, duckie.

BRIAN (*Introducing CYNTHIA*): This is Cynthia, Miles's fiancée.

RITA: That's nice. Brian and I are engaged. (*Holding out her left hand*) Look.

CYNTHIA (*Dryly*): I didn't know Woolworth's sold engagement rings.

MILES: What was all that about a ticket?

BRIAN: Ah yes – well, it's for a football match. Isn't that right, Rita?

RITA: Yes.

CYNTHIA (*Suspiciously*): Who are you going to see?

BRIAN: Arsenal.

RITA: Spurs.

BRIAN (*Hastily*): They're playing each other. Arsenal and Spurs.

The WAITER enters with the drinks.

WAITER: One gin and tonic – one pint of bitter.

BRIAN (*Taking the gin and tonic*): Thank you, very much.

CYNTHIA: Those are *our* drinks.

BRIAN: I'm sure Miles wouldn't begrudge his own brother a glass of beer.

CYNTHIA: Yes, he would.

MILES: It's all right, Cynthia. (*Picking up the beer*) If Brian wants a beer he can have a beer.

MILES pours the pint of beer over BRIAN'S head.

CUT TO.

15. STOCK FOOTAGE OF LONDON HEATHROW AIRPORT MIX THROUGH TO.

16. STOCK FOOTAGE OF QANTAS 747 JET STANDING AT GATE

ANNOUNCER (*voice over*)

This is the third and final call for passengers on Qantas flight QF1 for Sydney. Please proceed to gate twenty-four.

MIX THROUGH TO.

17. INTERIOR. QANTAS 747 BOARDING AREA. DAY

A uniformed AIR HOSTESS is at the doorway. MILES and CYNTHIA enter, carrying hand baggage.

AIR HOSTESS: Good morning.

MILES: You're a woman.

AIR HOSTESS: Yes, sir.

MILES: I didn't think they had lady drivers.

CYNTHIA: She's not the pilot. She's a hostess.

(*To the AIR HOSTESS*) You'll have to forgive him. He's never flown before.

AIR HOSTESS: I'm sure you'll enjoy it, sir.

MILES (*Anxiously*): Have we got a good pilot? Only I wouldn't like to have a learner driver.

AIR HOSTESS: Captain Roberts is one of our most experienced pilots. He'll be with us as far as Bombay.

MILES (*Alarmed*): Bombay? What are we supposed to do the rest of the way – take it in turns to fly it ourselves?

AIR HOSTESS: We change crews, sir.

CYNTHIA: Do stop worrying, Miles. Travelling by plane is safer than crossing the road.

MILES: I hope so. I've been knocked down twice.

AIR HOSTESS: If you'll follow me, I'll show you to your seats.

MILES and CYNTHIA follow the AIR HOSTESS down the aisle, with MILES bringing up the rear.

MILES: It's big, isn't it?

The AIR HOSTESS stops, CYNTHIA stops. MILES who has been looking round, cannons into CYNTHIA.

CYNTHIA: Do you mind?

MILES: Sorry, Cynthia?

AIR HOSTESS (*Indicating two seats in the centre*): Here you are.

MILES: Can we go a bit further back?

AIR HOSTESS: If you wish.

They all proceed a few rows further along.

AIR HOSTESS: Is this better?

MILES: I'd rather go a bit further back if you don't mind.

CYNTHIA: What on earth for?

MILES: In case we crash.

CYNTHIA: Don't be stupid. It's no safer at the back than at the front.

MILES: Yes, it is. Have you ever heard of a plane backing into a mountain?

CYNTHIA (*To AIR HOSTESS*): We'll sit here, thank you.

AIR HOSTESS: Very well. (*To MILES*) You can put your things in the overhead locker.

The AIR HOSTESS leaves frame.
CYNTHIA takes the second seat in from the aisle. MILES reaches up to an overhead locker just behind their seat and opens it. A duty-free bag and a jacket fall out onto a MAN sitting behind CYNTHIA.

MILES: Do forgive me. I'm terribly sorry.
MAN (*In obvious Australian accent*): That's all right, mate. No harm done.
MILES (*Handing him the articles*): Oh – what an unusual accent.
MAN (*Rising*): Yeah. I'm from . . .
MILES (*Putting his own things in another locker*): Don't tell me. Let me guess. I'm very good with accents. Birmingham.
MAN (*Putting his things back*): No.
MILES: Well, give us clue.
MAN: I'm from a beautiful city on the harbour.
MILES: Got it. Southampton.
CYNTHIA (*Turning*): He's from Australia.
MILES: You're not, are you?
MAN: Too true.
MILES: Well, cobber, my old sport, it's real beaut to meet a fair dinkum bruce like you. Good on you, mate.
MAN: Are you trying to be funny?
MILES: I'm speaking to you in your native tongue.
MAN: I've got news for you. We don't speak like that in Australia.
MILES: Of course you do. I used to listen to the *Flying Doctor*. 'Flying doctor to Wagga Wagga. Come in, sport'.
MAN: Aw, nick off, you Pommie poofter.
MILES: Charming.
CYNTHIA: Come and sit down, Miles.
MILES: Oh, very well.
MILES sits on the aisle seat. The AIR HOSTESS enters frame down the next aisle and stops at the two empty seats next to MILES and CYNTHIA.

AIR HOSTESS (*Calling*): This way please.

BRIAN enters frame as the AIR HOSTESS exits.

He stares at MILES and CYNTHIA.

BRIAN: What are you doing here?

MILES: Never mind that. What are *you* doing here?

BRIAN: The same as you. Going to Sydney to claim my inheritance.

MILES: It's mine.

CYNTHIA: Don't start arguing. There'll be enough for the three of us.

BRIAN: Three of us?

CYNTHIA: Yes. When Miles and I are married I'll be one of the family.

BRIAN: In that case there'd better be enough for four of us.

MILES: Pardon?

BRIAN: Rita's with me.

MILES: How did you manage to get enough money for two fares?

BRIAN: I didn't. Rita's travelling half fare.

18. INTERIOR QANTAS 747. BOARDING AREA

RITA enters. She is dressed as a schoolgirl. Black gym slip, and pigtails. We follow her down to where BRIAN is standing.

CYNTHIA (*Reacting*): Good heavens.

RITA: Oh, this *is* a nice surprise.

CYNTHIA: You look positively grotesque.

RITA: It's very uncomfortable. I can't wait to get out of this gym slip.

MILES: From the look of it, you're halfway out of it already.

BRIAN (*Sitting next to CYNTHIA*): I must say, Rita, you look very sexy. If they'd had girls like you at school I'd never have left.

MILES: You didn't have much choice – you were expelled.

BRIAN: It was victimisation. All I did was call Specky Williams a big four-eyed perve.

RITA (*Sitting next to BRIAN*): It doesn't seem fair to expel you for that.

MILES: He was the headmaster.

BRIAN: Rita . . .

RITA: Yes, Brian?

BRIAN: Can you help me get it in?

RITA: Not on the plane, Brian.

BRIAN: I'm talking about my seat belt. She's got a one-track mind – I'm happy to say.

(*Fiddling with the seat belt*) It's all right – I've done it.

The AIR HOSTESS passes.

RITA: Excuse me, could I have a vodka and tonic, please?

AIR HOSTESS: At your age?

BRIAN (*Hastily*): She was ordering it for me.

AIR HOSTESS: The bar will be open as soon as we take off.

The AIR HOSTESS leaves frame.

BRIAN: Well, this is cosy, isn't it?

MILES (*Dully*): Wonderful!

CYNTHIA (*Equally dully*): Fantastic!

RITA: Cheer up – it may never happen.

MILES: Too late. It already has.

RITA: You don't like your brother much, do you?

MILES: No. He used to bully me when I was young. I remember one day he jumped off a ladder right on to me new sailor hat.

RITA (*To BRIAN*): That was naughty of you, Brian.

MILES: I wouldn't have minded, but I was wearing it at the time.

CYNTHIA (*To RITA*): How long have you known Brian?

RITA: We met last year on holiday.

BRIAN: She was a topless waitress.

MILES: You mean you waited on men with nothing on?

RITA: Oh no. All the men were dressed – I just wore black leather tights.

CYNTHIA: How disgusting. Didn't you feel degraded?

RITA: I didn't feel anything – but the customers tried to, including Brian.

MILES: Dirty beast.

BRIAN: I told you, Rita – I thought you were offering me a couple of melons. I was only squeezing them to see if they were ripe.

CYNTHIA: Men are like animals – obsessed by sex.

MILES: Steady on, Cynthia. I'm not like that.
BRIAN: She was talking about men.

GRAMS. Noise of engine starting up.
MILES reacts and clutches CYNTHIA.

MILES: What was that?
CYNTHIA: Calm down, Miles – it's only the engines.
RITA: We're moving.
MILES: I feel sick. (*He tries to rise – can't*) Help – help – Miss.

The AIR HOSTESS enters frame.

AIR HOSTESS: What is it, sir?
MILES: My legs have gone numb. I'm paralysed. I can't stand.
AIR HOSTESS: You've got your seat belt fastened.
MILES (*Relieved*): Thank goodness. Where's my parachute?
AIR HOSTESS: We don't have parachutes.
MILES: No parachutes? I knew we should have flown British Airways.
AIR HOSTESS: There's a life jacket under your seat, sir.
MILES: A life jacket? That's no use. What are we supposed to do if we have to bail out at forty thousand feet? Blow it up and hope that it will break our fall? I'm getting off.
CYNTHIA (*Crossly*): Oh for goodness' sake, shut up. We're taking off now. There's nothing to be frightened about.

MILES (*Alarmed*): Oh – he doesn't seem to be going very fast.

CUT TO.
19. STOCK FOOTAGE OF QANTAS 747 TAKING OFF

MILES (VO): He'll never get us up at this speed. We're going to crash.

We see the 747 rise off the ground.

CUT TO
20. INTERIOR QANTAS 747. DAY

MILES (*Happily*): We're up – we're up. Nothing to it, really. I don't know why people are afraid of flying.

MILES smiles weakly and passes out.
21. STOCK FOOTAGE OF 747 IN FLIGHT MIX THROUGH TO.

22. INTERIOR QANTAS 747. DAY
CYNTHIA, BRIAN and RITA are all asleep. RITA has changed into more normal attire. BRIAN has a scowl on his face. He is dreaming. He starts to mutter and groan. He wriggles about in his seat and puts his hand on CYNTHIA'S bosom. CYNTHIA opens her eyes and screams. RITA and BRIAN both awake.

CYNTHIA (*to BRIAN*): You filthy swine.
RITA: What's the matter?
CYNTHIA: He had his hand on my ... (*Putting her hand on her bosom*) Here.
RITA (*Accusingly*): Brian!
BRIAN: I was asleep.
RITA (*to CYNTHIA*): He must have been dreaming.
BRIAN: If I had my hand there it must have been a nightmare.
CYNTHIA: Don't be so rude.
BRIAN: It *was* a nightmare. It's all coming back to me. It was horrible.
    I dreamt I was in a harem, surrounded by hundreds of naked women.
RITA: What's so horrible about that?
BRIAN: I was a eunuch!
CYNTHIA: Serves you right. (*Looking round*) Where's Miles?
BRIAN: He went to shake hands with the unemployed.
CYNTHIA (*Blankly*): Pardon?
RITA: He went to spend a penny.
CYNTHIA: That was ages ago. I hope he hasn't flushed himself away.

CUT TO.
23. INT. QANTAS 747 GALLEY AREA. DAY
A STEWARD is making coffee. MILES enters frame. He has a pained expression on his face.

MILES (*Groaning*): Oh . . .

STEWARD: Something the matter, sir?

MILES: Those loo seats are very painful.

STEWARD: We've never had any complaints before.

MILES: You probably haven't had anyone who fell asleep for an hour in there before. I've got pins and needles in the most peculiar places.

STEWARD: How do you fancy something long and cool?

MILES (*Raising his eyebrows*): That sounds divine.

STEWARD (*Warily*): I was referring to a drink.

MILES: I should jolly well hope you were.

STEWARD: Well, you never know. There's a lot of it about.

MILES: Well, I assure you, there's none of it about *here*.

STEWARD: Champagne and orange juice OK?

MILES: Yes, please. I'll just have a little walkabout first to get some feeling back into my legs.

As MILES moves off in the direction of the First Class section, a SENIOR STEWARD enters. He is carrying a plastic bag of ice cubes.

SENIOR STEWARD (*to STEWARD*): Here's the ice you wanted.

STEWARD: Thanks. How are things up front?

SENIOR STEWARD: Since the Sheik got on it's been like a flying harem.

STEWARD: How many wives has he brought with him?

SENIOR STEWARD: Twenty – they've taken over the whole of First Class.

STEWARD: Where's the Sheik?

SENIOR STEWARD: He's up in the cabin in the sky, having a kip.

STEWARD: I might take a stroll up later and look his harem over.

SENIOR STEWARD: They'll tear you to pieces.

STEWARD (*Frowning*): What do you mean?

SENIOR STEWARD: Well – think about it. If he has a different one every night, they're only getting it once a month. They must be desperate for a fellow.

CUT TO.
24. INTERIOR QANTAS 747 FIRST CLASS AREA. DAY
The curtain is drawn across. MILES enters frame, and stands stamping his feet. Suddenly a pair of hands emerge from behind the curtains and drag him inside.

25. INTERIOR QANTAS 747 FIRST CLASS CABIN. DAY
A startled MILES is being held by a dusky Arabian beauty. A further bevy of beauties are looking at them.

1ST ARABIAN BEAUTY: Look what I've found.
With squeals of delight the other girls fall upon him.
MILES (*Fearfully*): Help!

CUT TO.
26. INTERIOR QANTAS 747. ECONOMY SECTION. DAY
BRIAN is listening to music, with his headset.

CYNTHIA (*to RITA*): I'm worried about Miles. Something awful might have happened to him.
RITA: I'll ask Brian to go and find him.
(*Turning to BRIAN*) Brian. (*He doesn't reply*) Brian.
(*Still no reply, RITA unplugs his headset and bellows down the connection*) Brian!

BRIAN almost leaps out of his seat.

BRIAN: Cor blimey, you nearly burst my lughole. I was enjoying myself with Shirley Bassey then. What do you want?
RITA: Cynthia's worried about Miles.
BRIAN: I'm not surprised. I'm his brother and even I don't know which side of the fence he's on.
CYNTHIA: I'm not worried about that.
BRIAN (*Grinning*): Hello – hello – don't tell me, he's had his leg over at last?
CYNTHIA: Don't be so vulgar. I'm worried about where he is – what he's doing.
BRIAN: Well, he can't be far – unless he stepped outside for a walk.

RITA: Go and look for him, Brian.

BRIAN (*Grumbling*): Oh, all right.

BRIAN rises and moves towards the First Class section.

RITA: Don't worry, Cynthia. I'm sure he's all right. He's probably having a lie-down somewhere.

CUT TO.

27. INTERIOR. QANTAS 747 FIRST CLASS CABIN. DAY

MILES is lying across two seats surrounded by Arabian girls.

1ST ARABIAN GIRL (*Introducing another girl*): This is Jasmine – from Turkey.

MILES (*Weakly*): Hello.

JASMINE (*Seductively*): How would you like a bit of Turkish delight?

MILES: If it's all the same with you, I'd rather have a Bounty.

JASMINE leans over him and kisses him. BRIAN pokes his head inside the curtains.

BRIAN: Oh, sorry. I'm looking for a man.

1ST ARABIAN BEAUTY: So are we.

Two of the girls lead BRIAN forward.

BRIAN (*Dazed*): It must be my birthday.

MILES's head appears from behind a seat.

MILES: Help!

BRIAN (*Surprised*): Miles. You've got hidden talents.

MILES: Yes, and I want to keep them hidden. Brian, aren't you going to help me?

BRIAN (*Happily*): You must be joking. I'm going to help myself. (*To the two girls either side of him*) I'm all yours, girls.

They giggle and push him down on a seat.

CUT TO.
28. INTERIOR QANTAS 747. ECONOMY CLASS SECTION.
DAY

RITA: They've vanished.
CYNTHIA: People can't vanish on a plane. Did you look in all the toilets?
RITA: Yes.
CYNTHIA: No luck?
RITA: No. Apart from one, where a man had forgotten to lock the
    door.
CYNTHIA: Was it Miles?
RITA: I didn't look at his face. I could see it wasn't Brian!
CYNTHIA (*Rising*): They must be somewhere. Come on, we'll look
    together. You go up that aisle – I'll go up the other.

We follow RITA up one aisle in the direction of the First Class
section. A middle-aged MAN is standing in the aisle near a toilet
station, holding a can of beer.

RITA: Excuse me.
MAN (*Tipsy*): Hello, you beauty. How about a tube of Fosters?
RITA: No, thank you.
MAN: Aw, c'mon. Be a sport. Don't go away.

The MAN moves to his seat to get another can of beer. RITA
crosses through the toilet section to the other aisle where she meets
CYNTHIA.

RITA: You do that aisle. I'll carry on up here.
CYNTHIA: Very well.

CYNTHIA comes through the toilet section to the other aisle. The
MAN turns, with another can of beer in his hand.

MAN: Here you are, gorgeous.
(*Sees CYNTHIA and reacts*)
Jeeze – I must be drunker than I thought.

CUT TO.
29. INTERIOR QANTAS 747. CABIN IN THE SKY. DAY
The Sheik is lying on a couch. He is a muscular bearded man, wearing the full Arab robes. He stirs, wakens, yawns and stretches. The FLIGHT ENGINEER is sitting nearby, doing some paperwork.

FLIGHT ENGINEER (*Looking across*): Have a good sleep?
SHEIK (*Sitting up*): Excellent. Most refreshing.
(*Rising*) What time do you serve dinner?
FLIGHT ENGINEER: Any minute now.
SHEIK: Good.
FLIGHT ENGINEER: You can have it served up here if you wish.
SHEIK: No. I feel the need for some feminine company.
(*Moving towards the stairs*) I'll dine with my wives.

CUT TO
30. INTERIOR QANTAS 747. FIRST CLASS AREA. DAY
CYNTHIA and RITA are standing outside the curtains.

CYNTHIA: Any sight of them?
RITA: No.

From behind the curtains we hear a happy groan from BRIAN.

BRIAN (*OOV*): More – more.
RITA (*Reacts*): That sounds like BRIAN.
MILES (*OOV*): Stop it – you're tickling.

CYNTHIA and RITA exchange glances. CYNTHIA pulls the curtains aside.

31. INTERIOR QANTAS 747. FIRST CLASS CABIN. DAY
A happy BRIAN is sprawled across a seat, with a girl feeding him grapes. On another seat MILES is lying, a girl stroking his forehead. Both are stripped down to their underpants.

RITA: Brian!
CYNTHIA: Miles!

BRIAN and MILES smile weakly.

BRIAN: Hello, my pet.
RITA (*Angrily*): Don't you 'Pet' me.
CYNTHIA: Miles Gay – how *could* you?
MILES: I haven't. Anyway, I can't.

The SHEIK comes downstairs. He takes in the scene and bristles with anger.

SHEIK: What is going on?
CYNTHIA: There's nothing going on. It's all coming off.

MILES and BRIAN rise and start to gather up their clothes.

SHEIK: I'll have you punished for this.
BRIAN: There's a perfectly simple explanation.
SHEIK: What?
BRIAN: Tell him, Miles.
MILES (*Flustered*): Er – well – er – it's all been a terrible mistake.
RITA: Yes, and *you*'ve made it.
SHEIK: It's a pity you're not in my country – we have a way of
  dealing with people who offend the law. If somebody lies we cut
  off his tongue – if somebody steals we cut off his arm. And if
  somebody seduces our women we cut off his head!
RITA: Oh – for a moment I thought he was going to say cut off
  his . . .
CYNTHIA (*Hastily*): Yes, Rita – so did I. And quite frankly it's no
  more than they deserve.
RITA: Steady, Cynthia. There's no reason to punish ourselves!
SHEIK: You have insulted me and my country.
MILES: All right – all right. Keep your shirt on.
CYNTHIA: It's a pity you didn't keep *yours* on.

MILES and BRIAN dash out of frame.

32. STOCK FOOTAGE OF QANTAS 747. IN FLIGHT ANNOUNCER (VO)

In a few minutes we shall be landing at Sydney Kingsford-Smith Airport. For those of you on the left of the aircraft, there's a very fine view of the Harbour Bridge and the Opera House.

33. STOCK FOOTAGE OF AERIAL VIEWS OF SYDNEY HARBOUR

34. STOCK FOOTAGE OF QANTAS 747 LANDING AT SYDNEY AIRPORT

35. INTERIOR SYDNEY AIRPORT. INTERNATIONAL ARRIVALS. DAY

MILES, CYNTHIA, BRIAN and RITA are emerging from the Customs and Immigration Section. CYNTHIA and BRIAN are both pushing trolleys.

MILES: It's hot, isn't it?

BRIAN: Yes – let's find a bar and cool off.

CYNTHIA: You can do what you like. Miles and I are going straight to the solicitors. It's the last day to claim our inheritance.

BRIAN: We've plenty of time. They won't be open yet. It's only seven o'clock in the morning.

RITA (*Pointing*): According to that clock it's only five.

MILES (*Checking his watch*): It's wrong – it's definitely six. I'm as regular as Big Ben.

RITA (*Pointing*): There's another over there that says five o'clock.

PORTER: Yes, Bruce.

MILES: The name is MILES.

PORTER: Good on yer, Miles. You're a Pom.

MILES: No. I'm English.

PORTER: What can I do for you?

MILES: I think you've got something wrong with your clock.

PORTER: Are you trying to be funny?

BRIAN: What time is it?

PORTER: Five o'clock.

MILES: Are you sure? My watch says seven.

PORTER: I don't care what your watch says – it's five o'clock.

MILES (*Stubbornly*): It's very light for five o'clock in the morning.

PORTER: There's a very good reason for that – it's five o'clock – p.m.

CYNTHIA (*Shocked*): P.m.?

MILES: You mean it's afternoon?

PORTER: That's right. We're eleven hours ahead of you Pommies.

The PORTER moves off.

CYNTHIA (*Panicking*): Did you hear that? It's five o'clock in the evening.

BRIAN (*Reacts*): The solicitors.

CYNTHIA and BRIAN both charge out with their trolleys followed by MILES and RITA.

36. EXTERIOR. SYDNEY AIRPORT. DAY

CYNTHIA: I can't see any taxis.

MILES rushes up to a PORTER.

MILES: Excuse me – porter.

PORTER: Oh, it's you again. What do you want?

MILES: Where can we get a taxi?

PORTER: You won't get a taxi anywhere in Sydney.

CYNTHIA: Well I heard Australia was primitive but I didn't think it was *so* bad.

PORTER: They're all on strike, lady.

BRIAN: How can we get to Sydney? Is there an airport bus we can catch?

PORTER: Depends how fast you can run – it left five minues ago!

MILES: You're a big help, you are.

RITA (*Pointing*): Look, Brian – there's a coach.

ANOTHER ANGLE

A coach further along with people getting on. CYNTHIA and MILES, BRIAN and RITA enter frame, and try to board the coach. A burly male PASSENGER stops them.

PASSENGER: There's a queue here, mate.

BRIAN: We haven't time to queue.

PASSENGER (*Threatening*): What did you say?

BRIAN: We'll go to the end of the queue.

BRIAN and RITA join the queue, directly behind MILES and CYNTHIA. MILES and CYNTHIA get on the coach. BRIAN and RITA are about to do so when the DRIVER stops them.

DRIVER (*Slightly camp*): Sorry. Full up.

The DRIVER closes the door. The coach pulls away with a happy MILES and CYNTHIA grinning and waving from the window.

RITA: We've had it, Brian.

BRIAN (*Determinedly*): Oh no we haven't.

BRIAN moves to where an Italian, GIUSEPPE, is just about to get into his car.

BRIAN: Excuse me.

GIUSEPPE (*Eyeing RITA*): Santa Madonna.

BRIAN: We want to get to Sydney.

GIUSEPPE (*To RITA*): You a beautiful girl.

RITA: Thank you.

BRIAN: Look, never mind her.

GIUSEPPE (*To BRIAN*): Silenzio.

(*To RITA*) I take you home. We make love. We drink champagne.
  We make love again. We eata spaghetti – we make love again.

RITA (*To BRIAN*): Cocky with it, isn't he?
BRIAN: Please – can you take us to Sydney?
GIUSEPPE: I take *her* anywhere.
BRIAN (*Opening the back door*): Right – get in, Rita.
GIUSEPPE (*Opening front door*): She sit inada front with me.
RITA: Can I trust you to keep your hands to yourself?
GIUSEPPE: No.
RITA (*Grinning*): Oh good.

RITA climbs into the car. BRIAN opens the boot and starts to put the luggage in. GIUSEPPE gets in on his side. BRIAN slams down the boot lid. The car roars off, leaving BRIAN running after them. The car stops, BRIAN catches up and gets in the back.

38. INTERIOR. AIRPORT COACH. DAY
MILES and CYNTHIA are sitting at the front just behind the DRIVER.

MILES (*Gleefully*): Poor Brian. I feel quite sorry for him.
CYNTHIA: So do I.
(*They both laugh*)

39. INTERIOR. GIUSEPPE'S CAR. DAY
GIUSEPPE has one hand on RITA's knee.

BRIAN: I'd feel safer if you kept two hands on the wheel.
RITA: So would I.
GIUSEPPE: Hey. Giuseppe Gandolfo canna drive with a-no hands.

GIUSEPPE takes his hands off the wheel. The car swerves alarmingly. A car behind sounds its horn. GIUSEPPE leans out of the window and swears at him.

RITA: Brian – look.
BRIAN: What?
RITA (*Pointing*): In front. It's the airport coach. We've caught it up.

The car passes the coach. BRIAN and RITA wave to MILES and CYNTHIA.

40. INTERIOR. AIRPORT COACH. DAY

MILES (*To DRIVER*): Can't you go any faster?
DRIVER: Are you trying to get me into trouble?
CYNTHIA: I'll make it worth your while.
DRIVER: No, thank you. I prefer your boyfriend.

41. INTERIOR. GIUSEPPE'S CAR. DAY

GIUSEPPE (*Staring at RITA*): You havada most beautiful bosoms.
RITA: Do you think so?
GIUSEPPE: Fantastico.
BRIAN: Never mind about her bosoms. Keep your eyes on the road.
GIUSEPPE (*Half turning to speak to BRIAN*): You keepa quiet.
RITA (Alarmed): Look out!

42. EXTERIOR. ROAD. DAY
GIUSEPPE'S car hits a car in front that has stopped. GIUSEPPE gets out and he and the other driver start to argue. The airport coach passes, and we see a happy MILES and CYNTHIA gleefully waving.

RITA: We've really had it this time.
BRIAN (*Getting out of the car*): We'll see about that.

BRIAN climbs into the driver's seat. He reverses the car, then pulls out and drives off past the still-arguing GIUSEPPE who waves, then reacts.

43. EXTERIOR. ROAD. DAY
The coach is drawing up at the kerb.

44. INTERIOR. AIRPORT COACH. DAY

MILES (*To DRIVER*): What are you stopping for?
DRIVER: It's tinkle time.
CYNTHIA: Pardon?
DRIVER: Nature calls.
CYNTHIA (*Groaning*): Oh no. Can't you go later?
DRIVER: No, I can't
(*Calling*)
Anybody else want to spend a penny?
(*Several passengers alight. The DRIVER turns to MILES*)
How about you? Would you like to come with me?
MILES: You're a bit old to need someone to hold your hand.
DRIVER (*Winking*): It's not my hand I'm thinking about.
MILES: How dare you! I'm not a man like that.
DRIVER: You could have fooled me. Still, please yourself.

The DRIVER alights and moves off.

CYNTHIA (*Annoyed*): This is ridiculous. We're never going to get to
the solicitors in time.

45. EXTERIOR. ROAD. DAY
BRIAN and RITA pass in GIUSEPPE'S car. BRIAN holds up two
fingers to MILES and CYNTHIA.

46. INTERIOR. AIRPORT COACH. DAY

CYNTHIA: They're going to beat us to it.
MILES (*Rising*): No, they're not.

MILES moves to sit in the driver's seat.

CYNTHIA (*Alarmed*): Miles – you can't drive. You haven't passed
your test.
MILES: It's not my fault. I've taken it six times.

47. EXTERIOR. ROAD. DAY
The coach, with MILES at the wheel, pulls jerkily away.

ANOTHER ANGLE.
The DRIVER emerging from a Gents' toilet. He reacts.

DRIVER (*Waving his arms*): Come back – come back.
(*Turning to a passer-by*)
My coach has been hijacked.

48. INTERIOR. GIUSEPPE'S CAR. DAY

BRIAN: Have you found it yet?
RITA (*Trying to read the Sydney street guide*): I can't. You're going too
    fast. Everything's jiggling up and down.
BRIAN: So I've noticed.
(*Glancing in his rear-view mirror*)
Oh, oh.
RITA: What's the matter?
BRIAN: Here comes that blasted coach.
RITA (*Turning to look*): Miles is driving it.

49. INTERIOR AIRPORT COACH. DAY
A grim-faced MILES is at the wheel.

CYNTHIA (*Urging him on*): Faster, Miles – faster.
MILES: I've got my foot through the floor now.

(An elderly Italian woman, all in black, crosses herself.)

50. INTERIOR GIUSEPPE'S CAR. DAY
RITA (*Looking back*): They're gaining on us.
BRIAN: I'm practically flat out.

51. EXTERIOR. ROAD. DAY
A uniformed Police Sergeant (CARLTON) is standing by his police
car. He reacts as GIUSEPPE'S car goes speeding by and again as
the coach goes by. He climbs in his car and gives chase, sounding
his siren.

52. INTERIOR. AIRPORT COACH. DAY

CYNTHIA: Do something, Miles – they're getting away.

MILES: Try pushing a few people out, to lighten the load. (*Suddenly*) What's that noise?

CYNTHIA: It's a police car.

MILES: Perhaps there's an accident somewhere.

CYNTHIA: Yes – and I think we're it.

53. EXTERIOR ROAD. DAY

The police car pulls in front of the coach, and signals MILES to stop.

54. INTERIOR GIUSEPPE'S CAR. DAY

RITA: The police have stopped them.

BRIAN (*Half turning to look*): Lovely.

RITA (*Looking ahead and reacting*): Look out.

55. EXTERIOR ROAD. DAY

An empty transporter is stopped at traffic lights. GIUSEPPE'S car drives up the ramp onto the transporter. The lights change and the transporter pulls away.

BRIAN (*Shouting out of the window*): Help – stop, you Australian fool.

The transporter heads towards a road junction. We see a road sign with an arrow pointing right to Sydney and another arrow pointing left to the Great Western Highway. The transporter turns left.

56. INTERIOR. AIRPORT COACH. DAY

MILES: Leave all the talking to me. Just lie on that seat and groan.

CYNTHIA: What for?

MILES: Never mind what for – do as I tell you.

57. EXTERIOR. ROAD. DAY

SERGEANT CARLTON is approaching the coach. MILES leans out of the window.

CARLTON: Where's the fire?
MILES: We've got an emergency.
(*Indicating CYNTHIA*)
This poor woman's having a baby.
CARLTON: I'm not surprised, the way you were driving.
MILES: We've got to get her to a hospital.

CYNTHIA groans. CARLTON peers in at her.

CARLTON: From the size of her I think it could be twins.
CYNTHIA (*Sitting up*): Don't be personal.

(*She lies down and groans again.*)

CARLTON: Right – follow me. I'll give you a police escort.

CARLTON moves back to his car, gets in and pulls away, his sirens going.
MILES follows him.

58. INTERIOR. GIUSEPPE'S CAR. DAY
BRIAN is sounding his horn.

BRIAN (*Stopping*): It's no good. He's stone deaf. I'll just have to reverse off when he stops at those lights.

59. EXTERIOR. ROAD. DAY
The police car, followed by the coach, is approaching the road junction. The police car turns left towards the Great Western Highway – the coach turns right towards Sydney. We follow the police car which slows down as it nears the transporter. At that moment, BRIAN reverses GIUSEPPE's car off and backs into the police car.

60. INTERIOR GIUSEPPE'S CAR. DAY
BRIAN and RITA react.

BRIAN: Bloody Norah.

61. EXTERIOR. ROAD. DAY

CARLTON gets out of his police car, and starts to walk towards BRIAN.

BRIAN (*Calling out of the window*): Sorry, officer – we can't wait.

(BRIAN does a U-turn. Unfortunately his rear bumper is locked with the police car's rear bumper and the police car is towed away behind it. An irate CARLTON flags down a motor cyclist, commandeers his motor bike and sets off in pursuit.)

62. INTERIOR SOLICITOR'S OFFICE (SYDNEY). DAY

BURKE is sitting behind his desk. SANDRA enters.

SANDRA: Excuse me, Mr Burke. I'm just going across to Circular Quay for a bit.

BURKE: You naughty little girl.

SANDRA (*Sighing*): Mr Burke – you're always thinking of sex.

BURKE: When you get to my age, Sandra, that's all you *can* do – think about it! Go on – off you go. I'll lock up.

63. EXTERIOR SOLICITOR'S OFFICE. DAY

SANDRA emerges from the office. She is about to cross the road when she hears the blaring of horns.

64. EXTERIOR ROAD. DAY

The coach is speeding towards the solicitor's, followed by GIUSEPPE's car, followed by CARLTON on the motor bike. The coach screeches to a halt. GIUSEPPE's car smashes into the back. CARLTON swerves to avoid colliding and he and the bike go sailing over the jetty into the harbour.

65. INTERIOR. SOLICITOR'S OFFICE (SYDNEY). DAY

BURKE is getting ready to go. He moves to the door.

66. INTERIOR. CORRIDOR. DAY

BURKE emerges, locks the door and moves to the lift. He presses the button. The lift doors open and MILES, CYNTHIA, BRIAN and RITA emerge, almost bowling BURKE over.

BRIAN (*Pushing him aside*): Get out of the way, you silly old Burke.
BURKE: Have we met?
BRIAN: Pardon?
BURKE: You obviously know my name.
CYNTHIA: Just a minute. Are you the solicitor?
BURKE: Yes. I'm Burke. Of Burke, Burke, Burke and Burke.
MILES: Just the Burke we're looking for.

67. EXTERIOR. ROAD. DAY

A dripping CARLTON is climbing out of the water, watched by a crowd of people including SANDRA.

CARLTON.: Did anyone see where those people went?
SANDRA: We were all too busy watching you.
CARLTON (*Grimly*): I'll find them – if it takes me for ever.

68. INTERIOR. SOLICITOR'S OFFICE (SYDNEY). DAY

MILES, CYNTHIA, BRIAN & RITA are sitting facing BURKE who is at his desk, holding a document.
BURKE (*Clearing his throat and reading*): 'I, Charles Gay, being of sound mind and . . .'
BRIAN: Never mind all that rubbish – get to the bit about the opals.
BURKE: Quite so.
(*Reading again*)
'Hereby bequeath my opal mine to my only son and/or his rightful heirs.'
MILES: That's us.
CYNTHIA: Where *is* this opal mine?
BURKE: I've no idea.
BRIAN: What do you mean – you've no idea?
RITA: Doesn't he say where it is?
BURKE: No. As far as I can surmise, he didn't want anyone else to find it.

MILES: Well, that's a nice state of affairs – we can't go wandering all over Australia looking for it, can we?

BURKE (*Picking up a piece of paper*): I think we could narrow it down a little. It must be somewhere near Sydney, and he did leave a clue as to its whereabouts.

(*Reading*)

> 'Wealth and fortune will be thine
> When you discover Old Charley's mine
> Surrounded on all sides by sea,
> A fishy spot 'tis said to be
> Look beside a dried-up creek,
> And you will find there what you seek.'

RITA: That's nice. I like poetry.

CYNTHIA: What sort of clue is that?

MILES: A damn stupid one, if you ask me.

BURKE: There's just one other point you should know.

(*Reading*)

'In the event of there being more than one heir the opal mine shall go to the first to discover it.'

BRIAN: It's not an inheritance. It's a bleeding treasure hunt.

BURKE: And may the best man win.

69. INTERIOR. CORRIDOR. DAY

CARLTON is just emerging from the lift. He looks round and moves down to an office, knocks and enters. As he disappears, MILES, CYNTHIA, BRIAN and RITA emerge from the solicitor's office, move to the lift and press the button. The lift door opens and CARLTON emerges and sees them.

CARLTON: Stop – in the name of the law.

MILES: Quick – into the lift.

CARLTON runs towards them as they get into the lift. He manages to catch hold of RITA's dress and tries to drag her out.

RITA: Help!

BRIAN pulls RITA by the arm. There is a ripping sound as her dress is torn off and we see her pants and bra for a brief second before the lift door closes. CARLTON starts to run downstairs.

70. EXTERIOR. SOLICITOR'S OFFICE. DAY
MILES, CYNTHIA, BRIAN and the still scantily clad RITA emerge, climb into the coach and drive off.

80. ESTABLISHING SHOT OF GOLDEN PUSSYCAT NIGHT-CLUB. DAY

81. INTERIOR. FRANCO'S OFFICE. GOLDEN PUSSYCAT NIGHTCLUB. DAY
FRANCO, a swarthy Italian dressed in the best Mafia tradition – dark suit, black shirt and white tie – is watching TV. His girlfriend MARIA, a voluptuous Italian, is sitting sipping a drink.

MARIA: You wanta drink, Franco?
FRANCO (*Silencing her with a wave of his hand*): Silenzio.
He concentrates on the TV screen.
MCU of TV Screen
A NEWSCASTER is reading the early-evening news.

NEWSCASTER: State police are trying to find two men and two women recently arrived from England in connection with an incident on board their flight where the men are alleged to have raped several wives of a foreign minister. The people in question are in Sydney to claim an inheritance of a large fortune of opals left to them by their great-great-grandfather.
In Canberra today, the Prime Minister . . .
FRANCO rises and switches the TV off.

FRANCO (*To MARIA*): Get me Luigi.

MARIA moves to open the door.

MARIA (*Calling*): Luigi – the boss wants you.

LUIGI enters. Another Italian; wearing a slouch hat.

LUIGI: You want me, boss?

FRANCO: Attsa right. I want you to do something.

LUIGI (*Eagerly*): Who do you want rubbing out?

FRANCO (*Sighing*): How many times I got to tell you, Luigi. We in Australia now. We not rub people out. We maybe break a few arms – a few legs – but no rubbing out.

LUIGI (*Disappointed*): My gun, she's-a getting rusty.

FRANCO: Never mind. I want you to find four people who come from England. Two guys – two girls. They come in today. Ring up the airline – see if you can get their names.

LUIGI: Sure, boss.

FRANCO: Is Giuseppe back from da airport yet?

LUIGI: He's-a on his way. He's-a been delayed. Somebody stole his car.

FRANCO: Santa Maria. You can't trust anybody these days. Take him witta you when he comes back.

LUIGI: Okey-cokey, boss.

LUIGI exits.

MARIA: What you want to find these people for?

FRANCO: You hear what the man said. They come to collect a fortune in opals. Only Franco's gonna collect them first. Itsa not right they should take our opals – bloody foreigners!

82. ESTABLISHING SHOT OF BELLAVISTA MOTEL. DAY

83. INTERIOR MOTEL RECEPTION AREA. DAY

MILES, CYNTHIA, BRIAN and RITA are talking to SALLY, a pretty young receptionist. RITA is now wearing BRIAN'S jacket.

SALLY: I'm afraid all we've got are two doubles.

CYNTHIA (*To BRIAN and MILES*):

You two can share.

BRIAN: I'm not sleeping with him. I like a kiss and cuddle in bed.

MILES: In that case *I*'m certainly not sleeping with *him*.

RITA: Brian and I are sleeping together. You two will have to share.

MILES: I don't like the idea of that. You know what's likely to happen. Especially in this hot weather. A man and a woman of opposite sexes together in a bedroom. Passions could get inflamed. Lust could rear its ugly head.

RITA: I'm sure you wouldn't behave like that.

MILES (*Indicating CYNTHIA*): No, but she might!

CYNTHIA (*To SALLY*): We'll take the rooms.

SALLY: Very well.

(*Handing over some keys*)

Here are your keys. I'll get someone to carry your bags up.

CYNTHIA: I fancy a nibble.

MILES: You see, she's started already.

CYNTHIA: Something to eat.

SALLY: We serve sandwiches in the bar.

MILES: I'm going to have a bath.

MILES moves off, out of frame.

RITA: I'd like a drink.

(*To BRIAN*)

How about you, Brian – do you fancy a drink or something?

BRIAN: Well, let's have a drink first, then we can have the something after.

CYNTHIA (*To BRIAN*): Don't you ever think of anything but sex?

RITA (*Grinning*): As far as Brian's concerned there *isn't* anything but sex.

84. INTERIOR MOTEL BEDROOM 1. DAY

MILES emerges from the bathroom, wearing only a towel. He looks at himself in a mirror and poses like a muscle-man. He hears a noise from outside the French windows and goes to investigate.

85. EXTERIOR. MOTEL. DAY

The coach driver is arguing with BRUCE, a muscular bronzed young man in his early twenties.
COACH DRIVER: I tell you this is my coach.
BRUCE: How do I know it's your coach? Prove it.
COACH DRIVER: Don't be stupid.

ANOTHER ANGLE
MILES peering over his balcony.

86. INTERIOR MOTEL BEDROOM 1. DAY
A maid enters the room, moves to the bed and turns the covers down. She is about to go out when she notices the French window is ajar. She moves across, closes it and locks it.

87. EXTERIOR. MOTEL BALCONY. DAY
MILES turns back and tries the French window. It won't open. He rattles the door, then glances over the balcony.

88. EXTERIOR MOTEL. DAY
The COACH DRIVER and BRUCE are still arguing. A crowd has gathered. The Italian lady staggers off the coach and begins shouting in Italian.

89. EXTERIOR MOTEL BALCONY. DAY
MILES looks desperately round. He sees that the gap between his balcony and the adjoining one is about three feet wide. He climbs onto the balcony rail, and with his back firmly pressed against the hotel wall, slowly and carefully extends his left leg until his foot finally finds the adjoining balcony. He is now straddled with one foot on each balcony rail. He takes a look down and gulps.

90. EXTERIOR MOTEL. DAY
BRUCE and the COACH DRIVER are still arguing.

BRUCE: Look, if you don't push off, I'll thump you.
COACH DRIVER: Bully.

A bath towel slowly flutters down from above. BRUCE catches it and everybody's eyes turn upward. ANOTHER ANGLE: MILES, his legs apart, and his hands strategically placed between his thighs. ANOTHER ANGLE: BRUCE, the COACH DRIVER and the crowd react.

COACH DRIVER: Ooh, I say.

The Italian lady sinks to her knees and makes the sign of the Cross.

ANOTHER ANGLE: MCU of MILES. He sways and we see his arms raise to balance himself. ANOTHER ANGLE: BRUCE and the crowd's reaction.

OLD LADY (*To OLD MAN*): What is it, Cyril? I can't see without my glasses.
OLD MAN: Oh, it's nothing, Lily.
COACH DRIVER: I wouldn't say that.
OLD LADY (*Peering upwards*): It looks like a bird's nest up there.
OLD MAN (*To placate her*): Yes – that's what it is – a bird's nest.
OLD LADY: Is there a bird in it?
OLD MAN: Yes.
OLD LADY: Oh, that's nice. Is it a cock or a hen?
OLD MAN: Definitely a cock!
COACH DRIVER (*Excitedly*): It's him – it's him. He's the one who hijacked my coach. I recognise his face.
BRUCE: It's taken you long enough.
COACH DRIVER: I've only just looked at his face!

[THE SCRIPT WAS INCOMPLETE WHEN THE PROJECT WAS ABANDONED.]

iv)

Carry On Sergeant

The cast and crew on the *Carry On* films were renowned for their expeditious working methods. There was no idling and everyone worked flat out in order to wrap up each film within the stringent six-to-eight-week production schedule. Tight deadlines, though, weren't just forced upon those working on the film set: even the scriptwriters were under intense pressure and one could almost detect smoke rising from their typewriters and pencils as they beavered away preparing the script. For example, Norman Hudis was still finalising the treatment for *Sergeant* at the end of January 1958, but by 24 March filming was under way. Yet, despite the pressure and the tight deadlines, the following documents are an indication of how much thought and preparation was invested by the meticulous Norman Hudis, the attention to detail almost belying the seemingly rapid-fire, one-take reputation associated with a *Carry On* movie.

CARRY ON SERGEANT
First Treatment and Development Ideas

NH – for Beaconsfield Films Ltd

Development Ideas
The foregoing should be held within one reel – a reel to set the situation and characters and stamp the picture unmistakably as a light-hearted comedy with a trace of guts.

From this point, the film can naturally resolve itself into a series of comedy sequences – *but,* because there is a central idea, each situation and character can be related, however lightly, to the basic story of GRIMSHAWE, and the film cannot fall into the trap of being an unrelated play-off of Army-life sketches.

The following comments on the above are made immediately, before other ideas for development are presented:

– The size of the squad – 12 men – is quite arbitrary. One man of awkward outlook can louse up a unit of 100 men. There is no reason, of course, why the squads at Heathercrest shouldn't consist of any number of men: 12, here, seemed to be manageable. But our six characters can be trusted to create confusion whatever their numerical ratio to the squad as a whole. Any number can play . . .

– The opening scenes of a GRIMSHAWE squad failing and falling all over the place in final tests and pass-out parade could be scaled down, less exaggerated if it's desired to save the picturing of *real* incompetence for the central section of the film when our boys get to work. On the other hand, a slap-up comedy opening might have something to commend it.

– The training-plan at Heathercrest is seen as follows. Each squad is under a Sgt, with Cpl assisting, for drill and arms-drill. Other training (PT, weapons, Tough Tactics, anti-gas, fieldcraft etc) is given by various specialists, officers and NCOs. But each squad is known by the Sgt who not only takes it for basic drills but is responsible for its behaviour and general turn-out. Thus, our boys are unmistakably GRIMSHAWE's squad, and any kudos, or other-wise, from their efficiency or lack thereof, falls in his lap or on his head.

– Because of the bets laid, GRIMSHAWE's dependence on this squad is only known to his fellow Sgts. And as GRIMSHAWE is not the type to shout about his impending discharge, only his fellow-Sgts and a couple of disinterested clerks in the Orderly Room know that he's only 12 weeks off being a civilian.

* * * * *

A.

THE RECRUIT WITH A GUITAR

He can be established as the draft arrives at the railway station and can be placed in any of the other squads, or in GRIMSHAWE's squad as a subsidiary character, or, perhaps most fruitfully in GRIMSHAWE's squad as one of the principals. The immediate value of this character is that he is available at any time for music-spots – <u>one of which should certainly carry the title of the film</u> – say in hut, NAAFI or local pub. If he's built into a full character, he can tip the balance of the squad 7–5 in favour of disaster, for he'd be a real jazz kid, with all the jargon misapplied to the Army-life (square sergeant, cool corporal, gone-cat Captain, dig those crazy trenches etc). He'd be an amiable character, a liability to the squad not because he's against Army life but simply because he's not with it. He's hardly of this world at all. The character could take on more of a story-value (for example) if there's a Talent Competition in a nearby cinema and he, convinced like so many of his type that success is an overnight affair, is unable to enter for it, not being allowed out of camp during training. This could lead to obvious complications if it's thought worthwhile to extend this character this far.

B.

The first element which needs to be disposed of is CHARLIE SAGE. The previous scripts demonstrate that this situation will not hold indefinitely, so it seems best to play it for all it's worth as quickly as possible. MARY hiding in the laundry truck, getting a 'job' in the NAAFI, CHARLIE thinking he's suffering from hallucinations etc – all this is good stuff, provided it's bowled over at speed. It seems a good idea also to tie this situation in with TINKER: I can see a good comedy-effect in MARY arranging to meet CHARLIE somewhere on the camp (implication: consummation of marriage) – but having to leave the rendezvous for some reason, CHARLIE finding TINKER there instead.

<u>Resolution:</u> When the maximum comedy-effect has been extracted, CHARLIE gets his interview for special leave, it's granted and he

accepts it. He and MARY go off together, charged with the duty of returning TINKER to the farmer who will meet the train by arrangement.

Relation to Grimshawe: He loses one recruit straight off: CHARLIE will have a week's training to catch up on when he returns. DUCK-WORTH soon gets over pining for TINKER and settles down to Army life.

C.

HORACE STRONG is a valuable character for a running gag – reporting sick. It may well work out that every single sequence FADES IN on HORACE waiting his turn in sick bay. Waiting his turn? – He's first in the queue. The feeling one should have about this character is not that he's trying to work his ticket: this is old stuff, and like old stuff, tastes musty at best and nasty at worst. HORACE firmly and fully honestly believes he's always ill, suffering from every conceivable illness.

The MO will therefore be an important supporting character: I see him as young, good-humoured and sympathetic – not a blood-wagon sawbones with a vocabulary consisting entirely of the words 'Number Nine'. The most he gives HORACE, however, is medicine and duty.

Resolution: Finally, defeated and forlorn, HORACE does not report sick one day. This is what the MO has been waiting for. He summons HORACE urgently to sick bay, right off the parade ground. There is an air of grave tension: HORACE, mystified and somehow expectant, is not examined there and then. Instead, the MO escorts him, in a staff car, to a nearby civilian hospital. En route, the MO tells HORACE he has been worried about HORACE's constant reporting of terrible symptoms, mistrusts his own judgement and is now taking immediate action to save himself from the possible errors of his own misjudgement. At the hospital, HORACE is overjoyed: twelve specialists are assembled to give him a thorough going-over: at last, his poor pain-racked body will receive the respect and attention it cries for. Utilising an impressive array of the latest appliances, textbooks at the ready, so that HORACE can check for himself the readings against the reading, the specialists get to work on him. It's a hypochondriac's paradise – until, result by result, HORACE is shown up as someone almost abnormally normal. He has lungs like a vacuum cleaner, a heart like Big Ben, eyes like a hypnotic hawk and a digestive system like an atomic incinerator. The shock is colossal: the foundations of HORACE's life, one by one, are struck from beneath him. With tears of incredulous horror in his eyes, he learns that there isn't even one good medical reason for the removal of his appendix: and his last hope goes when he passes the psychiatric-associations test with the flying colours of a man without even the hint of a complex. They practically write him into medical history as HOMO HORACE – a phrase he indignantly misunderstands, but which, they explain is merely a synonym from now on for perfect health. Once the shock passes – well, nothing can hold HORACE now. A 100% personality in whatever he does, he becomes a fanatic for physical fitness, slays the girls, drills like a machine, zooms through the Commando course like a terrorist who enjoys his work – and winds up being recommended for further training as a PT Instructor.

Relation to GRIMSHAWE: To begin with, HORACE is not on parade: he's always reporting sick. To GRIMSHAWE, HORACE is nothing less than the old-fashioned lead-swinger. This exasperates him so much, he tries to trap HORACE in well-tried ways – but (and this is the whole point) HORACE really believes he's ill and the ruses don't succeed. When HORACE becomes a changed man – this is towards the end of the film, of course, as simultaneous with the climax as is possible, and GRIMSHAWE's exhausted emotions are just capable of resolving themselves into astonished gratitude.

D.

BAILEY rides high. He's not to know, of course, but GRIMSHAWE has his reasons for apparently letting BAILEY get away with unpunctual, uncooperative – everything but untidy, which, characteristically, he finds impossible to achieve. And yet, GRIMSHAWE doesn't chase him: GRIMSHAWE puts up with him: GRIMSHAWE even protects him when he tries the same tactics on other senior personalities. This is the hardest test of GRIMSHAWE's declared policy of keeping his men out of disciplinary trouble, and GRIMSHAWE has a hard time swallowing his bile. Thus, far from enjoying the grim martyred satisfaction of winding up in a military prison, BAILEY finds himself in an Army paradise: he just does as he pleases, even to the extent of breaking out of camp when this is disallowed, meeting GRIMSHAWE in a pub and still not suffering any disagreeable guardroom consequences.

BAILEY egotistically misinterprets the situation. He figures you only have to show you're not going to be pushed around, and nobody pushes – not even a Sgt with a cannibal reputation where recruits are concerned. And his ego is further varnished by the way in which HERBIE THE GOON latches on to him.

Pte. HERBERT BROWN of the Chits may appear to amble through life in a daze of his own, but he is not without appreciation for those better-endowed upstairs than himself. In fact he's inclined to hero-worship the more obvious examples of coordinated human existence – such as BAILEY. This adulation BAILEY at first impatiently rejects. But HERBERT is a limpet and won't be shaken off. BAILEY finds himself one time discussing the events of the day's training with this dimwit and, much to his astonishment, finds that he has absorbed all he's been taught and, moreover, is able to communicate the knowledge to HERBERT to such a degree that some of it evidently lodges in his sieve-brain. I see a scene, for example, in which BAILEY actually triumphs where experts have failed, and instructs HERBERT successfully in the stripping and reassembly of a rifle. The curious relationship develops apace from this point, BAILEY nightly passing on to the suddenly receptive HERBERT all the knowledge he has acquired during the day – and enjoying doing so.

The facts about BAILEY are really, after all, very simple. He just can't help doing well if he applies himself. His war-with-the-Army is, fortunately for him, canalised harmlessly (in the special circumstances) in his running with GRIMSHAWE, and is not carried negatively into technical training sessions (where he'd receive short shrift). Out of sheer boredom, he takes in what he's taught. Out of sheer force of personality, and ultimately responding to HERBERT's admiration, he uses up his final restless energy handing on his knowledge to this unexpectedly receptive quarter. By accident, he is given just what such personalities need – an objective plus a chance of self-expression and self-esteem. In short: GRIMSHAWE, about to leave the Army, paradoxically saves BAILEY from leaving the Army his way – via desertion.

Resolution: Though he mentally resists almost to the end, BAILEY is transformed from a negative rebel into a positive asset. He winds up being recommended for further training as a gunnery instructor – and is instrumental in giving HERBERT some stature as well, in a way in which emerges later.

Relation to GRIMSHAWE: bile-swallowing – through faint hope – to incredulous watching of the BAILEY-HERBERT relationship (faithfully reported by a dumbstruck Cpl. COPPING) – to ultimate tunic-busting pride.

E.
STARKE seems absolutely hopeless. At home with a pen, he's at sea with a grenade. He doesn't have the faintest idea of drill in any shape or form, achieving at best a dogged out-of-step as if on spring heels. He's inclined, with bland gravity, to doubt the ethics of bayonet-fighting, and the validity of gas-drill in a world bristling with H-bombs. He's known as The Brain, and while GRIMSHAWE may hold on to the hope that somehow he'll manage to mould the others into shape, this one is plainly impossible.

STARKE could have either or both of the following qualities: mathematical genius and a photographic brain. A great deal of comedy-effect could be gained from these factors.

<u>Mathematical genius:</u> in collaboration with HORACE (who could be a bookies' clerk in civilian life as in one of the scripts), STARKE could while away the evenings working out a foolproof system of playing the odds so that a sizeable profit must result. (The system needn't make sense: better in fact if it's impressive-sounding gibberish – 'all you have to do is select three odds-on cross-doubles both ways, doubling up against quarter average odds last time out.') GRIMSHAWE's squad, while not the most efficient militarily, certainly and suddenly becomes the most prosperous, able to finance the wildest parties the NAAFI can offer. Inevitably, the system one day fails – the very day GRIMSHAWE is roped in as a participating punter.

<u>Photographic memory:</u> this stands STARKE in good stead in written tests of all kinds during training. He can rattle off any instruction manual after reading it a couple of times, but it might as well be in Sanskrit for all it means to him. He can talk straight from the book about synchromesh gun-loading equipment, but will get his fingers jammed if he actually tries to operate the mechanism in question. There is a perfect pay-off to this, based on a true story within my own experience, too long to tell here – about How to Become An Entertainment Officer by Memorising the Radar Manual. (RAF story, but applicable.)

At any rate, STARKE's role in the story is that of an amiable, if slightly argumentative intellectual misfit, who's finally fitted – triumphantly and by accident.

<u>Resolution:</u> STARKE acquits himself not too disgracefully in drill etc, at pass-out, and goes on to further training in some administrative or abstruse capacity – junior adjutant or cyphers.

<u>Relation to GRIMSHAWE:</u> STARKE is very, very trying indeed: too clever to argue with, too owlish to bully. A constant source of worry who finally ambles into his own solution and victory.

F.

MILES HEYWOOD is our romantic interest. So far as he's concerned, Army training provides only a slight and slightly irritating distraction from romantic opportunities, presented by NAAFI girls and WRACE (clerks, cooks, etc). He's frequently baggy-eyed in the mornings, invariably glint-eyed at night. The only time he goes sick is when a new WRAC Medical Orderly arrives at the camp. There's also his girlfriend of the sports car who's prepared to risk a lacerated face for the chance of a Heywood-Special Kiss through the barbed wire.

MILES's success and otherwise with the girls is another running gag and could be productive of much feminine intrigue – as well as supplying a continuous light-romantic interest which the film needs and, in this way, can legitimately have. He should be an almost irresistible rogue.

Resolution: There's practically a band of keening women at the station to see him off when training's over. He turns into a reasonably good soldier – nothing special, certainly not officer material. (I'd like him to stick to his resolution in this matter – but perhaps he'd find, as a result of his Army experience, some hint of a career he'd like to follow when his service is over.)

Relation to GRIMSHAWE: In view of his experience with the rest of the boys, GRIMSHAWE practically develops an obsession about making MILES into an officer. More and more, as story and disasters develop, MILES seems to be his only hope – and this feeling persists in GRIMSHAWE right to the end.

When the denouement is reached, MILES is all that GRIMSHAWE has left – no matter what happens on pass-out and examinations, he must at least see MILES recommended as a cadet so that all is not lost. But MILES, really the least troublesome of all the men – and the least worth troubling with – only turns out as an average soldier and, the way things turn out, doesn't break GRIMSHAWE's heart or spoil his chances.

<u>Note:</u> About romance: on reflection, and in the way romantic interest suggests itself now, I think the idea of the NAAFI girl who wants to get married no longer, unfortunately, suggests itself as a major plot-factor. It would be quite wrong for any of the girls to take MILES seriously. Such an angle might be dealt with fleetingly – at the obvious risk of the humour involved being rather cruel.

G.

If all the above – story setting-up and character-factors – is substantially agreed, then it seems necessary to judge each sequence-idea for the film against this thematic material, and to reject, quite ruthlessly, any idea or angle which goes over the top. Elements from the other scripts which seem, to me, to be worth so judging are:

– Quotes from the Army's 'Welcome to Recruits' Manual (if genuine).

– Kit and rifle issue. DUCKWORTH could wind up with three rifles.

– Inoculations. A natural for HORACE.

– 'My Job in civvy street' essay: pay-off, LIEUTENANT is a punter.

– Recruit taking over drill. A natural for STARKE.

– Fire extinguisher in hut.

– Firing range and grenades could be combined into one sequence. I think the old lady's phone getting jumbled with the Army phone, and the whole sheep routine are less funny than the humour-tension which could naturally arise from the situation and setting, with such characters as STARKE, BAILEY, HORACE and DUCKWORTH in possession of firearms and explosives.

– Commando training.

- Night manoeuvres. Again: means should be sought to create confusion-comedy from the situation and not to impose comedy from the outside by such devices as Mitchelmore and Gertrude. Tinned soup exploding is good.

- Dance at which MILES triumphs despite his Army boots – or (my preference) the dance which is transformed into a military exercise. This could be very useful for a lead into the finale.

- Weapon training: CHARLIE able to assemble gun at speed, because he helped make them in civilian life.

- Bayonet training. This could make HORACE sick. (It did make *me* sick.)

- Gas training – but not just a lecture. More comedy could be extracted if the boys go through the tear-gas chamber and it somehow gets locked.

- Music spot(s).

H.
One more character, outside the squad, needs to be dealt with – the efficiency-mad LIEUTENANT who speaks the same way as Jingle in 'Pickwick Papers' but (at the moment) with less coherence. He certainly clamours for inclusion – on a less farcical level.

I.
THE DENOUEMENT
Recapping: on this basis, we'd have six (possibly seven) squad-characters' stories to follow interlocking and separately: in (G) there are fourteen suggested sequences, and the whole range of Army life from which to draw other sequence-ideas – all to be played against the central idea of GRIMSHAWE'S LAST SQUAD. I don't think, therefore, that there'll be any difficulty concerning screen time, and a fast, convincing film should result.

The finale suggests itself as follows:

As many of the individual stories as possible are screwed-up to climax-pitch – especially GRIMSHAWE's, which is the focal point of all stories – by the time the eve of training examinations and passing-out parade is reached. So far as GRIMSHAWE is concerned, the morrow can only bring shame, sorrow and ruin to . . .

Carry On, Sergeant!

31 JANUARY 1958
N.H. for Beaconsfield Films Ltd

* * * * *

1 Story Basis
2 Characters
3 Screenplay Plan

Story Basis

This is the story of a Sergeant on the verge of retirement, determined to achieve his life's ambition by heading a Star Squad of National Servicemen.

Fate sees to it that his last squad of preliminary-trainees includes six human obstacles to the realisation of this ambition: any one of them would be sabotage personified – taken together they present him with a Herculean task: they are the original men who, if laid end to end, it would be a good idea.

The Army invariably orders 'Carry On, Sergeant!' at moments of crisis. This film tells how one sergeant doggedly obeyed this time-honoured order – and what a carry-on it turns out to be.

Characters

<u>AROUND THE RECRUITS</u>
SERGEANT GRIMSHAWE: As mentioned
CORPORAL COPPING: His sidekick
LIEUTENANT POTTS: Efficiency-mad Platoon Officer
COMPANY COMMANDER
INSPECTING GENERAL
SGT-MAJOR BRITTAIN: I/C passing-out parades
NORAH: Love-lorn NAAFI girl
PRIVATE HERBERT BROWN: The unteachable
MARY: Newlywed
CAPTAIN CLARK, M.O.: A lady

THE RECRUITS

CHARLIE SAGE: Newlywed (Former engineering worker)
HORACE STRONG: Hypochondriac (former bookies' clerk)
JIMMY BAILEY: Rebel (Former Student)
DENNIS DEAN: Jazz-kid (Former jazz-kid)
MILES HEYWOOD: Dreamboat (Independent means)
PETER GOLIGHTLY: Heavy going (Former *anything*)

SCREENPLAY PLAN

Passing-out parade at Heathercrest. GRIMSHAWE established marching at head of so-so squad: Sgt Major BRITTAIN bawling orders. GENERAL on inspection rostrum. HERBERT sweeping-up.

Establishment of GRIMSHAWE situation, and bets in Sgts' Mess.

Introduction of recruits:
CHARLIE (Wedding reception, to train).
STRONG & BAILEY join train at last minute.
DEAN & GOLIGHTLY picked up en route.

GRIMSHAWE meets squad at station. Discouraging start, probably involving GOLIGHTLY locked in carriage (or elsewhere).

MILES HEYWOOD in sports car with girl at gate of camp. Mistaken for officer, simultaneously with CHARLIE's first 'hallucination' (MARY in laundry truck).

Recruits settle in Hut 40. HERBERT, their hut-mate, established as a heap of chits.

Simultaneously MARY infiltrates into NAAFI with aid of NORAH (established as love-lorn).

GRIMSHAWE, en route to Hut 40 for preliminary pep-talk with boys, confides his policy to COPPING.

Pep-talk. Discouraging response by recruits – especially CHARLIE and HORACE.

Boys in NAAFI (in civvies). MUSIC SPOT by DEAN. During it some distance from the counter, CHARLIE suffers another MARY 'hallucination': NORAH falls for HORACE. CHARLIE realises MARY is an hallucination. Marriage-consummation rendezvous arranged.

Mix-up. CHARLIE finds himself confronted at the rendezvous by SERGEANT instead of MARY.

So ends the first day . . .

* * * * *

Kitting-out. GOLIGHTLY, utterly confused, finishes up with three rifles and no trousers. GROSSCUT with HORACE going sick – establishment of woman M.O., CAPTAIN CLARK.

In uniforms for first time, recruits paraded for first meeting with LIEUTENANT POTTS, established as efficiency-mad and possibly just plain mad as well.

This is followed by hut and kit inspection by POTTS and COMPANY COMMANDER (?). Fire-extinguisher routine, GOLIGHTLY and HEYWOOD perhaps both running off to get extinguishers, both succeeding, both contrived into releasing foam for finale.

* * * * *

First drill session. Very discouraging. BAILEY argumentative, GOLIGHTLY bemused, HORACE made of glass, CHARLIE preoccupied, MILES only with eyes for passing WRACS. DEAN, as the least stupid (apparently) invited to take over, try his hand at simple drill-orders. He does so: finds jazz-rhythms more readily springing to his tongue than march-rhythms. Squad ends up practically jiving.

First gunnery instruction. CHARLIE sees MARY through window. Assembly-of-gun pay-off.

PT in gym, under COPPING, anxiously watched by GRIMSHAWE. General disaster. HORACE (to quote only one example) claims rack-paining seizure of the intestines as a result of undue exertion.

CHARLIE marched in by GRIMSHAWE for his interview with Company Commander (applied for on the moment of his arrival). Sergeant and Officer react suitably to his unique request. It is granted. GRIMSHAWE thus loses a recruit for a week. Nice touch: when CHARLIE and MARY leave, HERBERT only one allowed out of camp, is a lone confetti-thrower at the station.

GRIMSHAWE in Sergeants' Mess. Very gloomy, doubtful about the outcome.

* * * * *

HORACE reports sick with ailments collected from previous sequence. Found fit for duty, he's plunged into . . .

Bayonet drill. Full comedy-value extracted. GRIMSHAWE and COPPING jointly in command (?).

Same night: HERBERT, after one or two previously seen attempts at friendship with BAILEY, succeeds in clinging to BAILEY who finds himself passing on some of his new-gained knowledge, successfully, to HERBERT.

Same night: MILES on a romantic escapade with girlfriend with sports car – out of camp. His adventures trying to get back inside the barbed-wire without being caught.

Same night: off-duty NORAH practically chases HORACE all round the camp, seeing an opportunity to declare her love for him.

* * * * *

HORACE reports sick – <u>very</u> sick after bayonet-drill. Pronounced fit for duty, he's pitchforked into . . .

Commando-type training. This lasts for a gruelling morning, after which there's a chance to relax at . . .

ABCA session. 'Manchester Guardian' BAILEY makes life hell – politely – for POTTS who, in this one particular, isn't especially efficient. Subject under discussion is something (ideally) non-controversial and timeless (The Structure of Parliamentary Government?) Session eventually finishes with graduate in social science BAILEY taking over, holding his listeners – including POTTS – spellbound. Finale pay-off: <u>POTTS</u> asking a question of <u>BAILEY</u>.

Same night: MILES romantically involved with a WRAC (cook? Grub-and-love session in darkened kitchen?)

Same night: BAILEY, restless, breaks out of camp (in civvies – to heighten the 'crime'), meets GRIMSHAWE in a pub without, astonishingly, ending up in the cooler. This encourages BAILEY to further defiance and argumentation in relation to GRIMSHAWE.

Same night: HORACE, terrified of tarantula-NORAH, refuses to go to NAAFI. HERBERT, at a loss without BAILEY around, tries to 'advise' HORACE on what to do when chased by a love-mad woman.

* * * * *

HORACE reports sick, but is pronounced fit enough for . . .

Firing-range and grenade practice. Full comedy-value extracted. By this time, CHARLIE has returned from his delayed honeymoon – so there's one more 'butt' on the range: CHARLIE.

GRIMSHAWE learns, through COPPING, of BAILEY's astonishing success in ramming knowledge through HERBERT's skull. GRIMSHAWE therefore contrives to make BAILEY responsible for helping CHARLIE to catch up on all he's missed during his honeymoon (militarily speaking).

While the boys are at the range, webbing-cleaning having previously been established, GOLIGHTLY's webbing is peaceably soaking away to nothing in the solution of chloride of lime that GOLIGHTLY has 'brilliantly' concocted to save himself work. Only the brass remains when they return from the butts.

* * * * *

New Suggestion: Initiative Tests! Recruits sent out of camp in pairs, with sealed orders. This could legitimately open out the picture and be productive of enormous, fast-moving, fast-switching comedy effect. With a screwball like POTTS thinking up the tests – with this lot assigned to them – with GRIMSHAWE biting his nails awaiting the results (he's prepared for anything from having to bail 'em out to dragging the rivers for 'em) – and with me bearing in mind NO night sequences and NO extravagant settings – can we see how this works out in the script? All ideas, of course, gratefully received!

* * * * *

Unifying Visual Device: Throughout the above, a chart in Sergeants' Mess graphs the progress or otherwise of the various squads at Heathercrest. At any point – and especially to bridge time without a tremendous montage of training shots – the chart is there to show the inescapably downward trend of GRIMSHAWE's men – and GRIMSHAWE's hopes. After the Initiative Tests, for example, a really catastrophic decline is shown.

* * * * *

<u>Running Theme:</u> GRIMSHAWE, convinced MILES is officer material and trying to salvage at least this from the inexorably predictable wreck, gets MILES interviewed by POTTS with a view to recommending MILES for cadet-ship. MILES's background and lack of interest in a commission comes out.

* * * * *

NORAH's pursuit of HORACE persists throughout, until in romantic situation, by the moonlit pyrotechnics shed, a kiss is finally exchanged and HORACE falls in love – and into greater hypochondria. He . . . reports love-sick. Asks M.O. about his fitness for marriage. M.O. leads him on, treats him seriously, gives as her snap opinion that if he's sick and weak all the time, marriage will almost certainly kill him – the excitement alone . . .
M.O. promises to think about it and do something for him. HORACE has to go off on a . . .
. . . route march. During it, staff car pulls up. GRIMSHAWE halts squad, staff car contains M.O. who hauls HORACE off to . . .
. . . civilian hospital and HORACE pay-off. Shock – followed by Tarzanisation of HORACE.

Same evening: HORACE going great guns with NORAH.

Same evening: HERBERT discovers the facts about GRIMSHAWE's imminent retirement, rushes to inform squad. (HORACE has left NORAH, weak but happy, by now, and is back in the Hut.) Squad unity belatedly established, decision to dare all for GRIMSHAWE's sake – and squad's pride – taken. HERBERT co-opted as honorary member of the squad.

Pay-off and finale of parade and success of the squad.

Station pay-off.

* * * * *

333

Notes

Apart from those listed below, all the quotes used throughout the book were taken from interviews carried out by the author while researching the *Carry On* films.

INTRODUCTION
1 Review of *Spying* in the *Observer*, 9/8/64
2 Review in *Variety*, 18/3/59

IN THE BEGINNING
1 Letter from Peter Rogers to Beryl Vertue, dated 31/3/58, re: *Carry On Sergeant – John Antrobus*
2 Ibid
3 Letter from Beryl Vertue to Peter Rogers, dated 8/4/58
4 Ibid
5 Letter from Peter Rogers to Beryl Vertue, dated 9/4/58
6 *Who's There? The Life and Career of William Hartnell*, Jessica Carney, p.136
7 From *Don't Lose Your Head* press pack
8 Ibid
9 Minutes of Pre-Production Meeting, Thursday, 20 March 1958
10 *High Spirits* by Joan Sims, p.149, Partridge
11 Ibid
12 Ibid
13 Article in *Film Review* by Catherine O'Brien, 11/78
14 Ibid
15 *High Spirits*, Joan Sims, p.122
16 Letter from John Nicholls to Peter Rogers, dated 25/3/58
17 Letter from Peter Rogers to Stuart Levy, dated 31/3/58
18 Review in *Monthly Film Bulletin*, 1/9/58
19 Ibid

20 Ibid
21 Review in *The Daily Cinema*, 6/8/58
22 Ibid
23 Review in *Kinematograph Weekly*, 7/8/58
24 Ibid
25 Review in *Variety*, 24/9/58
26 Ibid
27 Ibid
28 Review by Hollis Alpert, *Saturday Review*, 7/9/58
29 Review by Campbell Dixon, *Daily Telegraph*, 20/9/58
30 Ibid
31 Review by Penelope Houston, *Observer*, 21/9/58
32 Review in *News of the World*, 21/9/58
33 Review by Ernest Betts, *The People*, 21/9/58
34 Ibid
35 Interviewed for the Radio 2 documentary *The Carry On Clan*, broadcast 7/4/96
36 *High Spirits* by Joan Sims, p.90, Partridge
37 Review in *The Hollywood Reporter*, 15/3/60
38 Review in *Variety*, 18/3/59
39 Ibid
40 Review in *Monthly Film Bulletin*, 1/4/59
41 Review in the *Evening Standard*, 5/3/59
42 Review in the *Daily Herald*, 6/3/59
43 Review in the *Daily Worker*, 8/3/59
44 Review in the *Daily Express*, 6/3/59
45 Review in *The Sunday Times*, 8/3/59
46 Extract from Norman Hudis's preliminary notes for *Carry On Teacher*, 17/10/58
47 *Hello* by Leslie Phillips, p.212, Orion Books
48 *High Spirits*, Joan Sims, p.101
49 Letter from Peter Rogers to John Terry, National Film Finance Corporation, dated 26/11/58
50 Ibid
51 Ibid
52 Ibid
53 Review in *Kinematograph Weekly*, 20/8/59
54 Ibid
55 Ibid
56 Review in *The Daily Cinema*, 14/8/59

57 Review in *Variety*, 2/9/59
58 Ibid
59 Review by Derek Prouse, *The Sunday Times*, 6/9/59
60 Review in *The Times*, 4/9/59
61 Review in the *Daily Mail*, 5/9/59
62 *High Spirits* by Joan Sims, p.92, Partridge
63 Ibid
64 Review in *Kinematograph Weekly*, 25/2/60
65 Review in *The Times*, 29/2/60
66 Review by Campbell Dixon, *Daily Telegraph*, 27/2/60
67 Review in *Daily Express*, 26/2/60
68 Review in *News of the World*, 28/2/60
69 Review in *Monthly Film Bulletin*, 1/5/61
70 Review in the *Daily Cinema*, 20/3/61
71 Ibid
72 Review by Penelope Gilliatt in the *Observer*, 19/3/61
73 Ibid
74 Extract from promotional material for *Carry On Cruising*
75 Review in *Monthly Film Bulletin*, circa 1962 [exact date unknown]
76 Article in a supplement within *Kinematograph Weekly* by Derek Todd, 5/6/71
77 Review by critic named 'Rich' on 25/4/62. [Source unknown]
78 Ibid

THE ROTHWELL ERA

1 Letter dated 25/6/62 from Kevin Kavanagh, Kavanagh Productions Limited, to Peter Rogers
2 Ibid
3 *The Kenneth Williams Diaries*, Kenneth Williams (edited by Russell Davies), p.207
4 Extracted from publicity material produced in connection with *Cabby*
5 Review in *The Daily Cinema*, p.7, 28/8/63
6 Review in *Variety*, 28/8/63
7 *The Kenneth Williams Diaries*, Kenneth Williams (edited by Russell Davies), p.230
8 Review in *The Times*, 20/2/64
9 Review in *Financial Times* by David Robinson, 21/2/64
10 Review in *The Daily Cinema*, 15/2/64
11 Review in the *Daily Telegraph* by Patrick Gibbs (date unknown)
12 Review in *The Monthly Film Bulletin*, 9/64

13 *The Kenneth Williams Diaries*, Kenneth Williams (edited by Russell Davies), p. 228
14 Interview for promotional material issued by the studio, date unknown.
15 Ibid
16 Review in *The Times*, 30/7/64
17 Review in *The Spectator* by Ian Cameron, 7/8/64
18 Review in *The Sunday Times* by Dilys Powell, 2/8/64
19 Review in the *Daily Telegraph*, 31/7/64
20 Review in the *Guardian*, 31/7/64
21 Letter from Peter Rogers to Stuart Levy, dated 29/4/64
22 Article in *Film Review* by Mike Munn, 7/75
23 Peter Rogers Interview by Andy Davidson
24 Review in *Daily Express*, 13/12/64
25 Review in the *Guardian* by Ian Wright, 11/12/64
26 Review in the *Daily Mail* by Cecil Wilson, 8/12/64
27 Letter from Talbot Rothwell to Peter Rogers, dated 3/2/65
28 Ibid
29 Letter from Talbot Rothwell to Peter Rogers, dated 12/2/65
30 *Just Williams – An Autobiography*, Kenneth Williams, p. 137
31 Review in *The Times*, 24/3/66
32 Review in the *Guardian*, 25/3/66
33 Review in the *Daily Express* by Ian Christie, 25/3/66
34 Ibid
35 Review in the *Sunday Times*, 27/3/66
36 Interview for the *Screaming!* press pack
37 Ibid
38 Ibid
39 Review in *Monthly Film Bulletin*, 9/66
40 Review in *The Daily Cinema*, 15/8/66
41 Review in *Kine Weekly* by Graham Clarke, 18/8/66
42 Review in the *Sunday Express* by Michael Thornton, 21/8/66
43 Review in *Kine Weekly* by Graham Clarke, 18/8/66
44 Review in *The Sun* by Ann Pacey, 16/8/66
45 Minutes of Rank Pre-Production Publicity Meeting, 1/9/66
46 Review in the *Observer* by Penelope Gilliatt, 12/3/67
47 Ibid
48 Ibid
49 Interviewed for Radio 2's documentary *Carry On Carrying On*, transmitted 29/8/94

50 Ibid
51 Letter from Talbot Rothwell to Peter Rogers, dated 26/1/67
52 *The Kenneth Williams Diaries*, edited by Russell Davies, p. 304
53 Review in *The Daily Cinema* by Marjorie Bilbow, 24/11/67
54 Ibid
55 Review in the *Financial Times* by David Robinson, 5/12/67
56 Review in *The Sun* by Ann Pacey, 12/12/67
57 Article in *Photoplay*, 7/75, author unknown
58 Interview for the documentary *Carry On Carrying On*, transmitted 29/8/94
59 *Carry On Cleo* press pack
60 Ibid
61 Ibid
62 Ibid
63 Ibid
64 Article in *Cinema & TV Today* by Bill Hughes, 28/4/73
65 Article in *Saturday Titbits* by Douglas Marlborough, circa 1972
66 Interview with Sid James in publicity pack for *Doctor*
67 *High Spirits* by Joan Sims, p.129
68 Review in the *Daily Mail* by Cecil Wilson, 12/3/68
69 Letter from Peter Rogers to John Davis, 22/11/67
70 Review in *The Daily Cinema*, p.10, 29/11/68
71 Article in *The Daily Post*, Steve Bagnall, circa 9/68
72 *The Complete A-Z of Everything Carry On*, Richard Webber, p.89
73 *High Spirits*, Joan Sims, p.131
74 *Just Williams* by Kenneth Williams, p.186
75 Interview for the documentary *Carry On Carrying On*, transmitted 29/8/94
76 Review in the *Daily Express* by Ian Christie, 3/12/69
77 Interview for the documentary *Carry On Forever*, 1970
78 Review in the *Daily Telegraph*, 10/4/70
79 Note made by censor on 31/12/70, initials K. R. P.
80 Review in the *Daily Mirror* by Dick Richards, 4/11/70
81 Review in the *Daily Express* by Ian Christie, 4/11/70
82 Review in the *Sunday Mirror*, 8/11/70
83 Review in the *Morning Star* by Nina Hibben, 17/12/71
84 Note made by censor on document, 30/6/72
85 Review in the *Daily Express* by Judith Simons, 30/11/72
86 *The Kenneth Williams Diaries* edited by Russell Davies, p.423

87 Interview for the documentary *Carry On Carrying On*, transmitted 29/8/94

88 Original interview details unknown except it was an interview in 1980 with Brian Matthew. Used in documentary *Carry On Carrying On*, transmitted 29/8/94

89 Review in *Films Illustrated*, 12/73

90 Ibid

91 Review in *What's On*, 9/11/73

92 Article in the *Manchester Evening News*, 15/4/74

93 Ibid

94 Ibid

95 John Trevelyan writing in a brochure celebrating the 21st *Carry On*, title of publication and date unknown

96 Review in the *News Chronicle* by Paul Dehn, 6/3/59

97 Review by Nigel Gearing, source and date unknown

98 Review in the *Observer* by Russell Davies, 4/8/74

99 Review in *Financial Times* by Nigel Andrew, 12/7/74

100 Review in the *Evening News* by Felix Barker, 31/12/75

101 Review in *Films Illustrated*, date and critic unknown

102 Review in *Monthly Film Bulletin* by Verina Glaessner, date unknown

103 Article in *Film Review* by Mike Munn, 7/75

104 Interview released as part of publicity pack, circa 75

105 Note recorded on BBFC's Exception Form, 20/5/75

THE BEGINNING OF THE END?

1   Arthur Thirkell in the *Daily Mirror*, 29/10/76

2   Ibid

3   Ibid

4   Ibid

5   Letter from Gerald Thomas to Bernard Sheridan, 2/4/76

6   David Castell in the *Sunday Telegraph*, 31/10/76

7   Joan Sims, *High Spirits*, pp.154–155

8   Ibid

9   Joan Sims, *High Spirits*, p.154

10 Ibid

11 William Hill in the *Evening News*, 3/5/76

12 Ibid

13 *West Hertfordshire and Watford Observer*, 29/10/76, writer unknown

14 Ibid

15 Derek Elley in *Films and Filming*, circa 10/76.

16 *Gloucester Echo*, 11/6/76, writer unknown
17 Vincent Firth in *Film Review*, 9/76
18 Sue Summers in *Screen International*, 5/6/76
19 Ibid
20 *Gloucester Echo*, 11/6/76, writer unknown
21 Angela Haydon in *Monthly Film Bulletin*, date unknown
22 Nicholas Wapshott in *The Scotsman*, 1/11/76
23 Ibid
24 Russell Davies in the *Observer*, 31/10/76
25 *News of the World*, 31/10/76, writer unknown
26 David Castell in the *Sunday Telegraph*, 31/10/76
27 *Screen International*, 16/10/76, writer unknown
28 Nigel Andrew in the *Financial Times*, 29/10/76
29 Ibid
30 Ibid
31 Ibid
32 Swan in *Variety*, 3/11/76
33 Ibid
34 Joan Sims, *High Spirits*, p. 154
35 Article by Quentin Falk, *Screen International*, 3/12/77
36 Article in *Screen International*, Colin Vaines, 6/5/78
37 Ibid
38 *The Kenneth Williams Diaries*, p. 553
39 Ibid
40 Ibid
41 Barbara Windsor quoted in the *Daily Express*, 19/4/78, writer unknown
42 Ibid
43 Article titled 'Opinion' and written by Kenneth Williams, source unknown
44 Article written by Kenelm Jenour, *Daily Mirror*, 19/4/78
45 Article titled 'Opinion' and written by Kenneth Williams, source unknown
46 Article by Douglas Marlborough, *Titbits*, date unknown
47 Ibid
48 BBFC report dated 27/6/78
49 Ibid
50 Article by Colin Vaines, *Screen International*, 6/5/78
51 As stated in Suzanne Danielle's contract, held in BFI Archives
52 Article in *Barking and Dagenham Post*, 2/8/78

53 Article in *The Sun*, 20/4/78
54 Ibid
55 Review by Geoff Brown, *Financial Times*, 1/12/78
56 Review by Kenneth Baily, *Sunday People*, 3/12/78
57 Review by Richard Barkley, *Sunday Express*, 3/12/78
58 Review by Ian Christie, *Daily Express*, 2/12/78
59 Article in *Daily Mail*, Kenneth Eastaugh, 22/2/78
60 Interview for *What's A Carry On?*, a 40th anniversary documentary, transmitted 12/98
61 Review by Derek Malcom, *Guardian*, 1/10/92
62 Ibid
63 Review by Hugo Davenport, *Daily Telegraph*, 1/10/92
64 Ibid
65 Review by Nigel Andrews, *Financial Times*, 1/10/92
66 Article in the *Independent* by Sheila Johnston, 2/10/92

False Starts & Fresh Hopes

1 Norman Hudis's Introduction to *Carry On Again Nurse* published in *The Lost Carry Ons*, Morris Bright and Robert Ross, Virgin, 2000
2 *Carry On Is Back . . . And It's Capital Fun!*, an official press release from Carry On London Ltd, circa 5/07
3 Ibid
4 Ibid
5 Ibid

Bibliography

The following publications proved useful sources of information for the author while he was writing this book.

Parsons, Nicholas: *The Straight Man – My Life in Comedy*, Weidenfeld and Nicolson, London, 1994

Sims, Joan: *High Spirits*, Partridge, London, 2000

Webber, Richard: *The Complete A-Z of Everything Carry On*, Harper-Collins, London, 2005

Whitfield, June . . . *and June Whitfield: The Autobiography*, Bantam Press, London, 2000

Ross, Robert: *The Carry On Story*, Reynolds and Hearn, London, 2005

Williams, Kenneth: *Just Williams: An Autobiography*, Dent, London, 1985

Williams, Kenneth: *The Kenneth Williams Diaries*, HarperCollins, London, 1993

Index

2 point 4 Children (television) 176
20th Century Fox 88, 89, 107
1492: Conquest of Paradise 179
ABC Pictures 14, 49, 52–3
Above Us the Waves 15
Adams, Ray and Rosenberg (literary agency) 76
After the Ball (1957) 21
Air Force News 20
All in the Family (television) 73
Alpert, Hollis 41
The Alphabet Murders 148
Altman, Robert 186
American Officers' Club 137
Ammonds, John 188
Andrews, Nigel 136, 152, 179
Anglo-Amalgamated Film Distributors 15, 27, 38, 39, 48, 84, 89, 96, 98
Anglo-American Associates Limited 42
Antrobus, John 17–19, 25, 26, 58
Anvil Studios 79
Appointment With Venus 15
The Army Game (television) 18, 34, 90
Arthur and the Britons (television) 148
Askey, Arthur 77
Askwith, Robin 152
Associated British Cinemas 89
Associated London Scripts (ALS) 17–18, 114
Aston, Anne 150
Attenborough, Richard 42

Baily, Kenneth 174
Bain, Billy 96
Baker, Joe 124
Baker, Robert S. 20
Baker, Roy Ward 14
Ball, Vincent 68
Banks, Peter 153
Barker, Eric 19, 59, 60, 65–6, 84
Barker, Felix 138
Barkley, Richard 174
Baxter, Stanley 30
BBC 13, 34
Beaconsfield Film Studios 14, 15
Beaconsfield Films Limited 18
Beale, Jack 42
Berman, Monty 20
Betts, Ernest 41
Bevis, Frank 31
The Big Job (1965) 58
Bilbow, Marjorie 101
Billy (play) 168
Black, George 29
Black, James 192
Bless This House (television) 127, 188
Board of Trade 54
Bogarde, Dirk 78, 104
Bolam, James 149
Boulting brothers 42
Box, Betty 13, 14, 16, 84, 104, 113, 138
Box, Sydney 13, 42
Bresslaw, Bernard 28, 34, 149, 191

in *At Your Convenience* 121
in *Behind* 137
in *Dick* 134
early career 90–1
in *Girls* 130
in *Up the Khyber* 107, 109
Bresslaw, Liz 91
Brighton 130
British Board of Film Censors (BBFC) 38–9, 134–5, 170, 171
British Film Corporation (BFC) 15
British Film Institute 106
British Film Producers' Association 43
Bromley, Sydney 95
Brown, Geoff 174
Bryan, Dora 27, 40, 53
Buckley, Peter 119
Burton, Richard 88, 90
Bush Davies Dance School 168
Butlin's 124
Butterworth, Peter 3, 28, 77, 91, 110, 125, 149, 191
   in *Behind* 137
   in *Camping* 111
   in *Dick* 134
   in *Screaming!* 95, 97
Byrne, Peter 34–5

Callan (television) 149
Cameron, Ian 84
Candy, John 176
Cannon, Esma 66, 82
A Canterbury Tale 34
Capra, Frank 63
Cargill, Patrick 42
Carney, Jessica 26
Carry On Abroad (1972) 7, 131, 145, 148, 151
   cast in 126–8
   filming of 125–6, 127, 128–9
   first gay characters in 127–8
   full details of 238–9

reviews of 129
screenplay for 126
Carry On Admiral (1957) 15–16
Carry On Again Doctor (1969) 112–14
   full details of 230–1
Carry On Again Nurse 24–5, 29, 123, 186–7
Carry On At Your Convenience (1971) 120
   filming of 121–2
   full details of 235–6
   reviews of 122
Carry On Behind (1975) 49, 86, 147, 150, 173, 177, 187
   cast in 137
   censorship of 140
   full details of 242–3
   reviews of 138, 139
   screenplay for 136–7, 137–40
   strip scene in 139–40
Carry On Cabby (1963) 4, 31, 73, 104
   cast of 80–1
   full details of 214–15
   reviews for 81
   screenplay for 78, 80, 81
Carry On Camping (1969) 7, 38, 48, 60, 137, 182, 195
   bikini scene in 112
   filming of 111–12
   full details of 228–30
Carry On Cleo (1964) 3, 31, 67, 82, 83
   full details of 218–19
   funniest line in 3
   making of 88–9
   success of 89–90
Carry On, Columbus (1992) 7, 8, 113, 143, 148
   assessment of 179–82
   cast in 177–9
   full details of 247–9
   making of 175, 176–7
   reviews of 178–9

screenplay for 177

Carry On Constable (1960) 54, 151
  filming of 59
  full details of 209–11
  reviews of 59–60
  screenplay for 58–9

Carry On Cowboy (1965) 3, 77, 90, 97
  cast in 91–2, 93–4
  filming of 91–2, 93
  full details of 220–1
  reviews of 94
  screenplay for 92–3

Carry On Cruising (1962) 34
  cast in 66–8
  full details of 213–14
  reviews of 68–9
  screenplay for 65–6, 69–70

Carry On Dallas 188–9

Carry On Dick (1974) 5, 88, 103
  cast in 135
  and the censor 134–5
  filming of 134
  full details of 240–1
  reviews of 136
  screenplay for 133–4

Carry On Doctor (1968) 48, 112
  filming of 104–5
  full details of 225–7
  reviews of 105–6

Carry On . . . Don't Lose Your Head (1966) 32, 83, 88, 98–9, 104
  full details of 222–4

Carry On Down Under 189–90
  script 265, 269–311

Carry On Emmannuelle (1978) 8, 143, 148, 187
  cast in 167–8
  financing of 155
  full details of 245–7
  hullabaloo surrounding 169–71, 72–3
  making of 154–5, 168–74

reviews of 174–5
  scene cut from 157–67
  screenplay for 156–67, 172, 173–4

Carry On England (1976) 8, 134, 139, 140, 147, 173, 175, 187
  cast in 149–50
  failings of 148–9, 151–3
  filming of 144–5
  finance for 144
  full details of 243–4
  reviews of 143–4, 145, 148, 151, 152–3
  screenplay for 144, 148, 150

Carry On Escaping 188

Carry On films
  canon at a glance 203–4
  continuing popularity of 181–2
  convivial atmosphere on set 101–4
  in depth 205–63
  familiarity with 149
  future of 195–7
  and ideas for those never made 185–97
  music in 78–80
  schedules and costs of making 85–8
  success of 3–7
  and use of regular cast and crew 85, 115

Carry On Fleet Street 186

Carry On Flying 185–6

Carry On . . . Follow That Camel (1967) 37, 104
  and camel story 101
  cast in 99–100
  filming of 99–100
  full details of 224–5
  reviews of 100–1

Carry On Girls (1973) 146
  cast in 129–31
  and the censor 131–2

filming of 132
full details of 239–40
reviews of 132–3
screenplay for 129–31
Carry On Henry (1971) 83, 88, 120
    and chicken episode 119
    and cost of set dressing 118–19
    full details of 234–5
Carry On Jack (1963) 31
    failure of 81–2
    full details of 215–16
Carry On Laughing (television series)
    148, 177, 255
    And In My Lady's Chamber 261
    The Baron Outlook 255–6
    Carry On Again Christmas 252
    Carry On Christmas 251–4
    The Case of the Coughing Parrot
    259
    The Case of the Screaming
    Winkles 258–9
    Christmas Classics 263
    Lamp-Posts of the Empire 262
    The Nine Cobblers 258
    One In the Eye for Harold 257–8
    Orgy and Bess 257
    production team for 262
    Short Knight, Long Daze 260
    The Sobbing Cavalier 256
    Under the Round Table 259–60
    Who Needs Kitchener? 261
Carry On Laughing (theatre) 249–50
Carry On London (2008) 191–2
Carry On London! (play) 134
    full details 249
Carry On Loving (1970) 7, 48
    cast in 119–20
    food fight scene in 117–18
    full details of 232–4
    reviews of 119
Carry On Matron (1972) 114, 148, 155
    cast in 123–5

filming of 125
full details of 236–8
screenplay for 122–3
Carry On Nurse (1959) 4, 7, 62–3, 76,
    87, 112, 186
    cast of 48–50
    critical success of 50–1
    full details of 207–8
    memorable scenes from 46–7
    rough cut and trade showing
        47–8
    screenplay for 42–6
Carry On Nursing 190–1
Carry On Regardless (1961) 60, 69, 95,
    117
    cast in 63–5
    full details of 211–13
    reviews of 65
    screenplay for 61–3, 64, 65
Carry On Robin Hood 188
Carry On Screaming! (1966) 3, 90, 155
    cast in 94–7
    full details of 221–2
    reviews of 97–8
Carry On Sergeant (1958) 4, 7, 15, 62,
    69, 76, 107, 144
    cast in 26–36
    early rushes and private viewing
        39–40
    filming of 11
    first treatment and development
        ideas 313–33
    full details of 205–7
    inspiration for 17
    payments made to actors 36–9
    reviews of 40–2
    screenplay for 17–26
Carry On Smoking 185
Carry On Spaceman 188
Carry On Spying (1964) 31, 73, 155
    cast in 82–3
    cost of making 84–5

critical success of 84
full details of 217–18
last of the black-and-white films
83
Carry On Teacher (1959) 49, 50, 63, 87,
173, 186
cast in 52–4
critical success of 55–7
filming of 54–5
full details of 208–9
screenplay for 52, 57–8
Carry On Up the Jungle (1970) 37
cast in 114–16
filming of 115–16
full details of 231–2
and the powder puff incident
116
reviews of 116–17
use of flashback in 114
Carry On . . . Up the Khyber (1968) 182
considered Rothwell's finest
screenplay 105–6
filming of 106–10
full details of 227–8
Princess Margaret's visit to set of
110
Carry On Vicar 186
Carry On Yank 188
Castell, David 151
Castle, Roy 107
Causey, Jack 147
CBS 76
Central School of Drama 29
Chain of Events 15
Chamberlain, Cyril 54
Chekhov, Anton, The Cherry Orchard
153
Chessington Zoo, Surrey 101
Children's Film Foundation 15
Children's Hour (radio play) 34
Chrisafis, Chris 192
Christie, Ian 94, 114, 119

Christopher Columbus: The Discovery
179
Chrystal, Biddy 68
Cinema Today 66
Cinematograph Film Production Acts
(1949, 1952) 53–4
Circus Friends (1956) 15
Clary, Julian 177
Cleopatra 88–9, 90
Cleves Investments Limited 156
Clive, John 127, 128
Cohen, Mr 45
Cohen, Nat 39, 43, 50, 98, 154, 186
Cole, George 26
Colin, Sid 78
Collins, Joan 168
Columbia Records 34
Columbia Studios 63
The Comedy House 176
The Comic Strip 176
Confessions of . . . films 152, 171
Connor, Jeremy 46
Connor, Kenneth 87, 149, 187, 191
in Abroad 125
in Behind 137
in Cruising 66, 67, 69
in Dick 134
in England 144, 153
in Girls 129–30
in Nurse 46
in Regardless 62, 63
in Sergeant 27, 28–9, 37, 39, 42
in Spying 74, 82
in Teacher 53, 54, 55
Cooper, Tommy 106
Cope, Kenneth 121, 123–4
Corbett, Harry H. 95, 97
Corona Academy School 54
County School, Willesden (London)
58
Coupling 18
Cox, Jenny 139–40

Crazy Gang 77
Cribbins, Bernard 84, 177
Croft, David 152
Crosby, Bing 175, 176

Daily Cinema 40–1, 56, 81, 82, 97, 101
Daily Express 51, 61, 89, 94, 114, 119,
    129, 133
Daily Herald 51
Daily Mail 56, 90, 105
Daily Mirror 51, 119, 132, 143
Daily Telegraph 41, 61, 82, 84, 116, 179
Dale, Jim 107, 113, 177, 178, 179, 181,
    185–6
    in Cabby 81
    in Cowboy 92
    in Follow That Camel 99
    in Screaming! 95
    in Spying 84
Dallas, Granada Theatre 50
Daly, John 156
Dane, Alexandra 104, 113–14
Danger Man (television) 90, 91
Danielle, Suzanne 168, 171–5
Dann, Larry 54, 55, 173, 174
Davenport, Hugh 179
Davey, Bert 92
Davies, Russell 136, 151
Davies, Windsor 137, 139, 144, 149,
    150, 153
Davis, John 106
Day to Remember 15
Deadlier Than the Male (1967) 138
Dear Dotty (television) 77
Delderfield, R.F. 17, 20, 21, 25
Denham Film Studios 14, 15, 35, 79
Denham Laboratories 47
Dillon, Carmen 66
The Dirtiest Show in Town (play) 139
Disney, Walt 15
Dixon, Campbell 41, 61
Doctor in Clover 113

Doctor in the House 15
Doctor movies 104
Dotrice, Michele 150
Douglas, Angela
    in Cowboy 92, 93–4
    in Follow That Camel 100
    in Screaming! 96
    in Up the Khyber 108, 110–11
Douglas, Jack 177, 181, 195
    in Behind 137
    in Columbus 148, 178
    comment on Rothwell 134
    in Dick 135–6
    in Emmannuelle 148, 172
    in England 148, 149, 151, 153
    in Girls 131
    in Matron 124–5, 148
    on teamwork 103
    and working with Windsor
        Davies 139
Douglas, Sally 96
Drake, Charlie 76
Drayton Secondary School, West
    Ealing (London) 54
Driver, Harry 188
Duff, Leslie 112
The Duke Wore Jeans 15, 21

Eade, Peter 37, 50, 169
EastEnders (television) 192
Eaton, Shirley 27, 47, 59, 60
Educating Archie (radio) 28
El Cid 89
Elley, Derek 148
Emergency-Ward 10 (television) 91
EMI 154, 156
Emmanuelle (1974) 155
Emney, Fred 78
Evans, George 133
Evening Standard 51
Eyer, Rita 108

Faith, Adam 149
Fielding, Fenella 94–5, 97
Film Producers Association 188
Film Review 37
Films and Filming 119, 148
Films Illustrated 132, 138
Financial Times 82, 101, 136, 152, 174, 179
Four Weddings and a Funeral 50, 187
Franklin, Patricia 130, 138
Fraser, Liz 138
Freeman, Dave 136–7, 138–9, 148, 177, 179

Gainsborough Studios 13
Galton, Ray 17
Gardner, Jack 154
Gearing, Nigel 136
Geeson, Judy 149, 150
Geeson, Sally 126–7
George and the Dragon (television) 95, 188
The Ghost of St Michael's 34
Gibbons, Spencer K. 35
Gibbs, Patrick 82, 116–17
Gilbert, Lewis 78
Gilliat, Sidney 147
Gilliatt, Penelope 5, 98–9
Gilmore, Peter 177
Glaessner, Verina 139
Glen, John 179
Globe Theatre 131
Goddard, Roy 36
Golden Rendezvous (1978) 154
Goldstone, John 175, 176–7, 178, 180, 181
Good Morning, Boys 34
The Goose Steps Out 34
Gordon, Richard 113
Grainger, Gail 125
Green, S.C. 78, 80
Guardian 84, 90, 94, 178–9

Guest, Val 15
Guildford, Queen's Barracks 11, 36
Guinness, Alec 78

Halling, Pat 79–80
Hamlet 14
Hancock's Half-Hour (radio) 28
Harris, Anita 99
Harris, Julie 88
Harris, Richard 154
Harrison, Rex 88, 90
Hartnell, William 34
    film reviews of 40, 41
    in *Sergeant* 26, 37, 42
Harvey, Laurence 21
Hassall, Imogen 120
Hawkins, Carol 127, 150
Hawtrey, Charles 3, 4, 5, 66–7, 69, 187
    in *Abroad* 125, 126, 127, 129
    in *Again Doctor* 113
    behaviour on set 102
    in *Cabby* 80–1
    in *Camping* 195
    character of 33, 34–5
    comedic talent of 33–5
    in *Cowboy* 3
    and drunken mother on set 87–8
    early career 34
    effect of alcohol on 34–5
    film reviews of 40, 41
    in *Girls* 131
    in *Regardless* 64
    in *Screaming!* 95–6
    in *Sergeant* 27, 28, 37, 39, 42
    in *Spying* 74, 82, 84, 85
    in *Teacher* 53, 54
    in *Up the Khyber* 106, 108, 110
Haydon, Angela 150
Hayes, Melvyn 150
Hayes, Patricia 34

Heatherwood Hospital, Ascot 125
Hemdale 156
Herbert, Percy 82
Here is The News (satirical revue) 67
Here's Harry (television) 188
Hi-de-Hi! (television) 152
Hibbin, Nina 51, 122
Hill, Benny 137
Hills, R.M. 78, 80
His Majesty's Theatre, London 29
HMS Defiant 78
Hollywood 15, 43, 50–1
The Hollywood Reporter newspaper 50
Home and Beauty (play) 90
Hope, Bob 175
Hornchurch Rep 168
Houston, Donald 23, 82
Houston, Penelope 41
How Do You View? (television) 77
Howell, George 54–5
Howerd, Frankie 77, 104, 105, 106, 178
    in *Up the Jungle* 37, 114–15
Howitt, Peter 117, 118, 119
Hudis, Norman 4, 6, 7, 8, 12, 15, 16,
    117, 154, 196
        and the *Carry On's* never made
            185–7
        on death of Kenneth Williams
            30–1
        early scriptwriting career 19–20
        Here Is The News (play) 20
        invited to Hollywood 50–1
        moves to America 76
        as possible screenwriter for
            Matron 122–3
    screenplays: *Constable* 58–9
        Cruising 65–6, 69–70, 73
        Nurse 42–6, 47–8, 50
        Regardless 61–3, 64, 65
        Sergeant 17, 21–6, 41–2
        Spying 73–5
        Teacher 52, 57–8

working and writing technique 21–
    2, 23–5
Hudis, Rita 44, 48, 76
Hume, Alan 35–6, 39, 55, 81, 85–6, 87,
    93, 101, 180
Hyde-White, Wilfrid 46, 47, 53

Imperial War Museum 144
Independent 179
Intandern Films 192
Is it Legal? 18
Islington Studios 19
It Ain't Half Hot, Mum (television) 137
It Takes A Thief 47
Italia Conti School 34
ITMA (radio) 28

J. Arthur Rank 13, 14
Jacobs, Philip 89
Jacques, Hattie 50, 79, 82, 87, 191, 195
    in *Again Doctor* 113
    in *Cabby* 80
    in *Girls* 131
    in *Henry* 119
    in *Loving* 117
    in *Nurse* 48
    in *Sergeant* 27–8, 37
    in *Spying* 74
    successful career of 48–9
    in *Teacher* 53, 54, 56
James, Sid 3, 5, 28, 82, 95, 137, 189,
    191, 195
    in *Abroad* 125, 127, 128
    in *Cabby* 80
    in *Constable* 59–60
    in *Cowboy* 3, 91–2, 93, 94
    in *Cruising* 66, 69
    death of 100, 101, 134, 145–7, 151
    in *Dick* 133, 134
    in *Doctor* 104–5
    in *Don't Lose Your Head* 98
    early life and career 59

enjoyment on set of *Carry On's*
102, 103
in *Girls* 130, 131
in *Henry* 119
in *Loving* 117
in *Matron* 123, 125
in *Regardless* 61, 64–5
in *Spying* 74, 82
in *Up the Khyber* 106, 110
James, Valerie 93
Jenkins, Mr (teacher) 58
Johannesburg Repertory Players 59
Johnston, Sheila 179
Jones, Peter 105
Jones, Vinnie 192

Kavanagh, Kevin 78, 92
Keith, Penelope 150
Kentish Express 13
Kenwright, Bill 155
Kernan, David 127
Kine Weekly 97
Kinematograph Weekly 41, 56, 60
Kirkwood, Patricia 21
Knight, Rosalind 87
Koper, Ann 108
Kristel, Sylvia 155, 167

Lamour, Dorothy 175
Launder, Frank 147
Lavender, Ian 149–50
Lawrence of Arabia 89
Laye, Dilys 67–8, 69, 84, 111
Layton, George 187
Le Brock, Kelly 167–8
Lean, David 85
Leatherhead Repertory Company 20
Lee, Auriol 13
Leon, Valerie 115, 130, 131
Leveson, Brian 191
Levy, Stuart 15, 38, 39, 52–3, 84, 96,
186

Lewis, Ronald 23
Life of Brian 175
The Liver Birds (television) 148
Lock, Stock and Two Smoking Barrels
187
Locke, Harry 53
Lodge, David 144
Logan, Jimmy 128
The Long Good Friday 187
Longdon, Terence
in *Constable* 59
in *Nurse* 46, 47
in *Sergeant* 42
in *Teacher* 53
The Longest Day 148
The Lord Chamberlain Regrets! (play)
67
Lorimar Productions 189
Lost Horizon 63
Lowe, Olga 145–6
Lynn, Jonathan 187
Lyric Theatre, London 42

McGill, Donald 5
MacRoary Whirl (play) 90
Mad About Men 15
Madness of the Heart 15
Malcolm, Derek 178–9
The Man from U.N.C.L.E. (television)
76
The Man Who Haunted Himself 115
Marcus Welby, MD (television) 43
Margaret, Princess 110
Marks and Spencer 89
Marry Me (musical) 34
Marsden, Betty 195
Marshall, Andrew 176
M*A*S*H (film) 186
M.A.S.H. (television) 43
The Mating Game (play) 130
The Mating Season (play) 146, 147
Mayall, Rik 176, 177

Maynard, Bill 125
The Meaning of Life 175
Medwin, Michael 53
Men Behaving Badly (television) 18
Men of Sherwood Forest 90
MGM Studios 51, 154
Miller, Max 5
Milligan, Spike 17
Mills, John 14
Mills, Juliet 53, 82
Minett, Paul 191
Minter, George 15–16
Monkhouse, Bob 25, 26–7, 37
Montgomery, Bruce 78, 79
Monthly Film Bulletin 40, 51, 68, 97, 139, 150
Monty Python and the Holy Grail 175
Moore, Roger 115
More, Kenneth 94
Morecambe, Eric 168, 188
Morning Star 122
Morris, Keith 146
Mother's Little Murderer (play) 155, 156
Mower, Patrick 149, 150
Mozart, Wolfgang Amadeus 186
Mr Ten Per Cent 76
Murder at the Windmill 91
Murder Mystery 15
Murder She Said 91
Murphy, Stephen 131–2, 140
My Fat Friend (play) 131

National Film Finance Corporation 53
The Navy Lark (radio) 133
Nearest and Dearest (television) 188
Never the Twain (television) 188
New Faces (television) 35
News of the World 41, 151
Nicholls, John 38
Nolan, Margaret 121, 130, 131
Nurse On Wheels 15, 43, 53

Observer 41, 136, 151
O'Callaghan, Richard 115, 119–20, 121–2
October Man 14
Oh, Nurse! (television) 76
Oil Strike North (television) 148
Olivier, Laurence 14, 90
One Foot in the Grave (television) 176
One Over the Eight (play) 67
Osborne, Brian 128, 131
O'Sullivan, Richard 54, 149
Owen, Bill 26, 53

Pacey, Ann 101
Pandora and the Flying Dutchman 15
Paramount Pictures Corporation 175–6
Pardon the Expression (television) 188
Parker, Cecil 82
Parsons, Nicholas 63–4
Parton, Hugh J. 113
Pavlou, George 192
Penhaligon, Susan 150
The People newspaper 41
Percival, Lance 23, 66–7, 69
Perry, Jimmy 152
Peters, Lance 155–6, 157–67, 172, 173–4
Phillips, Leslie 177
   in *Constable* 59
   in *Teacher* 53, 56
Pieces of Eight (theatre revue) 55, 95
Pinewood Studios 15, 16–17, 20, 23, 29, 36, 39–40, 66, 80–1, 92, 93, 96, 106, 107, 111, 113, 123–4, 127, 128, 144–5, 146–7, 173, 191, 195
Pink Floyd 144
Piper, Jacki 103, 115–17, 119–20, 121, 125
Planer, Nigel 176, 177
Players' Theatre, London 27
Please Turn Over 15
Poole, Frank 137
Posta, Adrienne 150
Powell, Dilys 51, 84

Powell, Vince 95, 172, 173, 188–91
Powers, James 50
Priestley, J.B., *People at Sea* 13
The Prince and the Pauper (television) 168
Pritchard, John 110
Prouse, Derek 56
Public Eye (television) 91
Pursall, David 147–8
Pyjama Tops (play) 139

Raising the Wind 15
Randall and Hopkirk Deceased (television) 121
Rank Organisation 15, 19, 20, 98, 106, 137, 144, 152, 156
Rattigan, Terence 63
Ray, Andrew 23
Ray, Ted 28, 29, 52–3, 54, 56, 60
Ray's A Laugh (radio) 28
Reed, Carol 15
Regal Gramophone Records 34
Regan, Linda 152
Reid, Beryl 173–4
Renwick, David 176
Richards, Dick 119
Richards, Frank 24
Richardson, Peter 176, 191, 192
Richens, Peter 191
Richie, Shane 192
Ring for Catty 42, 43
Rivers, Stella 35
Road to . . . films 175
Road to the Fountain of Youth 176
Road to Hong Kong (1962) 176
Road to Singapore (1940) 176
Robinson, Cardew 106
Robinson, David 82, 101
Robinson, Ethel 46
Rodway, Geoffrey 31–2, 35, 116
Rodway, Nora 31–2, 116
Rogers, Eric 78–80

Rogers, Peter 4, 6, 74, 86, 195, 196
and assembling of new casts 149–50
birth and early career 12–13
and change of distributor 98
comment on Joan Sims 50
completes script for *Dick* 134
and *Constable* 58
continues to work at Pinewood 16–17
and *Cruising* 65–6
engages Rothwell as script writer 77
and making of *Carry On* films 11, 85–8
marriage 13
and *Nurse* 43–8
partnership with Thomas 14–16
relationship with critics 143
reunion lunch with Hudis 186–7
and *Sergeant* 18–26, 28, 32–3, 35–40
and *Spying* 73, 84–5
and *Teacher* 52–4
and *That's Carry On* 154
and *Up the Khyber* 106–7
writing talents 12–14
Cards On the Table (radio play) 13
Circus Friends 14
Cross Questions (radio play) 13
Dear Murderer 14
Here Come the Huggetts 14
Human Straws (play) 13
The Man Who Bounced (radio play) 13
Mr Mercury (play) 13
Mr South Starts A War (radio play) 13
Time Lock 14
To Dorothy a Son 14
When the Bough Breaks 14

Rosenberg, Lee 76
Rossington, Norman 26, 34, 42
Rothwell, Talbot 4, 4–5, 6, 7, 12, 51,
    59, 91, 147, 151, 153, 154, 188
    death of 134
    early career 77
    screenplays: *Abroad* 126
      At Your Convenience 120
      Cabby 78, 80, 81
      Camping 112
      Carry On Again Doctor 113
      Cowboy 92–3
      Dick 134, 136
      Don't Lose Your Head 99
      Follow That Camel 100
      Girls 132
      Loving 119
      Matron 123
      Spying 73, 74
      Up the Khyber 105–6
    style of writing 77–8
      Once Upon a Crime (play) 77
      Queen Elizabeth Slept Here
      (play) 77
Rowlands, Patsy 117–18, 132, 137
Royal Goat Hotel, Beddgelert 108
Royal Victoria Hotel, Llanberis 107–8

St John, Earl 20
Saturday Review (newspaper) 41
Sayle, Alexei 177
Schenck, Nicholas 51
The Scotsman 150
Scott, Ridley 179
Scott, Terry 107, 116, 195
Screen International 152
Seddon, Jack 147–8
Shakespeare, William
    Much Ado About Nothing 91
    Two Gentlemen of Verona 91
Silvers, Phil 37, 99–100, 101
Silvstedt, Victoria 192

Simons, Judith 129
Simpson, Alan 17, 18
Sims, Joan 28, 37, 67–8, 69, 80, 82,
    87, 149, 150, 154, 187
    in *Abroad* 125, 126
    in *Behind* 137
    character of 49–50
    on death of Sid James 146–7
    in *Doctor* 105
    early career of 49
    enjoyment on set of *Carry On's*
      102–3
    loneliness of 50
    in *Regardless* 63, 64
    in *Screaming!* 95, 96–7
    in *Spying* 74, 82
    in *Teacher* 53, 54, 56
    in *Up the Khyber* 108, 111
Sinden, Donald 23
Sky Movies Comedy 3
Snowdonia 107–11
The Solitary Child 15
Somerset Maugham, William 24
Sommer, Elke 86, 137, 138, 139, 150
Special Branch (television) 149
Spectator 84
'Stars in Battledress' 29
Steele, Tommy 21
The Stud 168
Sullivan, Michael 124
The Sun 97, 101
Sunday Express 56, 97, 174
Sunday Mirror 119
Sunday People 174
Sunday Telegraph 151
Sunday Times 56, 84, 94
Sunderland Empire Theatre 145
Sykes, Eric 17

Tavistock Repertory Theatre 30
Taylor, Elizabeth 88, 90
The Ted Ray Show (television) 77

Terpning, Howard 89
Terry, John 53–4
Terry-Thomas 77
Thames Television 189
That's Carry On (1977) 154, 156
  full details of 245
That's Entertainment (1974) 154
The Third Man 15
Thirkell, Arthur 132, 143–4
Thomas, Gerald 4, 6, 23, 24–5, 28, 32,
  33, 34, 68, 74, 85, 86, 101
  behaviour on set 101–2, 103, 119,
    132, 136, 172
  birth and early career 14–15
  and *Columbus* 175, 176–8, 179–81
  and *Cowboy* 91
  and *Cruising* 66
  experience of 12
  in Hollywood 15
  and making of *Carry On* films
    88, 153–4
  and *Nurse* 44, 45, 46, 48
  partnership with Rogers 14–16
  and *Regardless* 64
  relationship with critics 143
  reunion lunch with Hudis 186–7
  on scriptwriting 150
  and *Sergeant* 19, 35, 36, 40
  style 11
  and *Teacher* 53, 54–5
  and *Up the Khyber* 107
Thomas, Jeremy 155
Thomas, Ralph 14, 104
Thornton, Michael 97
Three Months Gone (play) 120
Till Death Us Do Part (television) 73
Tilley, Vesta 21
Time Lock 15
The Times 56, 61, 82, 84, 94
Titbits 171
The Tommy Steele Story (1957) 21
Tomorrow Never Comes 148

Toms, Donald 31
Tony Draws a Horse 15
Torrance, Sam 173
The 39 Steps 62
The Twenty Questions 15
Twice Round the Daffodils 15, 23, 43,
  67
Two Cities Films 14
Two Many Crooks 90

Under Thirty Theatre Group 20
Universal Aunts 61–2
Unwin, Stanley 62
Up Pompeii! (television) 77
Up in the World 90
Upmore, Linda 140

Valmouth (musical) 95
Van Ost, Valerie 104–5
Variety 7, 41, 51, 56, 153
Vasey, Eric 108–10
Venetian Bird 15
Vertue, Beryl 18, 114
Vetchinsky, Alex 107
The Vice (television) 90
The Vicious Circle 15
Victoria Palace, London 134
Viz magazine 5

Wagner, Robert 47
Wallace, Mr (headteacher) 58
Wapshott, Nicholas 150
Watch Your Stern 15
Watford, Peace Memorial Hospital 44
Wattis, Richard 84
West Hertfordshire and Watford Observer
  147
Westbrook, Danielle 191, 192
What a Carry On! (television) 254–5
What's On 132
Whitfield, June 125, 126, 128, 130
Wilder, Gene 176

Williams, Brock 58
Williams, Kenneth 3, 4, 5, 23, 67, 79,
    80, 87, 95, 131, 149, 150, 178, 187,
    191, 195
    in *Abroad* 125, 126, 127–8, 129
    in *Again Doctor* 113
    behaviour on set 102, 118
    in *Behind* 137, 138, 139
    in *Cabby* 82
    in *Camping* 111, 112
    character and bizarre behaviour
        of 29–30, 32–3
    in *Cleo* 3
    in *Cowboy* 93
    in *Cruising* 66, 67
    death of 30–1
    in *Dick* 103, 133
    in *Emmannuelle* 168–9, 170–1,
        172, 173
    film reviews of 40
    in *Follow That Camel* 100
    gives money to George Howell
        55
    in *Loving* 118
    in *Matron* 125
    in *Nurse* 45
    and payment for the *Carry On's*
        36–7
    in *Screaming!* 3, 95, 97
    in *Sergeant* 26, 27, 28, 39, 42
    in *Spying* 82, 84, 85, 101
    in *Teacher* 53, 54
    in *That's Carry On* 154

    in *Up the Khyber* 106, 109
Williamson, Shaun 192
Wilson, Cecil 90, 105
Wilson, Julie 78
Wilson, Richard 177
Wilton, Rob 185
Windsor, Barbara 28, 87, 137, 151, 189
    in *Abroad* 125
    in *Camping* 38, 111–12
    in *Dick* 134
    in *Emmannuelle* 169–70
    in *Girls* 130, 131
    in *That's Carry On* 154
Winston, Eric 124
Wise, Ernie 168, 188
Wolfe, Felix de 17
Wolverhampton, Grand Theatre 153
The Woman in Red (1984) 167
World Press News 13
Worth, Harry 188
Wot a Carry On In Blackpool (theatre)
    250–1
Wren, Percival Christopher, *Beau Geste*
    100
Wright, Ian 90
Writers' Guild of America 123
Wyman, Lawrie 133

York, Susannah 153
You Know What Sailors Are (1954) 27
You're Only Young Once 34

Zulu 89